Praise for Jeff Alt's A WALK FOR SUNSHINE

"A Walk For Sunshine kept me turning the pages. Alt had become a friend, someone I was pulling for everyday of the way...It's a quick read that introduces you to a cherished American Trail."

—Dick Peterson, *North West Herald*

"Jeff wrote a book on his 147 day hiatus from civilization, A Walk For Sunshine. [The Sunshine Home is] where the developmentally disabled...are cared for and where his brother Aaron has lived for over a decade. The trail became a fundraiser for the home and the home became the motivation for Jeff—without which he might have never reached the final chapter of his Appalachian tale, the peak of Mt. Katahdin, Maine."

—Steve Porino, Host, ESPN's *Inside America's National Parks*

"With humility and charm, Alt tells his tale with awe for the people and his surroundings. This book is inspiring and entertaining."

—*Today's Librarian*

"This easy-reading book is full of many tales of how Alt got through the daunting hike from Georgia to Maine with humor."

—Karen Chavez, *Asheville Citizen-Times*

"A WALK FOR SUNSHINE tells the tale of a man who trekked 2,000 miles to honor his handicapped brother. Mr. Alt gathered donations, turning the trek into a fund-raiser. That's all in the book. So is the now funny but then ugly story of the day he put his arch supports in the wrong boots and developed such enormous blisters he had to wrap his feet in duct tape."

—Jim Knippenberg, *The Cincinnati Enquirer*

"A Walk For Sunshine has touched numerous people in many significant ways."

—Douglas Siebenaler, Sunshine Incorporated

Turn the page for more praise

More Praise for Jeff Alt's A WALK FOR SUNSHINE

"Alt shares ample anecdotes about life on the trail and the personalities he met walking this unique swath of wilderness through the hubub of the 21st-century America. Alt quickly disabuses the reader of the notion that walking the trail simply involves awaking one morning, tying on a pair of shoes and hitting the road."
—Mary O. Bradly, *Patriot-News*

"A Walk For Sunshine ably tells Alt's tale of braving everything from freezing cold, driving rain, and a bear encounter to boredom, exhaustion, charging bulls, and trail angels who offer food and support."
—Steve Pollick, *The Blade*

"...I have thoroughly enjoyed reading A Walk For Sunshine. I could not put it down. It brought back many memories..."
—Gene Espy, the second person to ever hike the entire Appalachian Trail

"For anyone thinking about walking the Appalachian Trail, this book would be a wonderful addition, and for those of us armchair travelers, it is wonderful to sense the excitement, danger, and adventure as the pages unfold."
—Maureen Darby, *The Lebanon Daily Record*

"Surviving the 2,160 mile Appalachian Trail is as much a mental challenge as a physical one and gave Alt a new perspective. Life on the Appalachian Trail was non-stop nature. No television, no steak dinner, no fluffy pillow. Just trees and rocks and sky. Three walled shelters, dirty water, and mosquitos. It was blistered feet, a growling stomach and weary bones."
—Pamela Davis, *The St. Petersburg Times*

"AN AMAZING STORY...A humorous and inspirational portrait of a modern American adventurer fulfilling lofty dreams, while discovering what lies beyond the physical and mental boundaries."
—Art Lander Jr., *Lexington Herald-Leader*

A
Walk
For
Sunshine

A 2,160-mile expedition for charity on the Appalachian Trail

by Jeff Alt

BEAUFORT
BOOKS

A Walk For Sunshine

Fourth Edition 2015

Library of Congress Cataloging-in-Publication Data

Alt, Jeff.
 A walk for sunshine a 2,160-mile expedition for charity on the appalachian trail by jeff alt. -- Fourth edition.
     pages cm
 "Distributed by Midpoint Trade Books."
 ISBN 978-0-8253-0776-8 (pbk. : alk. paper)
 1. Walk-a-thons--Appalachian Trail. 2. Fund raising--United States. 3. Charities--United States.. 4. Alt, Jeff--Travel--Appalachian Trail. I. Title.
 HV41.9.U5A44 2015
 917.404'43--dc23

For inquiries about volume orders, please contact:

Beaufort Books
27 West 20th Street, Suite 1102
New York, NY 10011
sales@beaufortbooks.com

Published in the United States by Beaufort Books
www.beaufortbooks.com

Distributed by Midpoint Trade Books
www.midpointtrade.com

Printed in the United States of America

Interior Design by Hiestand Design
Cover Design by George Foster

To my brother, Aaron

Disclaimer

This is a true account of the author's adventure along the Appalachian Trail. Some of the names and details of individuals in this story were changed to protect their privacy. The Appalachian Trail maps throughout this book have been modified and are not true to scale.

Acknowledgments

This book would not have been written without the help of countless volunteers and sponsors who supported my expedition and made it a success. *A Walk For Sunshine* is a non-fiction account of my journey, of those who inspired it, and of those who helped make it a success.

I am indebted to my editors, Mary Richards-Beaumont, and Julie and Jason Szucs, for their tireless efforts in refining my manuscript into this book.

I would like to thank my family and friends for their support and counsel as I put my journey on paper: my wife Beth, for her unwavering belief in me and my dreams; my stepfather and mother, Ron & Rose Almendinger, my father and stepmother, Mike & Sue Alt; my sister and brother-in-law, Steph & Dan Pitts; my brothers, Todd & Larry Alt; my aunt, Ellen Emch; my in-laws, Kathy & Laur Richards, Paul & Carol Richards, Mike & Katie Richards, Brian Richards; my stepbrother and wife, Mark & Dawn Shoviak; the Director of Development at Sunshine, Douglas Siebenaler; a colleague, Dr. Ken Ruder; a friend, Liz Osborn; and trail friend, Zeb Blanchard.

My sincerest thanks to everyone who gave their time, money, and energy to support my hike and fundraiser.

Thank you to the residents, staff, and volunteers of Sunshine, Inc. of NW Ohio for their inspiration and support.

I would like to thank all news media for their coverage of my hike, especially Betsy Heil of *The Toledo Blade* newspaper for her follow-through in keeping the community apprised of my journey.

Many thanks to Brian King and Robert Rubin of the Appalachian Trail Conservancy for providing factual information and maps of the Appalachian Trail.

Finally, I owe a debt of gratitude to the volunteers who spend countless hours maintaining the Appalachian Trail, making my journey and the journeys of others possible.

Without the efforts of all these people, *A Walk For Sunshine* would have remained a passing thought.

Contents

Preface

For 147 days, I put one foot in front of the other at least five million times. Not only did I walk an unbelievable distance—2,160 miles, to be exact—but I also raised more than $16,000 for a home for the developmentally disabled and mentally retarded, where my brother lives.

On March 1, 1998, I began my northbound expedition along the Appalachian Trail. Four and a half months later, with a new perspective on life, a few scars, a beard, and a very lean body, I climbed the final summit, fulfilling a dream that I shared with several hundred individuals with disabilities, their families, and friends.

I did not realize the connection between the Sunshine Home and the Appalachian Trail until I set out on my quest. The Appalachian Trail and Sunshine each began with a vision of fulfilling needs. The Appalachian Trail fulfills a human need to interact with the wilderness and get back to a simpler life. Sunshine provides needed services to children and adults with developmental disabilities and mental retardation. Each was founded by courageous visionaries who intended to increase the quality of life for everyone involved. Both rely on support of communities and volunteers.

The Appalachian Trail, commonly called the AT, began as the ambitious vision of Benton McKaye in 1921 and was completed in 1937. McKaye envisioned a wilderness trail all along the eastern seaboard for citizens to escape from the cities. Similar to the meanderings of a lazy river, the AT winds through 14 states, from Springer Mountain, Georgia, all the way to Mount Katahdin, Maine. Thanks exclusively to the volunteers who maintain the trail, an estimated one million hikers at any given moment follow the footpath, which is marked with white blazes the size of school erasers on trees, rocks, and signs. The AT changes in length every year due to constant rerouting of various sections in order to prevent erosion or to accommodate new land acquisitions. The struggle to convert land from private ownership to national park status continues today, with more than seven trail miles remaining in private ownership. The AT traverses the ridgelines of the Appalachian Mountains, the most rugged terrain in the eastern United

States. It has become legendary worldwide and continues to attract new dreamers every year.

Sunshine Inc. of Northwest Ohio is located in Maumee, a small community near Toledo. Roy and Georgette Engler created Sunshine in 1949. The couple was raising five children with mental retardation, and they learned to appreciate the need for more services to support children with dependent needs. The Sunshine Children's Home grew from 27 children in 1952 to its current capacity. Today, Sunshine supports the needs of more than 850 mentally retarded and developmentally disabled residents and clients throughout northwest Ohio.

My brother Aaron was born in 1973 with cerebral palsy and mental retardation. When Aaron's condition became too difficult for my family to manage, we began our search for assisted care for the developmentally disabled. Sunshine has provided my brother with the best care that he could get with his physical and mental conditions, and he has lived at the home for more than a decade. He receives outstanding health care, social interaction, and even employment. My family is grateful for what Sunshine has provided.

These seemingly unrelated details in my life provided me with my most rewarding and satisfying experience to date. I decided that I would hike the Appalachian Trail not only for recreation but also as a fund-raiser for Sunshine. It motivated me, and the money that I raised provided the residents at Sunshine with communication devices and other equipment that improved their lives. Little did I know that my hike would inspire the adoption of a new annual fundraiser, "Walk With Sunshine."

I faced many challenges along the way. I walked through 15 consecutive days of rain, through 10-foot snowdrifts, subzero temperatures, 100-plus temperatures, constant pain, and torturous blisters. On the home front, I faced the challenge of finding sponsors to donate funds for Sunshine.

Still, the support I had during my journey kept my spirits high. I never once considered quitting. Along the way, I received hundreds of letters and cards from the folks at Sunshine and from family and friends. Through postcards, letters, and the help of Sunshine volunteers, I was able to keep my brother, family, and friends involved with my walk.

I established a support team that I came to rely on for supplies and morale. My team was composed mostly of family and a few close friends. My team mailed my supplies to towns along the way, took care of my bills, mapped out my journey, and kept me focused on walking to Maine. My team was also instrumental in my fundraising efforts by writing newsletters to keep my sponsors informed.

I met hundreds of people along the way who inspired me to complete my journey. I shared my mission with everyone I met. I developed some lifelong friendships that I will cherish always.

I have shared my story with thousands of people. I have spoken to groups and given slideshows about my journey. I am excited to share my *Walk For Sunshine* with you. Not only are you about to read about my journey, but a portion of the money that you paid for this book will benefit the residents of Sunshine. Thank you!

J.A.

Chapter 1

Stepping Out

Walk 2,160 miles and live in the woods for six months?

I stepped onto the Appalachian Trail for the first time as a 14-year-old kid on summer vacation with my family in the Great Smoky Mountains National Park. I had never been to the park before, nor had I ever gone on an overnight hike. My family and I set up camp at one of the national park campgrounds, Elkmont, at the foot of Clingmans Dome. At 6,672 feet, it is the highest mountain in the Smokies. My two brothers and I decided to hike up the mountain, leaving behind our parents, a cooler full of food, and a comfortable camper. Obviously, we weren't thinking clearly. We didn't have the proper backcountry gear essential to hiking, so we headed up with our sleeping bags in trashcan liners along with some candy bars, canned food, and two-liter pop bottles filled with water.

We intended to stay in the Double Spring Gap Shelter along the Appalachian Trail, a makeshift shanty for overnight hikers located only a short distance from the summit. Halfway up the mountain, the three of us lay down along the trail, not wanting to go a step farther. A ranger came hiking down the trail from the summit and advised us to get off our duffs and scramble up the mountain if we wanted to make it to the shelter by nightfall. We all stood up and began hiking as fast as we could in fear of being exposed to the bear-infested forest without light or shelter. That ranger gave us the firecracker—the motivation—we needed, and we finally arrived at the shelter at dusk. The hike was the toughest thing I had ever done physically, and I still felt it in my muscles a week later. I was never so happy to be back with our parents and a cooler full of food the next day. We learned to appreciate all of the simple luxuries of life after just two days in the woods.

Of course, we didn't appreciate the historical significance of the Appalachian Trail on that first hike. We were just proud of our physical accomplishment and the bravery that carried us through the bear- and snake-infested wilderness. We were thankful to be alive. We didn't realize that we had spent the night in a shelter along one of the oldest, longest footpaths in North America.

I did not venture out on backcountry excursions again until I entered the U.S. Army years later, at age 18. If I had any pleasant memories of hiking in the backcountry, the Army was efficient in wiping those thoughts away. Forced marches wearing a poorly designed rucksack, 3 a.m. wake-up calls, digging defensive fighting positions, and verbal abuse pretty much eliminated any notions of hiking for pleasure.

Years passed before I went on a hike again. In college, I acquired some basic hiking equipment and returned to the Great Smoky Mountains for a hiking adventure. I was in better shape than my teenage encounter with hiking, and I had appropriate gear this time. I actually began to enjoy the rigorous endurance required for backpacking. Throughout college, I hiked frequently during school vacations and led several college groups on weeklong hikes in the Great Smoky Mountains.

The Great Smoky Mountains National Park became my mountain playground. If I wasn't visiting family during college breaks, I was hiking somewhere in the Smokies. The Appalachian Trail runs right through the Smokies and forms the state line between North Carolina and Tennessee.

My parents, who live in Florida, planned to meet me in the Smokies for Labor Day weekend in 1992. I asked my stepfather, Ron, if he would be interested in an overnight hike during the weekend, and he enthusiastically agreed to give it a try. After coordinating our supplies and gear, we hoisted backpacks that were outfitted with enough food and clothes to supply an army. We waved good-bye to our family and headed up the mountain to spend the night. The weather was pleasant, and the terrain was not very difficult. We reached our destination—the Spence Field Shelter—with plenty of daylight left. We had hiked eight miles in four hours. Some other hikers who also camped in the shelter informed my stepfather and I that we had just hiked one of the most rugged sections of the Appalachian Mountains. We sat around the fire into the dark hours that night sharing stories with other hikers. At some point during that inspirational weekend, my stepfather and I decided that we were going to hike the entire Appalachian Trail.

Everyone who decides to hike the AT does so for different reasons. I wanted to get back to a simpler life. I grew up in the computer age. These electronic wonders are supposed to simplify our lives, freeing our time and enhancing the quality of our life. Indeed, computers have simplified many tasks, making it easier to bank, shop, and write this book, but computers have not simplified our lifestyles. Americans work longer hours than we did 20 years ago. We spend less time with our families, and many folks are in a constant, fast-paced routine. Fast food has become the norm in many households, while home-cooked meals are a thing of the past. Road rage has become a national problem. Is there an end in sight for the overworked, fast-paced, demoralized, lack-of-family-time madness in which we live? Will the idea of having a weekend off eventually be something that kids read about in history books? What would it be like to step back in time to an era without cars? What would it be like to walk every day for five months with my only worries being food, shelter, and sleep, similar to our nomadic ancestors? All of these thoughts went through my mind on a daily basis after that second hike. I hoped to gain a better perspective on life and to enhance my quality of life. Walking the Appalachian Trail had become a necessary goal.

Ron and I definitely were not the first team to set a goal of walking the whole 2,000-plus-mile Appalachian Trail. Earl Shaffer was the very first person to walk from end to end in 1948, shortly after returning to the states after serving his country in World War II. If walking can ease post-traumatic stress disorder and the Appalachian Trail doesn't cure a person of it, I don't know what will. In the 1940s, people walked as a mode of transportation, but prior to Shaffer's hike, going the full 2,000-mile distance from Georgia to Maine was considered impossible, imprudent, and even crazy. But he did it. And he completed a second thru-hike in 1965. In 1998, the year I hiked the trail, Shaffer did another end-to-end-hike at age 79, marking the 50th anniversary of his first thru-hike. His third hike has inspired me to stay in shape so that I can hike the whole trail when I'm 80.

Since Earl Shaffer's first hike, several thousand hikers have completed end-to-end-hikes and have become what are known as thru-hikers. The adventure of living in the wilderness for six months has become attractive to more and more folks. Each year, between 2,000 and 3,000 hikers attempt to hike the entire Appalachian Trail. Only an estimated 10 percent actually complete the journey, but millions of hikers take day hikes and overnight hikes each year.

Saying that I was going to hike the Appalachian Trail and actually doing it were two different things. At the time of my hike with Ron, I was working as a food-sales consultant and preparing to leave my job to go back to school. I decided to make a goal of hiking the whole Appalachian Trail after I graduated from college and before I jumped back into the work force. At the same time, my stepfather decided that he would begin hiking the trail in short sections.

And so it went. I left my job to go back to college, and my stepfather systematically began hiking sections of the AT. I hiked with him during breaks. All through college, I read books about the trail, talked with people who had walked the entire trail, and tested out hiking equipment in preparation for my eventual thru-hike.

Chapter 2

Aaron

Living your dream is one thing, but sharing it lets everyone live it with you.

The window of opportunity to hike the entire Appalachian Trail had arrived. Five years had passed since I had made a personal commitment to walk the AT. I was at the end of a master's program in speech pathology. I had left a marketing career five years earlier to pursue a new chapter in my life. Most of my colleagues were interviewing for jobs, but not me. I felt that I wouldn't really "graduate" until I had completed my goal of walking from Georgia to Maine.

Often, I think of what my brother Aaron might have done with his life had he been dealt the physical and mental opportunities that I take for granted. Born with cerebral palsy and mental retardation, Aaron has been dependent on others for all of his daily needs, including eating, bathing, and using the bathroom.

As I began to prepare for my journey, I thought about the challenges that my brother and I faced—for me, walking 2,160 miles through rugged mountain terrain, or for him, not being able to live his dreams due to physical and mental disabilities. Aaron would never let on that he has had a rough life. He is always laughing and smiling as if he were up to something. He does not communicate verbally or with any adaptive devices, which leaves his thoughts, dreams, and aspirations a mystery to us. He might be living a better life than most of us by not facing the stresses of paying bills, taking tests, and accounting for himself. I've never known much about what goes on in Aaron's mind, but I did know this: Walking the AT would be a big challenge, but for me, it would be far easier than having to use a wheelchair.

I appreciate everything that Sunshine Inc. of Northwest Ohio has done for Aaron. My family admitted Aaron to Sunshine so that he could receive quality care. Aaron lived with my family until he was 12 years old. Every one of my siblings and parents cared for him. We changed his diapers, gave him baths, ground up his food for dinner and fed him, took him for walks, played with him, and took him on and off the school bus, but it wasn't enough. Aaron grew too big for us to lift without hurting ourselves. In addition, he often became sick and had to be hospitalized. We began to realize that Aaron was too much for our family to handle. His needs would be better served by an organization with the proper equipment and expertise.

Aaron first lived in a county-managed home. Shortly after Aaron moved in, the county began shutting down its services. My parents panicked. But then we heard about Sunshine, and the rest is history.

The home has lived up to this awesome task. My brother has lived at Sunshine for more than a decade. The home's committed, competent staff is willing to go the extra mile to make the residents and their families feel at home. I learned that a good measure of quality care is the bedsore-ratio among residents. Last I heard, Sunshine did not have any.

I wanted to dedicate my journey to Aaron out of love, but I also wanted to give back to the home for all that it has done for our family and for Aaron. So I decided to turn my dream of hiking the Appalachian Trail into a fundraiser for Sunshine.

The administration at Sunshine liked my idea. I contacted the home's director of development. He shared my idea with the board of directors, staff, and residents of Sunshine, all of whom overwhelmingly supported my idea. I met with the director, and we set a goal of raising $10,000 to purchase some much-needed adaptive equipment, such as communication devices, lifts, and walkers.

I kicked off the fundraiser in September 1997, during my last semester in graduate school. To begin, I contacted several organizations on campus and scheduled speaking engagements. I sent out press releases to my college, Miami University, and to local newspapers. I would not begin my hike until March 1998, which gave me several months to plan my journey and to raise funds.

I began planning for my hike at the same time that I kicked off the fundraiser. I submitted requests to manufacturers for specific hiking gear. I knew what types and brands of equipment that I needed for my expedition from five years of field-testing gear during college breaks.

I requested a 7,000-cubic-inch internal frame backpack, two pairs of mountaineer boots, a six-month supply of energy bars, two sleeping bags with different climate ratings (0-degree and 20-degree), a backpacker's tent, synthetic clothing, a Swiss army knife, trekking poles, and a one-burner stove. The manufacturers donated 90 percent of the gear that I had requested.

My next task was planning my menu for six months. I didn't know what I was going to eat tomorrow, which made planning 150 days' worth of meals seem impossible. I decided to create ten meals that I liked and use the same ten in every box. I visited the same grocery store every day for a month. I would fill two carts at a time. The grocery store employees must have thought that I was stocking a fallout shelter.

My mom had given me a food dehydrator for Christmas several years before. She had seen it on an infomercial and thought of me. I never really thought that I would actually use it. But when I began preparing my food, I found the prepackaged meals for backpackers to be as costly as eating in a restaurant. So I decided to dehydrate grocery store food, including fresh fruits and vegetables. I found that a dehydrator preserves nutrients in fruits and vegetables but removes the moisture, making the food light and easy to carry. Five months before my expedition, I began preparing my dehydrated food, and, needless to say, my clothing always reeked of whatever vegetable I was drying.

I was planning to have twenty-some boxes sent to me along the way. I needed to decide where to send each box. The Appalachian Trail Conference puts out the excellent *Workbook For Planning Thru-Hikes*, which I used to plan my supply points. I spaced my supplies about 100 miles apart to post offices all along the trail. Post offices along the AT have grown accustomed to thru-hikers using the U.S. mail for logistics. The post offices will hold packages for hikers.

I lured my good friend and future wife, Beth, into driving with me to Florida, where my mom and stepfather live. I explained to her that we would be setting up supply boxes for my parents to send to me along the trail. She didn't quite register what I was saying. Beth packed her bathing suit in anticipation of a week of fun in the sun. We ended up spending eight hours a day packing my supply boxes during six of the seven days that we were in Florida. To prevent mutiny, I took a day off from packing boxes and took Beth to the beach. I still cannot believe she married me after her Florida vacation boot camp.

The last few months before embarking on my hike were jam-packed. Between fundraising efforts and packing, I was training for the physical rigors of hauling a 50-pound pack up and down rugged mountains. Because there are no mountains near Toledo, I utilized a treadmill at Gold's Gym to simulate steep mountain inclines. I filled my backpack with 50 pounds of sand, raised the treadmill to its highest level, and walked on it for two hours every day. Many people stared at me while I was walking on the treadmill with my pack. I did look a bit odd. But after I explained why I was training to a few of the curious folks, they agreed that my training was a smart idea.

My three years of experience as a marketing and sales consultant gave me a pretty good idea about how to get attention and ask for money. I carried my 50-pound backpack to every presentation. Student Senate, the Office of Residence Life, the speech and hearing department where I studied, and Greek affairs all heard my presentation. My pack stood out like a sore thumb. It was fire-engine red, which drew the necessary attention. I first would explain what I was raising funds for and why. I played a short video reviewing the mission of Sunshine and showed a few slides about the Appalachian Trail. Then I would ask for financial support. In exchange, all sponsors would receive a newsletter three times during my trek. Sponsors who pledged more than $100 would be recognized in the newsletter. Every presentation ended with questions about the trail:

"Are you going to carry a gun?"

"No!"

"How much does your pack weigh?"

"Fifty pounds. Here, try it on."

"Where will you sleep?"

"In my tent and in shelters."

"Why walk all that way?"

"I don't know, but I hope I have fun getting there."

I presented my idea all over campus. Everyone I spoke with supported my fund-raising idea. The Student Senate set up a table in every dining hall on campus to collect money. Most residence halls gave donations, and the student speech and hearing association held a pizza drive. When I graduated in December 1997, I had already raised $2,300. After the holiday season, I planned to resume fundraising back in Toledo, Ohio, which was my hometown and Sunshine's.

Walking alone from Georgia to Maine might seem like an individual effort, but a team of individuals helped make the charity and journey a success. I formed a "Walk for Sunshine" team to assist with my journey and the fundraiser. My mom and stepfather agreed to mail my maps and supplies to towns along the trail; my father and stepmother, Sue, agreed to open my mail and stay on top of my bills while I was away; my sister, Stephanie, agreed to submit press releases and update my web page; my Aunt Ellen agreed to publish a newsletter to keep sponsors informed of my progress; the Sunshine development department agreed to track funds, mail thank-you notes, and create a "Walk With Sunshine" website; and I committed myself to speaking to service organizations and walking that incredible distance. My team was extremely efficient and would prove to be beneficial every day of my walk along the trail. It was nice that Aaron's disabilities had helped my family come together to help take care of him as a young child, and now my walk had again brought together family and friends as a team to support Aaron.

In the months before my walk, I spent a few hours daily calling local businesses asking for their financial support. Sunshine Inc. had scheduled speaking engagements as an opportunity for me to present my plan. I spoke with the local Rotary and Kiwanis chapters. My aunt, a Rotarian, arranged for me to speak at the east Toledo Rotary. I spoke at a chamber of commerce brunch. Media would call and schedule interviews. I spent every waking hour promoting, training, and planning.

My fundraising efforts were paying off, but I had not accomplished my financial goal before starting on my journey. I had raised $7,000, which was $3,000 shy of my goal. Before I left, *The Toledo Blade* and several suburban newspapers printed stories about my walk. I had spoken to several civic organizations, done interviews with various radio stations, and filmed a news episode with a local network that would air the day that I began my journey. Finally, the day arrived to head out. On February 27, 1998, my dad and Sue drove me from Toledo to Georgia, where we were meeting my mom and Ron, along with my brother Larry and his wife. Everyone had planned to see me off on my journey.

On my way out of town to begin my expedition, I spoke to a morning radio show by cell phone while traveling down the interstate. I was so excited that I don't remember much of what we discussed. This was it! My active fundraising efforts were over. Now all I had to do was fulfill my commitment—and live my dream.

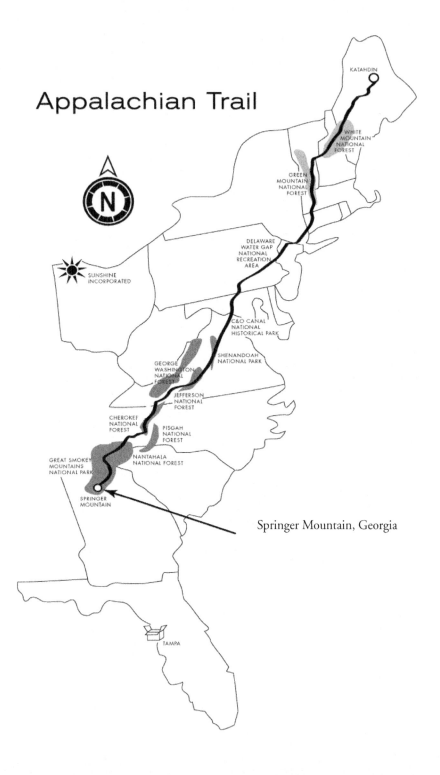

Appalachian Trail

KATAHDIN

WHITE
MOUNTAIN
NATIONAL
FOREST

GREEN
MOUNTAIN
NATIONAL
FOREST

DELAWARE
WATER GAP
NATIONAL
RECREATION
AREA

SUNSHINE
INCORPORATED

C&O CANAL
NATIONAL
HISTORICAL PARK

SHENANDOAH
NATIONAL PARK

GEORGE
WASHINGTON
NATIONAL
FOREST

JEFFERSON
NATIONAL
FOREST

CHEROKEE
NATIONAL
FOREST

PISGAH
NATIONAL
FOREST

GREAT SMOKEY
MOUNTAINS
NATIONAL PARK

NANTAHALA
NATIONAL FOREST

SPRINGER
MOUNTAIN

Springer Mountain, Georgia

TAMPA

Chapter 3

Only 2,159 Miles to Go

One mile from Springer Mountain, Georgia. March 1, 1998.

My family drove me from Toledo down to Amicalola Falls State Park, Georgia, the southern terminus of the Appalachian Trail. We spent the weekend there together before my departure. Earlier in the day, I had driven with Ron and my mom to the Walasi-Yi Center, an outfitter store 30 miles north of Amicalola Falls. We delivered my first re-supply of provisions. While dropping off my package, Ron, being the curious hiker that he is, struck up a conversation with some hikers at a picnic table outside the outfitter store.

The Appalachian Trail not only passes by this outfitter, but it goes right through the building, easily attracting hikers as they pass by to take a break. Two of the hikers had completed the AT in 1997. Their trail names were 180 and Rock Dancer. They were upbeat and had just completed a three-day hike from Amicalola Falls to the Walasi-Yi Center. Ron mentioned that I was to begin my thru-hike the following day. They began asking me questions, and they seemed to like my fund-raiser idea. As we talked, we discovered that we had a mutual friend, Broken Arrow, who hiked the AT in '97. Broken Arrow's parents lived in Oxford, Ohio, which is the location of my alma mater. An article about my hike in the *Oxford Press* caught the attention of Broken Arrow's parents. Broken Arrow had just finished her thru-hike and was visiting her parents. She became a great resource about hiking gear as I prepared for my journey.

Two other hikers, a middle-aged man and woman, were also sitting at the picnic table outside the Walasi-Yi Center. They decided to hike the entire AT for their honeymoon. Their hiking gear was dumped out on the picnic table, and they were trying to decide what items to eliminate in order to reduce their pack weight. I couldn't believe what they had decided to eliminate. They reduced their gear down to one sleeping bag. Now, I know that a honeymoon is supposed to be romantic, but two people in a one-person sleeping bag every night for six months? Especially considering the funk that you acquire in a day's walk, let alone a week at a time without a shower? No, thanks. After my encounter with the honeymooners, I began a mental inventory of everything in my backpack. What could I remove before I even started the hike? As Ron, Mom, and I drove back to Amicalola Falls State Park and the lodge where I would spend one last night with family before heading north, I considered various items that I could eliminate from my pack.

As we entered the park, I saw a ranger station with a sign in the window that read "Hiker Information." We stopped and went in. Standing in front of the ranger desk, I noticed a group of ten or so visitors of various ages and sizes who were standing outside of a glass wall adjacent to the souvenir shop. They all were looking up at a meat hook with a backpack hanging on it. The ranger saw my puzzled expression, grinned, and said, "Those are AT thru-hikers weighing their packs." Upon hearing this, I ran out to the car and grabbed mine. When I slung my pack up onto the hook, the scale needle rounded to 56 pounds. *Oh, no,* I thought. *That's more weight than I planned on.* I didn't even have water in my pack yet.

Less than a quarter-mile walk south from the lodge was a gorgeous overlook of the highest waterfall—Amicalola Falls—east of the Mississippi River. My family walked down to the waterfall after dinner that night. As I watched the water cascade down the mountainside, I couldn't help but wonder how many waterfalls I would see during my walk from Georgia to Maine. When we returned, my family sat in the lodge discussing the adventure that would begin the next day. The lodge was fairly new, in the style of a ski-resort chalet. The rooms opened into a central hall that led to a balcony overlooking a four-story, A-frame lobby. The structure itself was built of rock, mortar, and wood, which added a backwoods feel.

My family and I began considering possible trail names for me. Most thru-hikers get a trail name as part of the culture, just as boaters name their boats. This name will define your image among the thousands of hikers who will come to know you or know of you. I learned a good lesson that night. I will never again let my family help out with a trail name. The fate of my mystical thru-hike character was being decided by loved ones who were suggesting names like "Breaks Wind," "Stinky Man," and "Hyper Boy." I decided to postpone my trail name decision until I had actually embarked on the trail.

I went through my pack one last time, removing two pairs of socks to try to reduce the pack weight. It worked a little—by a mere five ounces. We all finally got to sleep about 11 p.m.

I hardly slept that night. This was it. I really was going to do this. OK, so I was a little nervous. All right, I was downright scared. I had hiked plenty of times before, but I had always hiked with someone else. This time I would be solo, by myself for 2,160 miles.

We were up at 6 a.m. We packed up, loaded the vehicles, and went down to the lodge restaurant for an all-you-can-eat breakfast buffet. After breakfast, I started giving and receiving hugs, kisses, and final words of motivation. The waitress said my meal was on the house since I was a thru-hiker, even though I had not yet set foot on the trail.

The guys were going to drive me up to the trailhead and hike the first mile to the sign initiating my hike, Springer Mountain. An 8-mile, near-vertical approach trail ascends from the lodge up to Springer Mountain, but it is not considered part of the Appalachian Trail. Driving to within one mile of the start did not sound like a bad idea, considering that 2,160 difficult miles lay ahead.

After about 45 minutes on a twisting, turning, gravelly road, we arrived at a stone parking lot. We all got out, and although we were going to come back to the truck, I insisted on wearing my pack that first mile up to the official starting point, which was south of the parking lot. Twenty minutes later, we came out to a little clearing. An iron plate bolted to a large boulder announced Springer Mountain. We took some pictures, and I signed the register located below the boulder in a metal container. It was a clear, sunny day, about 50 degrees. I sat down on the boulder, and from that rock I could see for almost 50 miles across the mountains. The excitement overwhelmed me, and I envisioned myself on the other side of those mountains. It was time to see my family off, so we hiked back down to the parking lot, where I fussed with my pack and posed for a few more pictures. My father, stepfather, and brother waved their final goodbyes as I took my first official steps. I walked into the tree line on the Appalachian Trail, turned, gave a final wave, and yelled, "Only 2,159 more miles to go!"

My journey had begun.

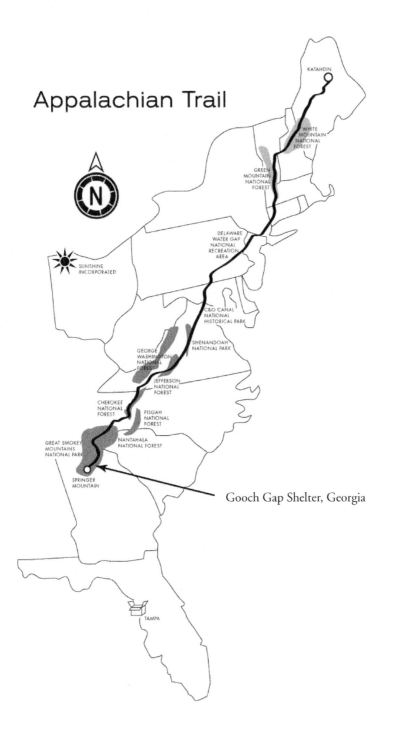

Appalachian Trail

KATAHDIN

WHITE MOUNTAIN NATIONAL FOREST

GREEN MOUNTAIN NATIONAL FOREST

DELAWARE WATER GAP NATIONAL RECREATION AREA

SUNSHINE INCORPORATED

C&O CANAL NATIONAL HISTORICAL PARK

SHENANDOAH NATIONAL PARK

GEORGE WASHINGTON NATIONAL FOREST

JEFFERSON NATIONAL FOREST

CHEROKEE NATIONAL FOREST

PISGAH NATIONAL FOREST

NANTAHALA NATIONAL FOREST

GREAT SMOKEY MOUNTAINS NATIONAL PARK

SPRINGER MOUNTAIN

Gooch Gap Shelter, Georgia

TAMPA

Chapter 4

Wrongfoot!

Gooch Gap Shelter, Georgia. March 1, 1998. 16 miles From Springer Mountain, Georgia.

The forest still had a ghostly winter appearance despite the upcoming spring, but the pines and rhododendrons provided some greenery. There I was, trekking my first miles on a solo thru-hike in the great outdoors. I didn't actively try to find a hiking partner. Early on, I had asked several of my close friends to join me, knowing full well that they would decline with some excuse about raising their children, paying the bills, or having already used their vacation time. Besides, I figured that hiking alone would force me to meet some new people. These first few miles seemed weird. I kept running into other hikers also beginning their journeys, but I had so much adrenaline going from all the pre-walk hype that I was lost in my own little world.

The Appalachian Trail is well-marked with painted white blazes on trees, rocks, or whatever is along the trail. I was carrying a map, data book, and portions of *The Thru-Hiker's Handbook*. The map had a topographical and profile view of the AT and was a great reference to preview the upcoming terrain. The mountains in Georgia have a reputation for being rugged. In fact, the terrain I was traversing has been used by the U.S. Army Rangers for mountain training. The profile view of the AT in Georgia resembled a heart-monitor machine attached to a fast-beating heart. There were no flat spots; it was either up or down for the next 80 miles. The data book provided mileage information about water, shelters, and towns. *The Thru-Hiker's Handbook* is the AAA of the AT. This book is a yearly publication that offers tips on recommended supply points, restaurants, hotels, hostels, laundromats, and water sources. My stepfather had photocopied the pages I needed for each section of trail so that I wouldn't have to carry the whole book.

The first few miles seemed to breeze right by. I had not really set a mileage goal yet. I knew there was a shelter eight miles from the road where my family had left me. By noon, I was beginning to feel the weight of my 55-pound pack, and my feet were giving me all the symptoms of newly formed blisters. I decided to stop for lunch at a waterfall. After snacking on some peanut butter and crackers, I took off my boots and socks. Sure enough, I had red hot spots on my upper heels and toes. From my pack, I removed some moleskin, which is a bandage-like adhesive that is supposed to remove the friction from your feet. I couldn't believe that I had blisters. I had worn these boots for three months on a treadmill with my pack. I had walked all over campus in them for a month. I was completely bewildered as to why I was blistering after only five miles.

After putting my socks and boots on, I hiked northward, but not as the crow flies. The trail wound up and down mountains. About two hours had passed before I came upon Hawk Mountain Shelter, offering lodging for up to six hikers. Shelters along the trail have three walls with no front wall, supposedly to allow hikers to fully experience the great outdoors. Most shelters are near a stream, lake, or river, and they have a designated privy. Eleven hikers were already staking out space in and around the shelter. I stopped and took a break.

Other folks who, like me, had fallen victim to the obsession of walking 2,000-plus miles to Maine soon began introducing themselves with their newly acquired trail names. Everybody was very friendly, and I decided to sit for a spell. I immediately removed my boots, only to find several new blisters on my toes, heels, and even the sides of my feet. I applied the rest of my moleskin supply and grew more concerned as to why my feet were turning into hamburger after only eight miles. While I was doctoring my feet, I noticed one man's voice dominating every conversation. One of the hikers next to me whispered, "This guy has been real annoying, offering everyone unwanted advice on how to hike from Georgia to Maine." There is an unwritten motto on the trail: *Hike your own hike.* This guy apparently did not understand that. His trail name was Burp. Apparently, Burp had set out on the trail yearly for the last several years. He didn't actually walk the whole trail. He just migrated along by hitching car rides, hiking small pieces until coming to a road and sticking the old thumb out. His physique made it quite obvious that he had not really hiked the trail any time lately. He stood about 6 feet tall and weighed at least 250 pounds.

Burp was criticizing everyone's gear, pointing out why the gear would not hold up. I felt his eyes stare down at me. *Oh great,* I thought, *now he's going to grill me.* He walked over to where I was seated on the edge of the shelter platform. He noticed my blisters and began to explain that I had the wrong boots for this kind of trail. Actually, the boots I was wearing were designed for extreme hiking and were rated by several sources as the boot of choice for the Appalachian Trail. I kindly invited him to research a product before criticizing it.

Burp then diverted his focus on the whole group of annoyed thru-hikers. He began to speak in a scolding fashion, waving his index finger in the air. "Hikers should leave mice alone," he said. "Mice are the lowest species on the food chain." You see, shelters are havens for field mice because they're attracted by the wide assortment of food that hikers carry into the woods. Hikers have to go through an elaborate procedure of hanging their food in a bag from the ceiling joists of shelters with a tin can tied to a rope. The mice cannot get beyond the can, so the food is safe, but the little critters are still annoying when they come out at night. Sometimes they can be so bold as to run right over your forehead in route to the buffet. There have been some deaths in the U.S. from the Hantavirus, which is a deadly airborne bacteria contracted from mouse feces. The last thing on my mind was a little mouse, and I did not want my mind polluted with this obnoxious man's opinions of how I should conduct myself for the next several months.

I looked at my watch. It was only 2 p.m. The map showed ten more miles to the next shelter, Gooch Gap. In spite of my blisters, I decided to press on. I figured nothing would be more memorable than the first night on the trail, and I wanted to keep Burp's opinions from entering the experience. I said goodbye to everyone, wished them luck on their journeys, and marched off, thinking to myself of some mouse stew recipes to write in trail journals along the way for Burp to relish.

The blisters were not subsiding. Three miles north of the shelter, the pain had overcome my anxiety about the first day on the trail. I was frustrated. I thought that there was no way I could walk all the way to

Maine with this blister issue. I took my pack off and sat down on it, removing my boots.

Since I was out of moleskin, I unraveled some duct tape secured to my water bottle and applied it to each new blister. I was ready to throw my boots down the mountain! I decided to take out the arch supports. As I pulled one support out of the left boot, I noticed that it was marked "right." Oh, no! In my excitement to begin hiking, I had put my arch supports into the wrong boots. Sure enough, the next few miles were more forgiving on my feet. Unfortunately, the damage was already done. Blisters take a long time to heal, and these would require constant doctoring. As I trudged along, I realized that I now knew my trail name: Wrongfoot.

***

Due to my shredded feet, I was moving at a slower rate than I had been earlier in the day. At 5 p.m., it started to get dark. I stopped for a snack and to look at the map. I had hiked only five of the ten miles to the next shelter, underestimating the terrain in Georgia. I had five more miles to go and only about 30 or 40 minutes of daylight. I wasn't going to make it to the shelter before dark. I pulled my light out of my pack. My light is a headlamp similar to those that miners use. I fixed it on my head so that when daylight ran out, I could travel by light.

One concern that I had was the large population of boars that lived in the southern Appalachian Mountains. Boars were brought to America from Thailand to hunt for sport in the early part of the 20th century. They originally were herded on gaming reservations, but over the years many escaped the hunters and adapted to the Appalachian environment. They have become overpopulated in recent years. Rangers hunt them regularly in the Smoky Mountains National Park because the boars tear up the hiking trails in search of food. I'm surprised Burp didn't speak up for the protection of boars. Boars travel in packs, sleeping during the day and becoming active at night. They have tusks that they use primarily to dig up the ground in search of insects, but these wild pigs have a history of attacking humans as well. They are stupid animals, and when they encounter people, they scatter in all directions. If you are in the path of one of them running, you could get gored.

So there I was, all alone, hiking in the dark with nothing to defend myself from boars or anything else except for two hiking poles. For two hours without incident, I trekked alone in the dark before stumbling onto Gooch Gap Shelter. What a wonderful feeling it was to end my hike knowing that I could finally give my feet a rest. Several hikers were in the shelter, already in their sleeping bags. I announced myself and asked if there was some space for me. Everyone rolled over, allowing me space to lay out my sleeping bag.

Without wasting time, I picked up my pan and walked down a path marked by painted blue streaks on trees to a little stream. With my flashlight illuminated, I filled my pan with water and brought it back up to the shelter. Next, I got out my stove and dug through my backpack for my food bag. I was so hungry that I ate two candy bars waiting for my dinner to cook. I boiled some water and made macaroni and cheese. I ate the entire four-serving portion in about two minutes. I decided that I would wait until morning to clean my dish. I hung my food from a rope tied to a ceiling rafter to keep the mice away and climbed into my sleeping bag. As I lay there, I began to realize that the temperature had dropped from 60 degrees during the day to the mid-30s. My feet were still pounding from my arch support mistake, combined with walking 16 miles the first day on the trail. What was I thinking? Wrongfoot, indeed!

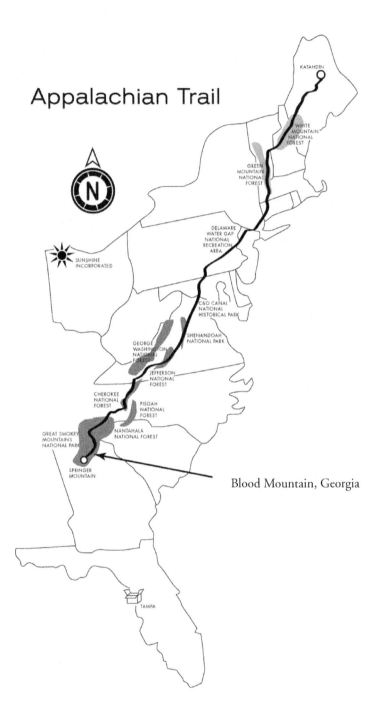

Appalachian Trail

KATAHDIN

WHITE MOUNTAIN NATIONAL FOREST

GREEN MOUNTAIN NATIONAL FOREST

N

SUNSHINE INCORPORATED

DELAWARE WATER GAP NATIONAL RECREATION AREA

C&O CANAL NATIONAL HISTORICAL PARK

SHENANDOAH NATIONAL PARK

GEORGE WASHINGTON NATIONAL FOREST

JEFFERSON NATIONAL FOREST

CHEROKEE NATIONAL FOREST

PISGAH NATIONAL FOREST

NANTAHALA NATIONAL FOREST

GREAT SMOKEY MOUNTAINS NATIONAL PARK

SPRINGER MOUNTAIN

Blood Mountain, Georgia

TAMPA

Chapter 5

Strange Bedfellows

Blood Mountain, Georgia. March 2, 1998. 28 miles from Springer Mountain, Georgia.

At sunrise the next morning, everyone immediately started moving about, and I could finally see the faces of the folks I had intruded on the night before. No one looked like an ax murderer, but then, what does an ax murderer look like? The group consisted of a retired minister and his wife (the Spoons), a retired gentlemen (Bevo), a college student between career/academic paths (Magaroni), and a man of about 50 (Packrat). It turned out that he was attempting a thru-hike for the fourth time and was not retired and hadn't taken a sabbatical from work. He had just plain quit his job in order to hike.

Everyone had assembled their gear into packs before I finished making coffee. I was moving slowly, and every step I took resulted in jolting pain from my blisters. Everyone said goodbye and good luck and was on the trail by 8 a.m.

My feet were pathetic. I sat there on my sleeping bag staring down at the most important asset for a hiker. My dogs were covered in square bits of flesh-colored moleskin and strips of duct tape. It looked like I had walked through a pile of confetti with glue on my feet. I squeezed painfully into my boots. My backpack was leaning against the side shelter wall, so I sat down on the shelter platform, leaned back, and slipped my arms through the pack straps. I stood up and immediately thought, *It's going to be a long day*. I trudged on. The temperature remained low, never breaking 40 degrees. I moved along all day, winding through the Chattahoochee National Forest, going up and down Georgia's finest mountains. By mid-afternoon, I arrived at a gap in the mountains called Miller Gap. Looking at the map unfolded on my lap, the profile showed a continuous five-mile climb straight up Blood Mountain, the highest peak of the AT in Georgia. This mountain was named after an Indian battle between the Cherokee and the Creek Indians. Supposedly, the battle was so fierce that blood dripped down the mountain.

I began my ascent after energizing myself with a candy bar. Every step challenged my balance. I felt like a roller-coaster car slowly approaching the top of the biggest hill, catching each chain link as I progressed closer to the top. As I approached the summit, it began to snow. The temperature had dropped significantly. Just the day before, it had been 60 degrees and sunny. The thermometer attached to my pack read 20 degrees, and when I stopped to take a drink, I noticed slush forming in my water. I was concerned. The profile map gave poor indication of how much farther I had to go in order to reach the shelter. I could stop and pitch my tent if the weather became severe, but there would be no water supply. Eventually, I summited Blood Mountain, which is a respectable 4,460 feet above sea level. The trail led smack into a four-walled gray stone shelter on the summit. Given the declining weather and a tough 12-mile day with raw feet, I decided to stop there for the night.

I stepped into the shelter and found one of the men that stayed with me the night before. His trail name was Bevo, and he was a Texan. Bevo is the name of the mascot of the University of Texas. The shelter had window cutouts but no panes of glass or shutters. The wind had picked up and was blowing snow into the shelter, which had begun to drift onto the sleeping platform. Bevo and I took the plastic ground cloths from our tents and some duct tape and secured it to the southern window, but the tape kept coming off. We collected some rocks from outside the shelter and used them as weights to hold the plastic. We then cut some slits in the plastic so that it wouldn't tear in the strong wind. I laid out my sleeping bag, put on all of my winter gear, and began cooking dinner. Since I was no longer walking and carrying a pack, my body got cold quickly. After dinner, I walked outside to answer nature's call and noticed that I could see the lights of Atlanta. It was too cold to appreciate the view, so I ran back into the shelter. As soon as I could, I climbed into my sleeping bag, pulled out my headlamp and some paper, and began writing in my journal: *March 2: 12 miles today, feet are hamburger. The temperature is around 20 degrees. The year of "El Nino" is not giving me the warm weather everyone predicted. Hopefully better weather tomorrow.*

Heading into Neels Gap for my first resupply.

I turned off my headlamp and burrowed deep into my sleeping bag to keep warm. In spite of the cold, I managed to doze off sometime later, only to be awakened by a heavy object moving across my feet and lower legs. I could hear my heart beating over the sound of an unknown creature moving around on top of my legs. Not knowing what to expect, I cautiously reached out, grabbed my flashlight, and turned it on. A skunk was lying on my sleeping bag! I cautiously nudged it with my foot, and it jumped off the platform, raising its tail. Great. The last thing I needed was a putrid scent on my gear and body, but the skunk didn't spray me. Instead, it ducked out of sight under the bunk platform, which was about eight inches off the ground.

I took out my candle and lit it. I figured the little critter would leave me alone, being afraid of flames. I was wrong. Twenty minutes later, I felt the weight drop on my feet and legs again, I sat up, and there he was, sprawled out on my sleeping bag again. The candle had given him enough light to precisely place his body between my legs on my bag. I decided that he just wanted to keep warm and that he was going to stay there, so I lay back down. Believe it or not, I actually fell asleep with a skunk on my feet.

The next morning, the skunk was gone. He must have gotten up at first light and scurried back under the platform. I poured some water into my pan and fired up the stove. The temperature had remained below 20 degrees all night. I made some coffee with the hot water and ate a granola bar.

I only had a two-mile descent to Neels Gap, my first resupply point. I packed up my gear more quickly than I had done on the previous day. My feet still hurt, but the cold weather kept me moving fast in order to keep warm. I figured that the quicker that I moved down the trail, the quicker I would warm up.

Appalachian Trail

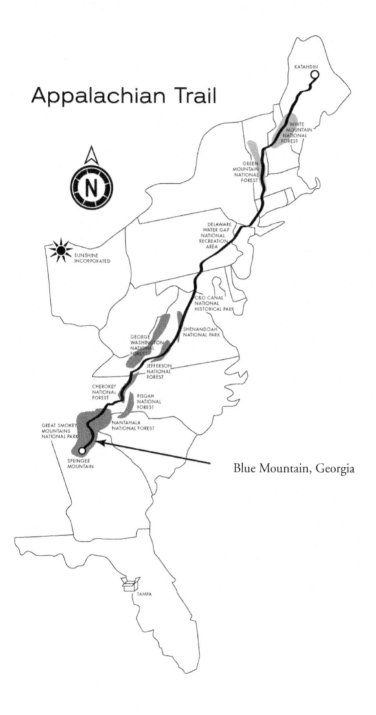

Blue Mountain, Georgia

Chapter 6

Lightening My Load

Neels Gap, Georgia. March 3, 1998. 30 miles from Springer Mountain, Georgia.

I descended Blood Mountain and arrived at the Walasi-Yi Center. The Appalachian Trail actually runs right through this rock building. The building is owned by the state, but a couple lease it for use as an outfitter store. They also provide a bunkhouse for hikers, but it was closed due to a problem with the plumbing. They did, however, have shower and laundry facilities.

This was the first supply point for me to receive food and provisions from my support team. I had planted this box of provisions in person with my mom and stepfather only five days ago, but it seemed much longer. The rest of my boxed provisions would be sent to post offices all along the way to Maine. This was my first opportunity to call home and update everyone on my progress and the events that had occurred so far. I wrote out a few postcards, making a brief mention of my painful foot error and my newfound trail name. I also included details of the night that I spent with the skunk. The outfitter had Ben & Jerry's ice cream, which I selected as my main entree for lunch, followed by a sandwich, a candy bar, and of course, coffee.

I spent the entire day there, taking a hot shower and doing laundry. On staff were two Appalachian Trail thru-hikers. They offered to look through my pack and provide suggestions for lightening my load. I brought my pack into the store. One of the thru-hikers had just finished hiking the 2,000-mile Pacific Crest Trail. He had also hiked the Appalachian Trail three years before, so I figured that he knew what he was talking about. He asked me to remove everything from my pack. After I did, he began separating my gear into two piles. I was getting nervous, wondering which pile he was going to recommend mailing home. After about 20 minutes he went in the back room and returned with a mini weight scale. Grinning, he placed one of the piles on the scale, which included my Walkman stereo. The scale needle tilted down to 4.5 pounds. I was shocked! One pound can make a big difference, but 4.5 pounds is equivalent to the weight of a hiker sleeping bag and stove, two of the heaviest items I carried. He said that I could do without everything sitting on the scale.

This guy had hiked more than 4,000 miles on two different mountain ranges, so I followed his advice. I took the empty box that had contained my re-supply provisions and plunked in my AM/FM stereo cassette player, an extra set of clothes, three pairs of socks, a can opener, and a spring-loaded candle lantern. I taped it closed, put my parents' address on it, and sent it home. I felt very comfortable taking advice from this guy as opposed to the mouse-loving loudmouth Burp. If I could do without these items for a week, then I wouldn't need them. I figured that if I wanted any gear back, I would have my parents mail it back to me. Yahoo! I was 4.5 pounds lighter.

I had spent most of the day at this outfitter store, something not hard to do considering that the temperature never reached above 20 degrees that day. Several other thru-hikers began dropping in by mid-afternoon. I began talking with four hikers who were planning to get a cabin for the night, and they asked me if I wanted to pitch in. I considered the idea and thought, *Why not?* I had spent most of the day at the outfitter already; it was cold, and I would get to spend some time with other hikers for the night.

There was one other item in my pack that I did not reveal to the gentleman at the outfitter store who had helped lighten my load. I had been carrying a plastic flask filled with whiskey in a sealed pouch of my backpack. I referred to it as my snakebite kit, but I no longer wanted to drink that rotgut. Growing up, I watched many John Wayne and Clint Eastwood movies, and in each there was always a scene with the tough guy drinking down a belt of gasoline, labeled "whiskey." Somehow my delusional thoughts had associated booze with the toughness of hiking. Now, come to think of it, I had never seen the Duke or Josey Wales throw on a backpack and head off into the woods for a few thousand miles. For that matter, they never veered far from their horses or the bar except for an occasional shoot-out. What had I been thinking? This was my opportunity to share the spirit of snakebite with the other hikers and to permanently lighten my load by another pound.

That night, we hunkered down in a rustic cabin warmed by an old electric heater that seemed to dry up any moisture left after the already very dry winter. The room became so arid that my tongue would occasionally stick to the roof of my mouth from lack of moisture. All of us had gathered around a kitchen table and were tinkering with our hiking gear. I pulled out the snakebite flask, spoke a few quotes from some Western movie bar scene, drank a belt down, and passed the flask to another sorry sucker. The flask emptied after being passed around the group two or three times. My mouth was now at least wet with whiskey. I pondered, *Should I never see these guys again, will they have that same vision of John Wayne or Clint Eastwood when they think of Wrongfoot?* Then I thought, *Who cares? My pack is a pound lighter!*

Appalachian Trail

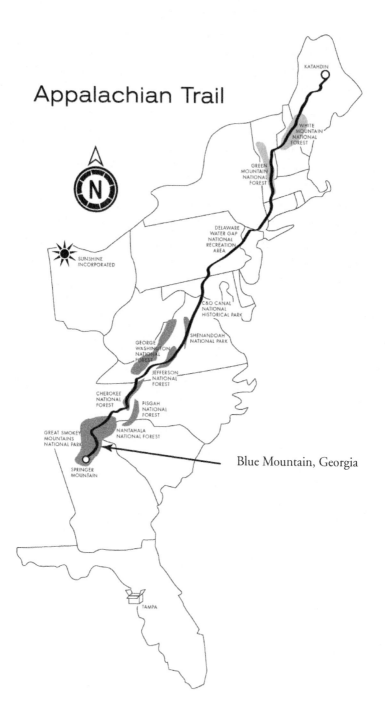

Blue Mountain, Georgia

Chapter 7

All Alone in the Woods

Blue Mountain, Georgia. March 4, 1998. 48 miles from Springer Mountain, Georgia.

The next morning, I awoke at first light. The other hikers in the cabin were still sleeping, probably from the late night and the shots of whiskey. As I quietly packed my gear, I wondered if I would ever see them again. The cabin owner pulled up out front in an old jeep to pick me up just as we had planned the night before. He drove me two miles down the road, back to the trail. I got out of the jeep in front of the Walasi-Yi Center outfitter, where I had left the trail the day before. The outfitter was still closed and would not be open for another hour. I felt refreshed after a good night's rest and with a lighter pack to carry, but the temperature remained in the 20s.

Slowly, I began my ascent out of Neels Gap. An inch of snow remained on the ground, and snow was falling from the sky as well. Every step I took left a boot imprint for the rest of the hikers to follow. My map showed an uphill climb of 1,400 feet in the first mile. As I stepped with one foot, I would strike my hiking pole of the opposite hand into the ground and push off, similar to using a railing when climbing a set of stairs. Ascending mountains in Georgia was like walking up a playground slide that seemed to last forever. Most of the trail that I had hiked in Georgia went straight up mountains without switchbacks. Switchbacks wind back and forth up mountains, making for a gradual climb to the top.

Within the first 10 minutes, I was wide awake from the early morning climb. Despite the low temperatures, hauling a 50-pound pack up and down the southern Appalachias resulted in me being constantly wet with perspiration. Cotton clothing is a major no-no in the backcountry. Cotton retains moisture and clings to your skin, and it can contribute to hypothermia, which can result in death. Hypothermia occurs when the body temperature decreases below 93.2° F. Early signs of hypothermia are confusion and nausea. In previous years, I had helped hikers who showed signs of hypothermia, so I knew the precautions to take. But hiking alone left me vulnerable if I needed medical attention. At one of my frequent rests, I removed my wind pants to cool off, leaving on a pair of shorts. I was wearing a synthetic hat, synthetic shirt, waterproof jacket, gloves, and shorts, but I was comfortable as long as I kept moving. Even when I stopped for just a minute, I would get cold in my sweat-laden clothes.

My feet still were very sore, a reminder of my first day on the trail. I had stocked up on extra moleskin to wrap them, but I had found that duct tape seemed to stick to my skin better. I had wrapped each entire foot in duct tape to eliminate friction on my blisters.

As the day wore on, the sun emerged and the snow let up. I felt warm as long as I kept moving. Around noon, I stopped for lunch in a valley at Low Gap and put my wind pants back on to keep warm while I sat still. I pulled out a jar of peanut butter and a Snickers bar, dipped the Snickers bar in the peanut butter, and took a bite. Wow! Not bad. I heard voices approaching. A group of eight came walking down the trail heading south. I had crossed a road a mile south and had seen some parked cars. The folks stopped and said hello. They were trail volunteers walking back to their cars after working on the trail all morning. The group of four couples was from the same church. Each person was holding a saw, shovel, or rake. I thanked them for clearing off the trail. They wished me luck and kept walking.

I started my hike alone, but I had yet to stay a night by myself. I walked a respectable 18 miles and arrived at the Blue Mountain Shelter around dusk. For the first time, I would be alone since beginning my hike. With that thought, I was happy and lonely at the same time. I rolled my sleeping bag onto the floor of the shelter and began to cook dinner. While I was waiting for the water to boil, it began to sleet. The wind blew the sleet into the three-walled shelter, leaving no place to stay dry. The roof was higher than in most shelters, and so it offered no overhang to block the sleet. In addition, the open side of the shelter faced south, overlooking a town below the mountain. It was a beautiful view, but with such a vista, there were no trees to block the wind. Not wanting to be cold and wet all night, I decided to set up my tent as protection from the elements. After getting into my tent, I lay there nervous about every noise outside of the nylon wall. My mind began to wander. With each noise I heard, I imagined a pack of wild boars gathering to stampede through my tent. Needless to say, these thoughts were not helping me to fall asleep.

Before leaving for my hike, I had received a free cellular telephone with unlimited airtime as a donation from a well-known cellular phone company. How could I refuse? What better tool to have in the backcountry for instant communication in case of emergencies, especially being on the trail alone? So, lying there alone, I turned on my phone. I found out later that the Appalachian Trail Conference frowns on the use of these high-tech communication devices because the cell companies are riddling the mountainsides with antenna towers. I have to agree that the towers take away from the aesthetic views, but I was out there alone and was not about to give up the opportunity of having unlimited free air time. In the meantime, this battery-operated device was doing a nice job of giving me a false sense of security. If a boar blasted through my tent, I could just call the nearest ranger station and have someone hike the 19 miles up to my camp to shoot the damn thing.

The phone rang. I was in shock, but I answered it. Some friends from Toledo had decided to call me and were just as shocked as I was that they actually were able to reach me in the middle of the woods.

"Where are you?" they asked.

"I'm on a mountain in the woods."

We chatted for a few minutes and signed off. I had mentioned in my first newsletter, which was sent out to all the sponsors, that I would have my phone turned on every Wednesday from 7 to 8 p.m. This was my first Wednesday on the trail, and sure enough, the darn thing worked!

Fund-raisers usually are held in communities, offering lots of advertising for the sponsors. A charity run, for instance, usually is held in or near a city or town. Big sponsors are recognized on T-shirts provided to all runners and walkers participating, and banners are posted at the beginning and end of the run. Raising money by hiking in the wilderness; however, changes the way sponsors are recognized for their contributions and involvement. I had mentioned all of my sponsors in a newsletter, which was being mailed to everyone involved. The cellular phone idea originated as an opportunity for my sponsors to have personal involvement by giving them a chance to call me and get an interactive low-down of life on the trail. If other hikers were camped out with me on Wednesdays, I planned on walking away from everyone so I would not disturb their escape from modern amenities. Most of the thru-hikers that I met, however, did not mind my cell phone. As a matter of fact, some of them realized the benefits of these devices and carried them as well. After my brief but welcome discussion with my Toledo friends, I fell asleep with the false sense of security provided by my phone in the woods.

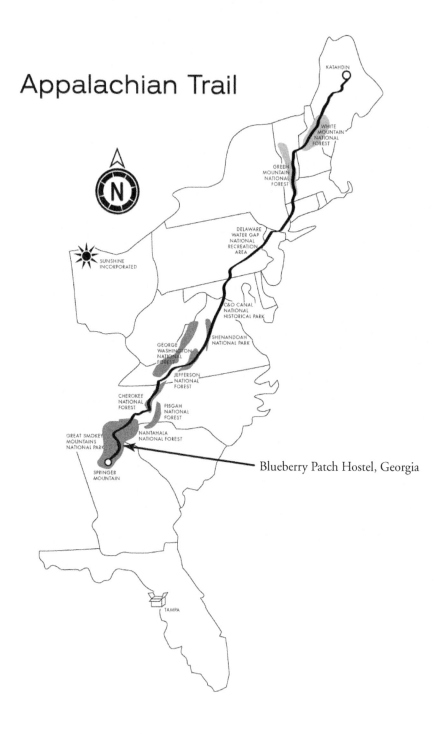

Appalachian Trail

KATAHDIN

WHITE
MOUNTAIN
NATIONAL
FOREST

GREEN
MOUNTAIN
NATIONAL
FOREST

DELAWARE
WATER GAP
NATIONAL
RECREATION
AREA

SUNSHINE
INCORPORATED

C&O CANAL
NATIONAL
HISTORICAL PARK

SHENANDOAH
NATIONAL PARK

GEORGE
WASHINGTON
NATIONAL
FOREST

JEFFERSON
NATIONAL
FOREST

CHEROKEE
NATIONAL
FOREST

PISGAH
NATIONAL
FOREST

GREAT SMOKEY
MOUNTAINS
NATIONAL PARK

NANTAHALA
NATIONAL FOREST

Blueberry Patch Hostel, Georgia

SPRINGER
MOUNTAIN

TAMPA

Chapter 8

Hitchhiking is for Hitchhikers!

Blueberry Patch Hostel, Georgia. March 5,1998. 67 miles from Springer Mountain, Georgia.

I woke up to a very crisp 20-degree morning. Sleet had fallen all through the night, and as I unzipped my tent, ice sheets broke off around my door. I fired up my stove for coffee and untied my food bag, which hung from the shelter cross beam. I was beginning to get into a morning ritual: light stove, fill pan with water, get food bag down from tree or cross beam, go to bathroom, brush teeth, wrap blisters with duct tape …

By 7 a.m., I had broken camp and was ready to head north. Most of the trail was beneath the canopy of the trees, so I could not see where I was going or where I had been. The maps were the only indication of progress. I hiked a steady pace all morning, achieving ten miles by noon. A constant sleet pelted my body. I took many short breaks instead of a few long ones so that my body temperature would remain high and keep me warm.

On one of these breaks, I sat on a log, ate lunch, and looked at maps. There was a shelter six miles north and a popular hostel nine miles north. At 4 p.m., I had reached the trailhead leading to the shelter. Hmmm. Only three extra miles to stay in a warm bunkhouse. Noting the chilly air and my wet, cold body, I decided that I deserved a little luxury since the weather was not what I had anticipated. So I kept moving north. I came out to a quiet highway—State Route 76, according to the map.

The Thru-Hiker's Handbook showed a hostel about three and a half miles down the road, but I was tired, and it was getting dark. I had hiked 19 miles already, my longest day yet on the trail, and I was afraid to find a full hostel after walking three additional miles down the road. I pulled out the cell phone and called the hostel keepers. A friendly man answered and said not to worry, that they had plenty of room. He told me that most hikers hitchhike down to his place. I said that I would give it a try and hung up. I felt a lump in my throat. I had never held out my thumb before except to let someone know that I was OK. All of my life, my parents had lectured about never picking up hitchhikers, and here I was about to hang the thumb out along the roadside.

After a few minutes, I heard a car motor approaching the top of the hill south of me. I could see its lights. I propped my pack against my legs put a smile on my face, and stuck out the thumb. Whoosh! A blue Chevy Caprice zipped right by. I sat down on my pack and waited. Five minutes later, I heard another vehicle approaching. The thumb went out; the smile went on, and whoosh! A pickup truck whizzed past. This went on for almost an hour, and it was completely dark by now. At least twenty cars and trucks had passed without pause. I even tried putting my baseball cap on to look more presentable and turned on my flashlight on so that drivers could see me. No one was going to pick me up if they couldn't even see me.

By now, I could have already walked to the hostel. I called Blueberry Patch and Gary, the owner, agreed to drive up and taxi me in for the night. Boy, was I grateful, but I think that I was even more grateful that I didn't have to actually hitch a ride.

After hiking a long, 19-mile day through the unforgiving mountains of Georgia in the sleeting rain, it felt good to know that I would be spending the night in a warm bunkhouse. Two days had passed since I had last visited comfortable accommodations, and I had hiked 37 miles in cold, wet weather. I had not anticipated the constant nasty weather, but I was determined to keep my spirits up in the early days of my hike by treating myself to a few luxuries.

Finally, a car approached from the direction of the hostel and pulled into the turnaround where I stood. The driver window came down and the friendly voice from the telephone shouted, "Hop in!" Five minutes later, we were pulling into a stone driveway and up to a building with a sign that read "Blueberry Patch." Many hikers to whom I had spoken raved about the accommodations offered here. The driver instructed me to drop my gear in the hostel and to bring all of my dirty laundry to the main house. He gave me a towel and directions to the shower house located behind the hostel in the blueberry field. I stepped into the bunkhouse.

Just inside the door, I immediately recognized two hikers with whom I had stayed in the shelter my first night on the trail—Packrat and Magaroni. A third hiker named Jeremy was also in the bunkhouse. Jeremy had not gotten farther than the first shelter on the trail when he developed flu symptoms. Jeremy had hitchhiked all the way to Blueberry Patch, 60 miles farther north, to rest and meet up with his group of friends. After chatting with the hikers for a few minutes, I began to warm up. The wood-burning stove was going full tilt.

The caretakers, Gary and Lenny, were a husband and wife who had hiked the entire Appalachian Trail in 1994. After I had showered, Gary and Lenny brought the homemade pizza and blueberry cheesecake that I had ordered when I arrived. They sat and chatted with us until I had finished my meal. They left the bunkhouse, and we thru-hikers continued to talk for another hour or so. We all agreed to hike out together in the morning. All of the bunks were fitted with straw-stuffed mattresses, and I must have fallen asleep as soon as I literally hit the hay. I was so tired that I had even forgotten to write in my journal.

The next morning, Gary hollered in the door that breakfast was ready in the main house. The four of us nearly got wedged in the doorway together with the excitement of eating a hot meal. Gary and Lenny served us an all-you-can-eat blueberry pancake breakfast with sausage, orange juice, and coffee.

After breakfast, we all piled into Gary's van and he drove us back to the trail, pulling into the turnaround where I had stood 12 hours earlier attempting to hitchhike. We thanked him for the awesome hospitality and shouldered our packs for our trek northward.

Appalachian Trail

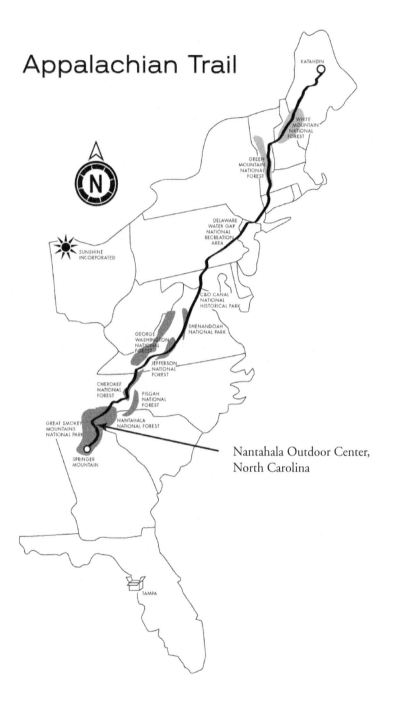

KATAHDIN

WHITE MOUNTAIN NATIONAL FOREST

GREEN MOUNTAIN NATIONAL FOREST

DELAWARE WATER GAP NATIONAL RECREATION AREA

SUNSHINE INCORPORATED

C&O CANAL NATIONAL HISTORICAL PARK

SHENANDOAH NATIONAL PARK

GEORGE WASHINGTON NATIONAL FOREST

JEFFERSON NATIONAL FOREST

CHEROKEE NATIONAL FOREST

PISGAH NATIONAL FOREST

GREAT SMOKEY MOUNTAINS NATIONAL PARK

NANTAHALA NATIONAL FOREST

Nantahala Outdoor Center, North Carolina

SPRINGER MOUNTAIN

TAMPA

Chapter 9

Some Make It, and Some Don't

Nantahala Outdoor Center, North Carolina. March 10, 1998. 134 miles from Springer Mountain, Georgia.

Shortly after leaving the road, Packrat, Jeremy, Magaroni, and I spread out at our own pace. Packrat and Jeremy were ahead of me, with Magaroni following. We marched up and down Georgia's most rough terrain. We were excited about crossing our first state line into North Carolina. For the first few hours, we were able to remain within visual and hearing range of each other. As the day wore on, a cold sleet began to fall, and the burst of energy from the blueberry pancake breakfast wore off. Jeremy was complaining about the rain, the wind, the inclines, and his aching knee. He had spent the past three nights at Blueberry Patch hoping to recover from the flu, and he already had skipped 40 miles of the trail. My gut feeling was that he would be the first thru-hiker I would see leave the trail.

The majority of hikers—85 percent to 90 percent, according to the Appalachian Trail Conservancy—who set out to complete the entire 2,160-mile journey quit before reaching the end. A mere 10 percent to 15 percent of the hikers—roughly 200 to 300—actually make it each year. Most hikers drop off in the first 500 miles. The rest trickle off all along the way. Some thru-hikers have quit as far as 2,000 miles into their journeys.

I wanted to be in the statistic of those who complete the AT. I had physically prepared for my hike. I had a well-planned supply route, a team to assist me, and a great cause to walk for. When I began the journey, I knew that it would be up to me to stay motivated. I needed to remain high-spirited and positive-minded if I was going to make it to the end of the trail at Mount Katahdin, Maine.

Just attempting a journey of this magnitude is an accomplishment, let alone going the full distance. Anyone who tries a thru-hike should be considered a hero for being bold enough and determined to give it a try.

Jeremy was a college student from Wyoming who had set out to hike the Appalachian Trail as an independent study project. I certainly hope it was worth more than one credit hour.

Magaroni was from Rhode Island. Prior to hiking the AT, he had worked in a hospital as a nurse's aide, and he now wore hospital scrubs as hiking clothing. Magaroni previously had hiked the Long Trail in Vermont, which covers almost 265 miles of craggy mountains. He was well prepared for the tough terrain of the AT. I put my money on Magaroni to be one of the 10 percent who make it to Maine.

Packrat could hike at an exceptional pace. He was 55 years old, with a marathon runner's build. Packrat had attempted to hike the whole trail four times, making this his fifth attempt. Each of his previous hikes had ended in Erwin, Tennessee, which is 340 miles north of Springer Mountain. Despite his appearance, perhaps Packrat was more of a sprinter than an endurance runner.

Packrat and I seemed to hold a comparable pace, and we soon had pulled quite a distance ahead of Jeremy and Magaroni. Just before noon, we summited a ridge. We were deciding if we should take a break to let the others catch up when Packrat hollered, "Hey Wrongfoot, we're in North Carolina!" A 4-by-12-inch wooden sign with engraved lettering that read "NC-GA" was nailed to a large oak tree. Yee-ha! Our first state crossing. Without much hesitation, I dropped my pack and put one foot in Georgia with my other foot in North Carolina. After going through this ritual, I took out my data book and realized I still had 2,083 more miles to go, with 12 more state crossings. I enjoyed my border crossing even more and decided that I must celebrate these little triumphs and treat them like milestones toward the ultimate goal of Mount Katahdin.

In the distance, Packrat and I could hear someone griping about not having any toilet paper. Sure enough, Jeremy appeared around a bend in the trail. I offered him some of my limited supply, but I was too late—he already resorted to using snow-covered rhododendron leaves. When Magaroni caught up, we looked at our trail maps and decided to call it a day at Muskrat Shelter a few miles ahead. We had hiked 12 miles through a constant, cold sleet. For the first time since beginning my journey six days ago, I had hiked an entire day with the same hikers.

Hiking with others had some advantages. Packrat seemed to know quite a bit about gear, and I was having some problems getting my pack to contour to my back. Carrying 50 pounds is inevitable on a journey like this, but I wanted to carry it as comfortably as I could. At the shelter, he took apart my pack and pulled out two metal bars called stays. I was a little nervous about being in the middle of the woods and looking down at what was essentially my house disassembled into 10 separate pieces. Packrat held the each stay up to my back and then walked over to a tree and bent it to the contour of my back. This went on for an hour as my pack slowly returned to one piece. When my pack was reassembled, a huge relief set in. It fit much better.

The next morning, everyone was awake at sunrise. We performed our respective morning routines and got onto the trail. It was only 25 degrees, and no one wanted to hang around after getting out of his warm sleeping bag. The sooner we started walking, the sooner we would warm up.

Over the next few days, Packrat and I pulled ahead of the others. We had entered the Nantahala National Forest, which recently had made national news. Eric Rudolph, the 1996 Olympic Park bombing suspect also wanted by federal authorities for several other bombings, was thought to be somewhere in the Nantahala National Forest. Every road we crossed showed a wanted poster offering a $1 million reward. The FBI was conducting the largest manhunt in history to apprehend the fugitive. We had heard rumors that government agents were questioning AT thru-hikers and were checking IDs.

I was glad to travel with others through this section just in case we encountered Rudolph. We all felt a sense of heightened concern for our personal safety. I decided that if I ran into Rudolph, I would pretend that I didn't know who he was and would befriend him. Then, while he was sipping on a cup of hot chocolate that I would prepare for him, I would spray him with pepper spray, duct tape him to a tree, and collect my million-dollar reward. I never ran into Rudolph, but having a crazy plan for how to capture him kept me from being preoccupied with the fear of actually running into him.

The weather was horrible. Temperatures stayed below freezing, and the sun had not appeared in several days. In my attempt to lighten my load, I had mailed home all but two pairs of socks, and I was regretting it. I had no dry socks left after two days of sleet and snow. Packrat suggested sleeping with my wet socks on at night, allowing my body heat to dry them. It worked, but it made my list of the most uncomfortable things that I have ever done. He also suggested putting my wet boots in my sleeping bag to prevent them from freezing during the night. I compromised and used my boots as a pillow—ouch! Just two weeks earlier, my car had taken me everywhere I needed to go, and now my feet and boots were the most important assets I had on the trail. I was determined to take care of them.

Six days had passed since my last supply point, and I still was miles from my next supply point, the Nantahala Outdoor Center (NOC). I left that morning from Siler Bald Shelter with Packrat. By lunch, we had traveled almost 12 miles. The temperature had not moved above 20 degrees. NOC boasted heated bunkhouses, a restaurant, and an outfitter store. I had been daydreaming about a big, hot meal and a warm bed. But what I really wanted were some extra socks. We decided to work hard for 12 more miles and make it to the NOC by nightfall. In all, we hiked 24 miles that day, my longest distance traveled up to that point. I had been walking in snow, sleet, and rain for eight days without a break.

By the end of the day, I was numb and seemed to be hiking in a trance, not even seeing what was going on around me. Without warning, we were heading down a very steep incline. The trail descended at a 45-degree angle for five miles. A natural momentum pushed me along. It was difficult to walk slowly. The weight of the pack made it difficult to keep from breaking into a run down the steep slope. At one point, when I rounded a bend in the trail, my intentions were to turn left with the trail, but my momentum carried me forward. I fell off the trail and landed on a rhododendron bush growing on the steep slope. Somehow, I managed to saddle a branch, which actually saved me from a plunge down the mountainside. I was stuck and looked quite ridiculous saddled up on a bush. Packrat helped me remove my pack and climb off the bush.

Dusk was upon us when I began to see lights ahead. The trail finally leveled off, and we emerged from the forest along a rural highway. Just across the road sat a complex. The trail continued across the road between the outfitter store and the restaurant and across a bridge over the Nantahala River. On the other side of the river, rows of bunkhouses with smoke swirling from the chimneys stoked our desire for a warm night out of the frigid weather. After paying an overnight fee, we dropped our gear in our room and made a beeline for the restaurant. We ate cheese sticks, a hearty casserole, and some ice cream for dessert. I fell asleep as soon as my head hit the pillow. Not having to worry about the cold was bliss.

The next morning, Packrat and I were standing in front of the outfitter shop, sipping some coffee and waiting for the store to open, when we saw Jeremy coming down the trail where it crosses the highway in front of the outfitter. He threw his pack down on the ground and hollered to us that we could have the food supply that was mailed to him here at NOC. He walked into the outfitter and arranged to get a shuttle to the bus station. I knew that he was going to quit, but watching him actually give up made me thankful that it wasn't me.

Note: Eric Rudolph, the Olympic Park Bomber, was caught in 2003 and is serving five consecutive life sentences.

Appalachian Trail

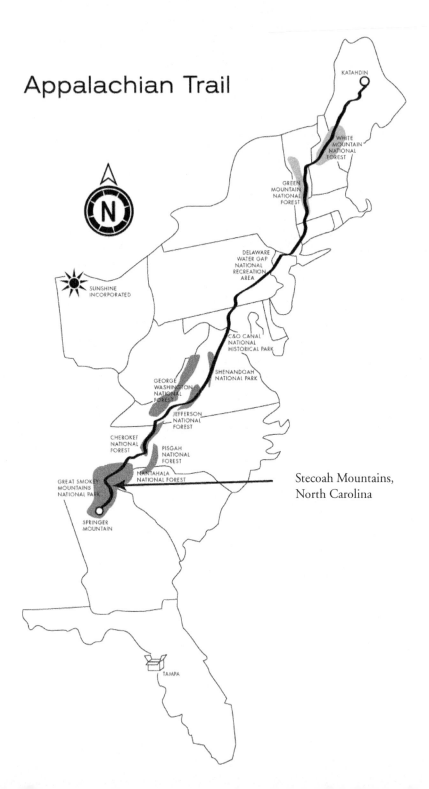

KATAHDIN

WHITE
MOUNTAIN
NATIONAL
FOREST

GREEN
MOUNTAIN
NATIONAL
FOREST

DELAWARE
WATER GAP
NATIONAL
RECREATION
AREA

N

SUNSHINE
INCORPORATED

C&O CANAL
NATIONAL
HISTORICAL PARK

SHENANDOAH
NATIONAL PARK

GEORGE
WASHINGTON
NATIONAL
FOREST

JEFFERSON
NATIONAL
FOREST

CHEROKEE
NATIONAL
FOREST

PISGAH
NATIONAL
FOREST

NANTAHALA
NATIONAL FOREST

GREAT SMOKEY
MOUNTAINS
NATIONAL PARK

Stecoah Mountains,
North Carolina

SPRINGER
MOUNTAIN

TAMPA

Chapter 10

I'm Still Alive

The Stecoah Mountains, North Carolina. March 12, 1998. 145 miles from Springer Mountain, Georgia.

With a full, supplied pack, I began my hike out of Wesser, North Carolina, from the Nantahala Outdoor Center. I had enjoyed a warm bunkhouse for two days, hoping that the weather would improve, but the forecast was calling for snow and sub-zero temperatures. An advisory was posted that warned hikers to avoid the backcountry unless they had "arctic gear." I already had packed the supplies mailed to me and sent postcards. I was so gung-ho to trek northward that I could not sit in a hostel for a third day. I decided to add some additional cold-weather gear: an extra ground mat, waterproof gloves, and a full-face mask. I also had purchased a few extra pairs of socks. I was heading into the Stecoah Mountain Range, which is considered the most severe terrain south of the White Mountains in New Hampshire. Wesser is located in a valley, so the AT could go in only one direction—up. The first seven miles out of Wesser was a consistent 3,000-foot climb. I had been hiking with Packrat since March 5. He, too, was stir-crazy in the hostel, so he chose to continue with me.

The sun was shining for the first half of the day, and it did not feel as cold as 20 degrees. As we ascended the Stecoahs, we would look back and watch the Nantahala Outdoor Center get smaller and smaller until we rounded the mountain, leaving behind the view of Wesser. About a mile north of Wesser, we crested our first of a series of ridges. Before us lay an awesome view of snow-capped mountains. The farthest mountain peak in view was Clingmans Dome, the highest along the entire trail. We soon would traverse the Clingman ridge. The next five days of travel would be amazing. The view was gorgeous, the snowy peaks sprinkled with green pines.

As long as we kept moving, we stayed warm. As we climbed, the trail became icier. Part way through the day, we were walking on a sheet of ice from melted snow run-off that had frozen solid. It was like trying to skate on an uphill ice rink with no skates. We stopped for a snack at Sassafras Gap Shelter, seven miles north of Wesser. Neither of us wanted to stop for the day because it was so cold, so we kept moving. After all, the sun was still shining. After refilling our water at the spring, we pressed on, intending to make it to the Brown Fork Gap Shelter another eight miles north. We left Sassafras Shelter about 12:30 p.m., and the snow began falling about a half-hour later. We had reached the ridge of the Stecoah Mountains, so the incline was not as drastic as the first part of the day, but our visibility was diminishing rapidly. The goal of reaching the next shelter became impossible. About three miles north of Sassafras Shelter, four inches of snow already had fallen, and we could not see ten feet ahead of us.

We stopped and put up our tents to get out of the elements. The temperature had fallen below zero. The wind was blowing dramatically and brought a biting wind-chill. Immediately after I took off my glove to assemble my tent, my fingers turned to Popsicles. I could barely move them at all, and they hurt. After getting the tents up, Packrat and I began the chore of cooking dinner. During the course of the day, our water had frozen solid, so we packed our pans with snow and melted it down. I cooked some macaroni and cheese and boiled more water for hot tea. I melted some additional snow, filled my water jug with it, and threw the jug in my sleeping bag to help keep me warm. It was only mid afternoon. It was so cold that we figured even the bears weren't moving about, so we didn't bother to hang our food bags high in a tree. Instead, we clipped our food to a bush next to our tents. We huddled in our tents for 15 hours. Every few hours, I would hit the roof to knock off the snow.

I had been carrying a cell phone to use for emergencies. I tried to rationalize that the possibility of freezing to death counted. Actually, I was just bored, so I called my sister. Even if it had been an emergency situation, my sister couldn't help. She lives in Florida. Still, it was really strange to be in this miserable cold on top of a mountain and be able to dial up someone hundreds of miles away. Steph could not believe that we were in sub-zero temperatures. As I was talking to her, I heard her doorbell ring. It was her pizza delivery—hot pizza, warm Florida. That night, I kept thinking to myself, *What the hell am I doing out here? I could be with my family in Florida—with pizza.* I didn't really sleep. I was too afraid that I would never wake up. I must have dozed off for a while, though, because the next thing I knew, it was morning. I still had a pulse. I hollered out to Packrat, "Hey, are you alive?"

He replied, "Yeah, but this is not the weather I ordered for my hike."

My boots were frozen solid in the position that I left them when I took them off the night before. The boot leather was bent as if I were taking a step up. The boots were so cold that they hurt my feet. Each step exacerbated my soreness. It took about two miles to melt the leather and warm up the boots.

A mile or so up the trail, we came into a clearing on the ridge of the Stecoah Mountains. The sun peeked out from behind a cloud. I leaped and raised my arms into a victory "V" and yelled, celebrating the fact that I was still alive and somewhat warm. There was a tourist town, Fontana Village, about 20 miles ahead. We originally had not intended to visit, but after our arctic experience the night before, we decided to walk to town and find a warm bunkhouse. I learned later that the night I spent in my tent on the Stecoah ridge was the coldest night of my entire journey.

Appalachian Trail

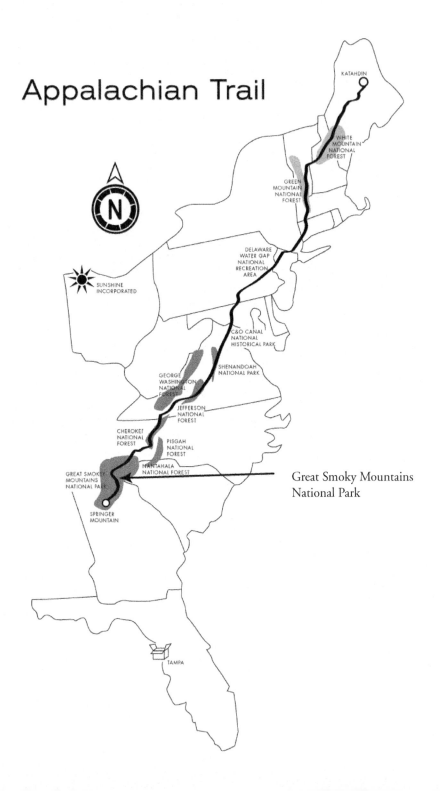

KATAHDIN

WHITE
MOUNTAIN
NATIONAL
FOREST

GREEN
MOUNTAIN
NATIONAL
FOREST

DELAWARE
WATER GAP
NATIONAL
RECREATION
AREA

SUNSHINE
INCORPORATED

C&O CANAL
NATIONAL
HISTORICAL PARK

SHENANDOAH
NATIONAL PARK

GEORGE
WASHINGTON
NATIONAL
FOREST

JEFFERSON
NATIONAL
FOREST

CHEROKEE
NATIONAL
FOREST

PISGAH
NATIONAL
FOREST

NANTAHALA
NATIONAL FOREST

GREAT SMOKY
MOUNTAINS
NATIONAL PARK

Great Smoky Mountains
National Park

SPRINGER
MOUNTAIN

TAMPA

Chapter 11

Hikers, 12
Mice, 0.

Mollies Ridge Shelter, Great Smoky Mountains National Park. March 13, 1998. 174 miles from Springer Mountain, Georgia.

Warming up in a cabin for the night rekindled my spirit and thawed my body. I felt better as I set out the next morning. Just north of Fontana Village is a large dam. The trail tiptoes along the ridge of a narrow dam corridor the size of a one-lane road as it heads into the Great Smoky Mountains National Park. All thru-hikers are required to register at a ranger station located on the edge of the dam.

For the next 70 miles, the AT rips along the mountain ridge through the national park. Ever since Springer Mountain, I had been walking through national forest. Yet the forests and mountains are the same in national parks as in national forests, despite the different designations.

The Appalachian Trail follows a constant 5,000-foot elevation through the Smokies and gradually climbs up and over the highest mountain along the entire 2,160-mile trail. The mountain is Clingmans Dome, a peak that measures 6,643 feet above sea level. Clingmans Dome also has a lookout tower dedicated to the geologist who measured the elevation and determined this to be the highest peak along the trail. As the AT enters the Smokies, it becomes the state line between Tennessee and North Carolina. My right foot would be in North Carolina and my left foot in Tennessee for the next 70 miles.

Nantahala outfitter employees had warned me that Clingmans Dome had 10-foot snowdrifts. I was several days away from Clingmans, but the trail already was covered with a sheet of ice below six to ten inches of dry powder snow. With every step I took, my foot slipped. I had been walking with trekking poles—which are similar to cross-country ski poles—since I began my journey. Now I wished that I had the skis to go with them. I fell a lot. The gentleman at the NOC outfitter had recommended instep crampons and snowshoes. Instep crampons are claws that clip onto boots to provide traction on ice. I hadn't realized how beneficial a pair of crampons would have been, and I didn't take his advice. It took all day to walk 10 miles. Snowshoes keep your feet from post-holing, which is sinking through the snow. For just a few days in snow, I hadn't wanted to invest the funds on equipment that I would have to mail home, never to be used again. I regretted that decision now.

My right ankle had become swollen up from being mangled and twisted during my frequent falls. Every time I slipped on the ice-covered trail, I would go into a balancing routine trying to keep the weight of my pack from toppling me over. I must have looked like a character in a Holiday on Ice show. I spent all of my energy trying to recover from slipping and sliding, but each little dance always seemed to finish with a fall. I wanted the day to be over. Every step was painful.

The sun was setting, and I was still on the trail. I kept trudging up an incline that never seemed to end. For every two steps up, one foot would slip back down. My whole focus was on balance. My eyes were glued to the trail. I began to notice wild boar tracks everywhere. *Great,* I thought. *Dusk will come, and I will be surrounded by wild pigs looking for dinner.*

Finally, I could hear voices, and I knew that I was near the shelter where I planned to stay. The Civilian Conservation Corps had built shelters in the Smokies during the 1930s. President Franklin D. Roosevelt assembled this workforce as one of many ways to jump-start America during the Depression. The shelter walls were made of rock and concrete almost two feet thick. It was a great symbol of the craftsmanship and work ethic of the era. A newer tin roof had been added later.

A chain-link fence stretched across the front of the shelter, serving as the fourth wall. The fence was added to keep the large population of black bears away from hikers. During the winter months, hikers attach plastic to the fence to block the wind and snow from blowing in. The funny thing about sleeping inside a fenced shelter is that you trek up into the Great Smoky Mountains backcountry to escape society, only to sleep in a cage for the animals to look at. Every year, millions of people flock to the Smokies hoping to get a glimpse of a bear. Many people feed the bears, which conditions the bears to expect to be fed constantly. In turn, bears become aggressive, expecting food from everyone. Over the years, bears have pursued hikers for food, destroying tents and backpacks.

The insides of the shelters contain lower and upper wood-plank bunks all along the back wall. In all, the bunks sleep twelve. I opened the gate and stepped inside. The shelters are dark even in the daylight because there are no windows or skylights. Packrat was sitting on the lower bunk. I hadn't seen him all day since we entered the park. He was boiling some water for dinner and had his sleeping bag rolled out, which indicated he had arrived much earlier.

Two other hikers were in the shelter. They introduced themselves as Coke and Mr. N. Coke was in his sixties, and he had recently retired from a steel mill—coke is an industrial term for the steel industry. Mr. N was in his thirties. They started their thru-hike on February 14, two weeks before my start. And I had caught up to them. After figuring out their daily mileage, I asked them if they realized that they would not get to Maine for two more years. Mr. N looked at Coke and then back at me and said, "Yeah, we need to pick up our pace a little." Then Coke pulled out a gallon-size bottle of Kentucky bourbon, took a big swig, and handed it to Mr. N, who also took a belt. Another Clint Eastwood movie scene ran through my mind.

Mr. N and Coke promised Packrat and me a peaceful night without the worries of the one animal that even a chain-link fence could not keep out: mice. Coke was cutting slices of cheese and placing the pieces in mousetraps. I looked over to Mr. N, who was baiting traps with beef jerky. Coke said they compete to see who can catch the most mice. Each had six mousetraps. I went outside in the snow to answer nature's call and to wash my dinner pan. I came back in and bundled up in my sleeping bag. I kept wondering what it would be like if these guys were in the same shelter with Burp, the mouse lover whom I encountered the first day on the trail. All through the night, the occasional snap of a spring would signal the end of another rodent's life. I slept well, despite the popping traps.

The next morning, I was the first one up. I put water on to boil for coffee. My stove made the sound of a distant train as it chugged out fuel to heat the water. Coke and Mr. N woke up before my water finished boiling. Mr. N thought he heard a train. They began lining up their mousetraps to compare the catch. Every trap was full. Twelve mice had met their fate that night. How many more got away? It dawned on me that I probably had slept well because the mice that usually run around the shelter making noise had fallen victim to these guys.

The deer mice that inhabit the shelters are bold and relentless. Since beginning the trail, I had woken up on several occasions after a mouse had pattered across my face en route to a crumb left by a hiker. Mice had chewed holes through several of my pack pouches while searching for food, and they also had chewed part of my bootlaces. One morning, I even found mouse feces in my coffee cup. Needless to say, hikers are helpless against one of the smallest species on the food chain. The 12 occupied traps lying before us represented a small victory for hikers.

After breakfast, I packed my gear and was ready to press on along the trail. Coke was shuffling around the shelter in a pair of purple furry slippers and arguing with Mr. N about one of the dead critters in the trap. It was difficult to take him seriously in that footwear. Apparently, Mr. N had caught a shrew, and he felt that he had won the competition because the shrew was a bonus rarity. Coke felt that he had won because the shrew was not part of the rodent family. I would have loved to have heard the end of that argument, but it was too cold to stand around. I knew that I would never see these guys again unless they picked up their pace three-fold.

As I walked down the trail, I realized that I had not read a newspaper or seen a television program in three weeks. Most of my adult years had included a morning ritual of reading the newspaper, and I usually caught the evening news on TV. Now, only three weeks away from civilization, the only news that I got each morning was a rough guess at what the weather would be like and a few entries in the trail registers. Every shelter has a notebook left by a volunteer or another hiker. Most hikers leave notes in the shelter registers. Some hikers talk about the weather or how their hike is going, or else they leave a note for hikers behind them. I had replaced my newspaper habit with trail registers. The headline in the shelter register that I shared with Coke and Mr. N read: "Shelter victory: hikers-12, mice-0."

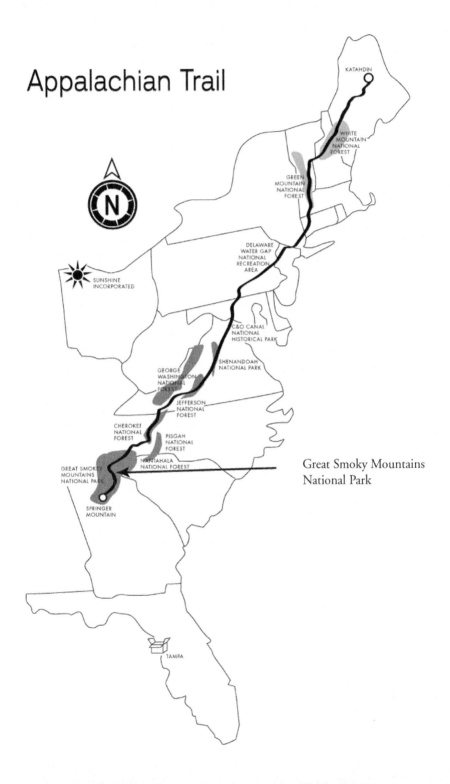

Appalachian Trail

KATAHDIN

WHITE MOUNTAIN NATIONAL FOREST

GREEN MOUNTAIN NATIONAL FOREST

N

SUNSHINE INCORPORATED

DELAWARE WATER GAP NATIONAL RECREATION AREA

C&O CANAL NATIONAL HISTORICAL PARK

GEORGE WASHINGTON NATIONAL FOREST

SHENANDOAH NATIONAL PARK

JEFFERSON NATIONAL FOREST

CHEROKEE NATIONAL FOREST

PISGAH NATIONAL FOREST

NANTAHALA NATIONAL FOREST

GREAT SMOKEY MOUNTAINS NATIONAL PARK

Great Smoky Mountains National Park

SPRINGER MOUNTAIN

TAMPA

Chapter 12

Ouch! It's Beautiful

Clingmans Dome, Great Smoky Mountains National Park. March 15, 1998.
196 miles from Springer Mountain, Georgia.

The Great Smoky Mountains National Park is the nation's most visited national park. Each year, millions of tourists invade the parks campsites, nature walks, and hiking trails. A growing proportion of tourists set out to experience the Appalachian Trail within the Smokies. Despite the terrible weather, I encountered several college groups enjoying their spring breaks. How many of these students would become thru-hikers? All throughout college, I had retreated to this awesome park.

The popularity of the park has damaged the trail, causing deeply eroded grooves about a foot wide and six inches deep. Even in good weather, sections of the AT are difficult to walk. As the snow melted, my feet sunk in and got twisted in these grooves. My ankle was swelling, causing pain from every little slip on the ice. Packrat stayed with me the whole day. He also was having a tough time walking through the snow.

We had been walking in the Smokies for three days. The closer we got to Clingmans, the deeper the snow was. Every few steps, one leg would sink into the snow, and the other would remain on the surface. My body was put into positions that were physiologically improbable and extremely uncomfortable. Not only was my ankle swollen, but also I now experienced sharp pains in my knee with every step. I had been taking ibuprofen daily since beginning my trek to reduce the pain in my feet. Ibuprofen is known as Vitamin I to thru-hikers because most hikers take it as often as daily vitamins.

We stopped for a rest on the approach to the Clingmans summit.

I sat on my backpack to elevate myself above the deep, wet snow. My ankle had swollen. It caused my boot to tighten and left me in more pain. I had taken four ibuprofen pills already that morning; any more and it would be toxic. Packrat and I fell silent as we heard the footsteps of someone approaching us from further up the trail.

A park ranger came around a bend in the trail with a shotgun slung over his shoulder. He stopped and asked us if we had seen any wild boar. We told him about the tracks and damage back at Mollies Ridge Shelter. He thanked us and kept walking in pursuit of the pigs. The rangers actively hunt the wild boar because of the damage they do to the park. The wild pigs dig up trails and contaminate the water. They have huge piglet litters, too, which has caused overpopulation.

After talking with the ranger, we saddled up our packs and kept heading north. The snow was becoming deeper with every step, but we were within a mile of the summit. In some places, the snow had drifted as high as 25 feet, burying whole trees. The tops of huge pine trees were sticking out of the snow, making them look like little pine bushes.

We reached Clingmans Dome by noon. There were no clouds for the sun to hide behind, and we could see for miles. At the summit, a concrete outlook surged stories above the trees. From a distance, it had looked like a 1950s UFO. I dropped my pack and wound my way up to the top. Wow! Majestic views in every direction. Snow-covered pines and blue spruce blanketed the mountainsides. To the north, I could see a town that most likely was Gatlinburg. I stood on the highest point of the entire trail until the wind chill became too uncomfortable.

If I had a sled, I could have taken it down the ramp of the outlook. The snow was at least 10 feet deep on the trail. I was walking on top of the snow, but every five or six steps, one leg would sink through, leaving one leg on the surface and putting me into an L-shaped, half-split position. I was in extreme pain and didn't want to take another step, but we were seven miles from Newfound Gap, the only access road open this time of year. The AT parallels a paved road all the way to Newfound Gap. The road had been plowed but would not open to traffic until April. A thin line of spruce trees separated the road from the trail. We blazed through the trees and onto the road to avoid any more twists and falls from stepping through the deep snow.

Newfound Gap was at the bottom of a seven-mile decent. My ankle and knee hurt with every step, but knowing that we were heading toward civilization lifted my spirits and blocked the pain. We reached the Newfound Gap parking lot by 5:00 p.m., having walked 19 miles in very difficult conditions.

Hitchhiking to Gatlinburg was the next feat. I needed some time off the trail to assess my ankle. The parking lot was full of tourists enjoying a clear, sunny day and the overlook of a valley of mountains. It was kind of strange walking into a crowded place after experiencing the drastically lonely trail conditions.

I positioned myself next to a billboard, which detailed the views and history of the area. I figured someone eventually would notice my pack and inquire about my journey, at which point I would ask for a ride down to Gatlinburg, 18 miles away. I noticed three young adults walking toward their car. I had only attempted hitchhiking one other time, and that attempt was unsuccessful. I had nothing to lose.

I raised my voice and approached them. "Excuse me, my friend and I are hiking the Appalachian Trail, and I've injured my ankle. Could you give us a ride down to Gatlinburg?"

The three tourists looked at each other, wanting to say no like their mothers had always told them to, but my hurt, puppy-dog face must have swayed the driver. "Yeah, we'll take you to Gatlinburg," he replied.

They didn't expect the awful smell that accompanies thru-hikers. We piled into the backseat with our packs on our laps. The three tourists crammed in. As the doors shut, the windows went down. I had grown accustomed to my awful odor in the last three weeks, but I had not been crammed into a car. Only then did I realize that I smelled like a pile of old, sweaty socks that had fermented in a dank basement for a few weeks.

On the ride down the mountain, we learned that our chauffeurs were college students on their way back from a weekend of gambling in the casinos on the Cherokee reservation. The female in the group told us that she worked at a hotel, The Inn at Afton, which is right on the AT near the Shenandoah Park entrance. I wrote down her name and said I would stop in and say hi when I got to that point, another 550 miles north.

Our taxi ride to Gatlinburg went quickly. The driver could have left the engine off and coasted all the way to town. Route 441, a roller-coaster track that splits the park in half, descends drastically from over 5,000 feet to the bottom of the mountain.

Gatlinburg can fulfill even the mightiest of thru-hiker cravings. It's a commercialized tourist town that began as a small logging and farm town and has grown in size and popularity since the creation of the national park. These days, plenty of people come to Gatlinburg just to shop, never even setting foot in the park. Every block has the equivalent of an entire shopping mall crammed into it, with wedding chapels, restaurants, and hotels scattered throughout. After living in the woods for three weeks, I found the endless restaurant choices to be tantalizing.

I asked the driver to let us out at the first intersection in town. We pulled into a gas station across from the hotel where we intended to stay. The driver hopped out and popped open the trunk, which was full of beer. "Do you guys want some beer?" he asked.

"You darn betcha, I'll drink a beer," I replied. I grabbed a six-pack of Budweiser from the trunk. I told our chauffeurs, "You are the first trail angels of my journey. Thank you!"

The little white Honda Civic drove off with all four windows down to air out the car. "Trail angel" is a name given to anyone who goes out of his or her way to help out a hiker. Every year, hikers' spirits are lifted by trail angels offering rides to town, food, shelter, and in this case, cold beer. I had not opened a beer since beginning my hike three weeks ago. For the past three weeks, the trail had wound in and out of dry counties, which prohibit the sale of alcohol. I couldn't have found a beer if I'd wanted one. I am apprehensive when I am prohibited from any rights provided by federal law. When I was in the Army, the old saying was, "If you're old enough to die for your country, you're old enough to have a beer."

Packrat and I checked into an old, rundown motel that offered discounted rates for thru-hikers. Tourists were gawking at me as I limped across the street to the motel. I was favoring my leg and was eager to get off my feet. As soon as we got into our room, I took off my socks and boots. My right ankle was swollen twice the size of the left ankle. I took the ice bucket down to the ice machine and filled it up. I poured half of the ice into a towel and wrapped the cubes up tight. I took one of the beers and set it next to the bed. I sat down on my bed, elevated my right leg with a pillow, and packed the ice-filled towel around my ankle. I cracked open a cold Budweiser and took a sip. Wow, that tasted good! I figured that I would take a day or two off the trail to let the swelling go down.

Packrat walked over from his side of the room and asked to see my ankle. "Wrongfoot, you may have a fracture," he informed me.

I was nervous that my journey might be over. The last thing I wanted to hear was the word "fracture." I didn't want to tell anybody about my injury until I knew how serious it was. I decided to see if the swelling would subside on its own. I was afraid that if I went to a doctor, he would tell me that I was done.

We stayed in Gatlinburg for two nights. The swelling in my ankle began to recede on the second day. I was relieved. The pain was subsiding. Knowing that my ankle was healing, I called my family and the Sunshine home to let everyone know about the extreme weather conditions. I didn't say a word about my ankle. I didn't want anyone thinking that I was going to quit.

Appalachian Trail

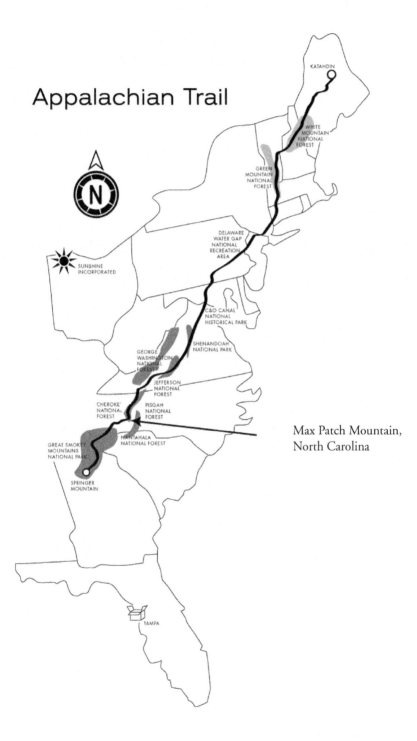

KATAHDIN

WHITE MOUNTAIN NATIONAL FOREST

GREEN MOUNTAIN NATIONAL FOREST

N

DELAWARE WATER GAP NATIONAL RECREATION AREA

SUNSHINE INCORPORATED

C&O CANAL NATIONAL HISTORICAL PARK

SHENANDOAH NATIONAL PARK

GEORGE WASHINGTON NATIONAL FOREST

JEFFERSON NATIONAL FOREST

CHEROKEE NATIONAL FOREST

PISGAH NATIONAL FOREST

NANTAHALA NATIONAL FOREST

Max Patch Mountain, North Carolina

GREAT SMOKY MOUNTAINS NATIONAL PARK

SPRINGER MOUNTAIN

TAMPA

Chapter 13

My Spirit Warmed by the Sun

Max Patch Mountain, North Carolina. March 19, 1998. 249 miles from Springer Mountain, Georgia.

After a day and a half of rest in Gatlinburg, I stood along the road on the edge of town, just outside the Great Smoky Mountains National Park. I held a piece of cardboard that read, "Thru-hikers, need a ride to Newfound Gap." Several vehicles went by before a van pulled over to pick us up. A middle-aged man, who owned a shop in Gatlinburg, offered to take us up the mountain.

Eighteen miles later, with an economics lesson from our chauffeur on making money in the stock market, we stepped out of the van. The AT stretched another 30 miles north through the Smokies. As soon as our ride drove off, a chartered tour bus with Canada plates pulled into the parking lot. The bus screeched to a halt; the door swung open, and fifty senior citizens climbed off. One of the senior citizens approached me.

"Son, where are you going with that pack on your back?"

"To Maine, ma'am."

"Where are you going?" she asked again, with a puzzled look on her face, as if she had misunderstood.

"To Mount Katahdin, Maine, 1,900 miles north."

Forgetting the gorgeous view the bus had pulled over for them to see, the senior citizens crowded around Packrat and me, snapping pictures and asking all sorts of questions. Finally, we said goodbye, noting that we still had many miles to complete that day.

Six inches of snow remained on the trail. We continued north from the parking lot under the Christmas tree-like spruce and fir canopy. Shiny green rhododendron leaves peeked out along the trail. Every step sunk through the melting snow. It made my ankle and knee hurt, but not nearly as much as they did two days earlier.

Sleet and rain fell on us for the next two days. The trail followed the ridge, but the clouds were so thick that I could not see any of the views along the way. Packrat hiked ahead, and we would meet up at the end of the day. Spring break groups of college students were huddled in every shelter along the trail, trying to duck out of the miserable elements. The trail follows a narrow ridge in many places. I could jump off the mountain six feet to my left or to my right. The wind was whipping the treetops and mountainside so hard that the roots of trees were pulling out of the ground beneath my feet.

Walking through the mountains in good weather is a totally different experience than walking in bad weather. When the weather was nice, I would stop and enjoy the views, snapping several pictures. When walking along in cold sleet and rain, though, I didn't stop to look at views, and I didn't take pictures for fear of ruining my camera. I just plodded on.

Two days after leaving Newfound Gap, I reached Davenport Gap, which is the northernmost point of the Smokies. A mountain country store called Mountain Mama's was a half-mile off the trail on a gravel lane. *The Thru-hikers Handbook* mentioned that the place had showers/washer/dryer/lodging. After two days of walking through icy slush and cold sleet, a hot shower was just the remedy. I needed to rejuvenate myself. Packrat agreed to share the cost of a room with me.

Mountain Mama's was built from mountain rock and concrete. Decrepit buses, trucks, and cars were scattered along the sides of the building. Stepping into the store was like walking back in time. It looked like a general store from *Little House on the Prairie*. I walked up to the counter and saw a grill behind it. A menu hung above the grill hood. To the left was a grocery section with three small aisles of canned foods. An ice-cream freezer stood at the end of the counter. In spite of the cold, ice cream sounded good. Restaurant tables filled out the right of the store. The end wall was packed from floor to ceiling with tobacco products——snuff, cigarettes, cigars, and chewing tobacco.

A woman behind the counter asked in her Appalachian twang, "Can I help ye?"

"We would like to stay for the night, if there's room," I said.

"Plenty of room," she replied. "There are two cabins out back, showers, washer, and dryer. Seventeen dollars a night."

We paid and went around back to drop off our gear. Two small 10-by-12-foot cabins with little front porches stood to the left of the store. We stared at our two options. One cabin was painted pink with a sign above the door reading "Honeymoon Suite." The other cabin was painted lime green. There was no question.

"Packrat, there is no way I am staying in a honeymoon suite with you."

"Good, Wrongfoot. You made me nervous with your delayed response."

We set our gear in the green cabin, took some hot showers, and put our wet hiking clothes into the dryer. We figured there was no sense washing them—they would just get dirty tomorrow, anyway. It sure felt good to warm up with a shower after the cold, wet weather.

After cleaning up, Packrat and I went into the store to order dinner. The trail guide said that the hamburgers were excellent, so that's what we ordered. We sat down at a table and waited for our food. The burgers were magnificent and vanished immediately. Cars and trucks pulled up all throughout our meal. Everyone walked over to the tobacco-filled wall, grabbing several cartons of cigarettes and assortments of other odds and ends. I had never seen people buy so many cigarettes. We definitely were in tobacco country.

Packrat and I retreated to our cabin after dinner for a night's rest away from the elements. In the morning, Packrat caught me completely off guard. He told me that he was sick of the weather and was getting off the trail. After pondering his decision, I suggested that the weather would improve the further north we went, but he seemed determined to quit. I suggested taking a day off the trail to think about it some more before giving up.

"Come on," I said. "You quit the trail four times before."

"The weather sucks, Wrongfoot. I'm sick of it." He had a point.

We went into the store for some breakfast. Packrat made arrangements with the storeowner for a shuttle to Hot Springs, North Carolina. Of course, the storeowner agreed to take him for the right price. After breakfast, we rolled up our sleeping bags and repacked our gear.

It seemed that every bit of my spirit had been challenged in the past three weeks, and I had not even hiked one-tenth of the total distance of the trail. I didn't want to lose focus on my goal just because Packrat was quitting the trail. He wished me luck, and we said goodbye. We had walked together for 17 days. Packrat was a walking encyclopedia when it came to hiking gear, which sparked many interesting conversations. He complained about the weather often, but his endurance over the miles had kept me motivated. I was disappointed that he had decided to quit.

I tossed my pack on my back, clipped my waist belt and sternum strap, and headed north. The AT crossed below a busy Interstate 40. After crossing to the other side, the trail weaved back and forth up switchbacks through barren, leafless oaks and maples. I ascended for several miles onto Snowbird Mountain. The trees were speckled with pine, rhododendron, and blue spruce at the higher elevations.

The sun appeared from behind some clouds, and the temperature rose rapidly. By noon, the thermometer clipped to my pack read 60 degrees. I was dripping in sweat from two hours of walking, so when I stopped for a snack and some water, I took off my jacket and wore just a T-shirt and shorts. The sun shone. Ironically, the day Packrat decided to leave the trail because of bad weather was the nicest day yet, with sunny skies and mild temperatures.

I reached Max Patch Mountain by mid-afternoon. Max Patch is a bald mountain; nothing but knee-high grass and seasonal flora grow there. The southern Appalachians are known for these unexplained balds. Scientists argue on the origin. One group claims that the American Indians and settlers cleared the mountains. The other group believes the drastic climate prevents trees from growing.

The trail follows straight up over the summit and down the other side, heading in a northeasterly direction. I reached the peak, which although bald was surrounded on all sides by forested mountains. The summit is a flat hill as wide as a football field. It's as if a giant stood on Max Patch Mountain and leveled it off with his weight as he turned in all directions to build the surrounding mountains. I could see for miles with every turn. At one point in history, Max Patch served as an airstrip for small planes. I took off my pack and sat down for more than an hour. For the first time since leaving Springer, I actually felt comfortable outside.

I had been to Max Patch once before with my family on an Easter day-hike. Being there brought back memories of my whole family standing right where I was sitting.

Finally, I packed up and descended Max Patch, arriving at Flint Mountain Shelter about 4:00 p.m. A mountain stream flowed in front of the shelter. I already had hiked 20 miles and was unsure whether I wanted to go another mile to Walnut Mountain Shelter. I took out my water filter and refilled my quarts.

While I pumped water from the stream, I heard footsteps approaching me. A gray-haired man with a thick beard and a red Appalachian Trail bandanna tied on his head appeared around the bend in the trail. He was wearing a backpack, green pants, and a long-sleeved shirt. His cheeks were chiseled. He introduced himself as Zeb. I had been reading his journal entries since beginning my hike. To see him here was a surprise to me. I hadn't expected to catch up to him. He was at least two days ahead of me every time I saw his name in a shelter journal. I introduced myself and explained my surprise. He explained that he and another thru-hiker, Briggs, had taken a few days of rest in Gatlinburg. Zeb said that he was going to hike another mile to Walnut Mountain Shelter. I told him that I would see him there.

The Appalachian Trail Conference left Walnut Shelter off the newly printed maps because it was considered substandard compared to some of the newer shelters. This shelter was one of the few remaining originals along the AT. It was made entirely of wood, and it had floorboards elevated off the ground on which to roll out your sleeping bag. It was a small shelter and could sleep only four. When I arrived, Zeb was sitting inside on his sleeping bag up against the left wall, and another hiker was sitting inside against the right wall.

Zeb and this other gentleman meshed with the rustic appearance of the shelter. Both men, like the shelter, were older and distinguished-looking. I introduced myself to the other hiker, who said his name was Ted. Ted was eating a cold MRE—military combat food. He was about 65 years old and had gray hair and a white beard. I set up my bed in the center of the shelter between them.

Zeb was an engineer and recently had retired from aerospace in Cape Canaveral, Florida. Zeb's engineering background was obvious from his customized hiking equipment. He had altered most of his gear from its retail state to personally fit his liking. Extra pockets had been sewn onto his rib-pack. He had sewn Velcro onto the ankle cuffs of his pants and cut a seam on each leg so that he could take his pants on and off without having to remove his boots. His hiking poles had been cut shorter to fit his height.

Ted had retired recently from the General Electric aircraft division in Cincinnati, Ohio. Later in the evening, Ted took out a weather radio and turned it on. We listened to it for a while, never really getting an accurate report for our area. From that day forward, Ted was known to me as Weatherman Ted.

The next morning, Ted was up and ready to hit the trail before I even got out of my sleeping bag. Zeb and I awoke about the same time Ted was leaving. I never saw him again.

***

Hot Springs, North Carolina, was only another 12 miles up the trail. I couldn't wait to get to town. Hot Springs is known for its natural springs, which are piped from the ground into hot tubs. For a reasonable price, one can soak in these healing mineral waters and even get a massage. I had knee pain and a sore ankle from my rough hike through the Smokies, so I planned to treat myself to a little holistic medicine.

The terrain was fairly easy. My maps indicated no elevation gains. As a matter of fact, the last few miles would descend several thousand feet into town. I zipped along the trail, conversing on and off with Zeb when we were within hearing range of each other. By noon, I could see Hot Springs down in the valley.

On the descent into town, I ran into Packrat walking up the trail. He explained that he got a shuttle to Hot Springs from Mountain Mama's, and after resting and enjoying a day of good weather, he decided to continue with his journey. He was eager to let me know of his decision to continue, so he walked south on the trail until he found me. I was glad that Packrat had decided to stick it out. We headed into Hot Springs together.

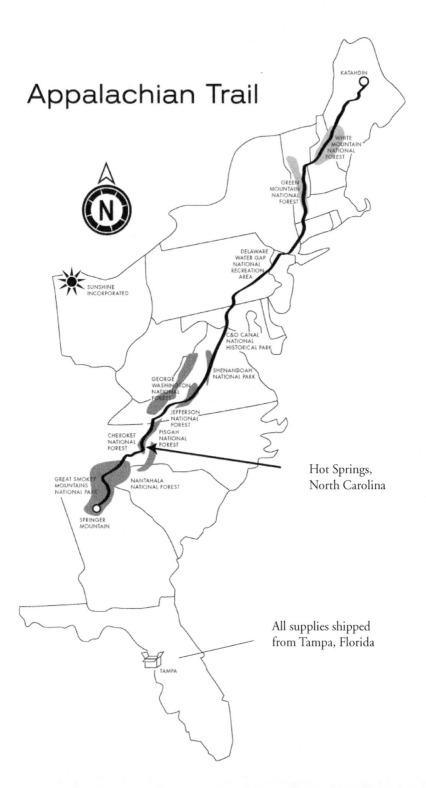

Appalachian Trail

KATAHDIN

WHITE MOUNTAIN NATIONAL FOREST

GREEN MOUNTAIN NATIONAL FOREST

DELAWARE WATER GAP NATIONAL RECREATION AREA

SUNSHINE INCORPORATED

C&O CANAL NATIONAL HISTORICAL PARK

SHENANDOAH NATIONAL PARK

GEORGE WASHINGTON NATIONAL FOREST

JEFFERSON NATIONAL FOREST

PISGAH NATIONAL FOREST

CHEROKEE NATIONAL FOREST

GREAT SMOKEY MOUNTAINS NATIONAL PARK

NANTAHALA NATIONAL FOREST

SPRINGER MOUNTAIN

Hot Springs, North Carolina

All supplies shipped from Tampa, Florida

TAMPA

Chapter 14

Meatless in Hot Springs

Hot Springs, North Carolina. March 20, 1998. 270 miles from Springer Mountain, Georgia.

Everyone I had talked to who thru-hiked the Appalachian Trail emphasized how the towns and people along the way are just as much a part of thru-hiking as the wilderness experience. The first trail town that the AT actually passes through is Hot Springs. The AT winds down the mountain, drastically dropping 3,000 feet in elevation to the little town of Hot Springs. The town is nestled in a valley on the French Broad River, which has become a popular rafting spot in recent years. Most of the buildings in town are originals of the late 19th and early 20th centuries.

During World War I, German merchant sailors were imprisoned in Hot Springs until the war ended. Throughout the war, the sailors were allowed to have their families live in town. The Germans tapped into the hot springs and made a bathhouse. They also built a little German villa and lived like royalty instead of as prisoners. When the war ended, the prisoners did not want to leave. Hot Springs was quite livable, compared to going home to a devastated Germany that had just been defeated in war.

The Appalachian Trail winds along Main Street into town and back up a mountain north of town. Hot Springs has become a trail favorite because of the conveniences of being able to walk everywhere without hitchhiking. The best part about Hot Springs is that it has remained commercial-free. There are no billboards or chain restaurants—just simple, local businesses. Of course, the town benefits greatly from the influx of hikers and rafters every year.

My trail guide recommended The Sunny Bank Inn, a hostel famous among hikers. Elmer, the hostel keeper, has been taking in hikers for more than 15 years. The hostel had been an old boarding house during the days of stagecoach travel. Packrat already had a room with an extra bed, so I dropped my gear in the room, and we split the cost.

The post office was my first order of business. I was going to collect a box of supplies that had been mailed to me from my stepfather and mom. Each supply box had ten days' provisions, and I had not resupplied in ten days. Here is the inventory list of one supply box:

Breakfast	Dinner	Liquids	Snacks
5 Kudos bars	2 freeze-dried din.	1 pwdr. milk	4 Cliff bars
4 gran. bars	2 Lipton din.	1 coffee	3 Reeses Cups
4 brk. bars	1 spaghetti din.	1 Kool-aid	1 Skor bar
4 Pop-Tarts	1 couscous	1 veg. oil	2 Snickers
2 cereal	2 mac & cheese	1 Butter Buds	2 Almond Joy
2 grits	2 rice		
Lunch	**Veggies**	**Essentials**	**Other**
1 smoke saus.	1 broccoli	1 wet nap	1 film
1 cheese	1 mushroom	1 detergent	1 nic wax
1 crackers	1 onion	1 t.p.	1 Gold Bond
1 dried apples	1 pepper	1 Kleenex	maps
1 dried banana	1 tomatoes	1 toothpaste	1 Q-tips

When I picked up my box, I mailed home my weekly journals, maps of terrain I had already walked through, and used rolls of film. My stepfather had put maps for each section of trail into the appropriate boxes with the rest of my provisions. I did not truly appreciate this until I ran into other hikers who had no maps at all or who carried every map of the entire 2,160-mile trail, which totaled about three pounds.

After the post office, I walked back to the hostel with my supply box. Zeb and Briggs had checked into the room next door. All of us gathered in their room. We were sharing stories and talking about the weather. Zeb had just showered and changed into a T-shirt. His left arm had some tattoos partly visible below the sleeve. Briggs had been hiking with Zeb since Springer Mountain. He pointed out one of Zeb's tattoos.

"Hey, Zeb, show them your AT tattoo," Briggs told him. Zeb pulled up his left sleeve. His lower bicep had a three-inch tattoo of the AT logo, a capital "A" with a capital "T" below, and a mountain background. To show loyalty and commitment, military personnel get tattoos of their branch of service permanently etched onto their bodies. Many folks get their spouse's names inscribed onto various parts of their bodies. But Zeb had the AT emblem permanently attached.

"Zeb, that's definitely a sign of trail loyalty," I told him.

"Actually, Wrongfoot, the AT tattoo is covering up my ex-wife's name." He said that he'd strategically designed his AT tattoo to replace his failed marital commitment with his current commitment to the trail. Ha!

In the morning, Elmer served a pancake breakfast. During breakfast, Elmer announced to everyone that dinner would be served at 6:00 p.m. that night. Elmer had quite the reputation for his vegetarian meals. I'd never really had a gourmet vegetarian meal and decided to reserve a spot for myself. Zeb, on the other hand, declined, saying that he was heading on. Shortly after breakfast, Zeb said good-bye to everyone and headed north on the trail.

After breakfast, I walked down the street along the river to the Hot Springs Spa. On the way, I saw Zeb ripping open a box outside the post office. "Hey, Wrongfoot!" he hollered.

"What are ya doing?" I asked.

"Picking up my supply box and mailing home my dirty laundry."

"You don't wash your clothes?"

"No!"

"Zeb, do you know how bad your socks smell?"

"Brenda doesn't mind."

"Zeb, I learned that the sense of smell has the strongest memory of all five senses. All your girlfriend has to remind her of you is your nasty clothes, paired with your voice on the phone once a week."

"Nah, she really doesn't mind. She's my support team. She volunteered to do my laundry."

"Well, take care. Maybe we'll trek some miles together soon?"

"Yep, see ya, Wrongfoot."

I never thought to mail my dirty laundry to someone to wash for me. As soon as someone opened the box and caught a whiff of socks worn for 50 miles, that person would probably tell me to shove it.

The spa was another two blocks down Main Street. I wobbled my stiff, sore body the rest of the way. I stepped into the office and inquired about a massage therapist to address my knee and ankle injuries. A woman behind the counter said the therapist would not be in for an hour. She offered a hot tub for soaking until the therapist arrived. This sounded just fine to me.

An employee walked me across the lawn into the tree line along the river's edge to a secluded tub surrounded by a tall wooden fence. A plastic dome had been placed over the tub to retain the heat of the natural spring water, which was pumped directly into the tub as it sprang out of the earth. I didn't have a bathing suit, so the birthday suit it was.

My hour in the hot tub seemed to go quickly. The therapist had arrived, but I didn't have a towel to dry off, and the morning was a bit cold for me to walk around wet. I hollered for a towel, hoping that someone would hear me, and I was thankful when one of the employees brought over a towel. I dried off and walked to a mobile trailer about 100 yards from my hot tub. The massage therapist led me into a room with a therapeutic bed. For the next hour, all of my aches and pains were pulled, rubbed, and stretched away. I was totally relaxed afterward. I did not have a worry in the world. As I walked back to the hostel, I began to realize that the pain in my knee was gone. Wow! Holistic medicine had won me over.

I spent the rest of the day doing my town chores: laundry, writing postcards, making phone calls, cleaning my boots, airing out my pack, and letting my gear dry. The massage had completely relaxed me. In the afternoon, I took a catnap.

Hot Springs had a public library, so I dropped in to see if it had Internet access. Sure enough, the librarian was online when I asked and was happy to let me use the computer. Sunshine had created a website for my sponsors, family, and friends to keep tabs on my progress. The site was not up when I left, so I was curious to see if it was online. I typed in the address www.sunshinefnd.com. The Sunshine homepage appeared. The bottom left side of the page had a link called "Jeff's Hike." I pointed the mouse at the selection and clicked. An introductory page sprang up, showing a picture of my brother and I and explaining my hike and fundraiser. The next page had a map of the entire trail with an arrow pointing to my approximate location. What a wonderful addition to my walk.

The rest of the day, I lounged around the hostel and browsed Elmer's extensive library. Finally, the dinner hour arrived. I walked downstairs to the dining room, which already contained a mixture of folks. Some were in town for rafting, and others were on retreat for the weekend.

Elmer employed a small staff of thru-hikers that had prepared the meal with his supervision. Elmer sat down and asked us to go around the table and introduce ourselves. He asked us to tell of an animal we would want to be and why. The meal started with a carrot soup appetizer followed by a salad. The main entree was pasta with garbanzo beans. Everything was very good. The only thing missing was the meat.

Elmer asked who would be having breakfast in the morning. I declined. The vegetarian meal was very good, but I was raised on meat and potatoes. After a meatless night, I had decided that I would go across the street in the morning to the diner for some greasy bacon and eggs.

Packrat and I once again were hiking together. We slung on our packs after breakfast and began our ascent north of town. The trail climbed several thousand feet in the first mile. Just before reaching the summit, we came to an overlook with a bird's eye view of the entire Hot Springs valley. This overlook was called Lovers Leap. As the story goes, an Indian woman jumped to her death after witnessing the murder of the man she loved and fearing her fate if the murderer caught her. I stepped up to the edge and looked down. About 20 feet below the edge was a thick forest of pine trees ornamenting the mountainside and stretching down to the French Broad River edge. It did not look as if a jump from this overlook guaranteed death. The pine trees would break the fall. The worst that could happen, as far as I could see, was a few cuts, scrapes, and a few broken limbs. Did the woman really leap to her death? Or did she run off with her lover's killer?

Snow blanketed the trail as we climbed away from town. The leaf-less tree branches were glazed with ice. The green rhododendron leaves peered out from beneath a dusting of snow, providing some color as I walked along. The snow on the trail mixed in with the dirt turned up from our boots. It looked like Oreo ice cream. The sun was breaking from behind the clouds. It felt good leaving town with nice weather, a well-supplied pack, relaxed muscles, and a friend.

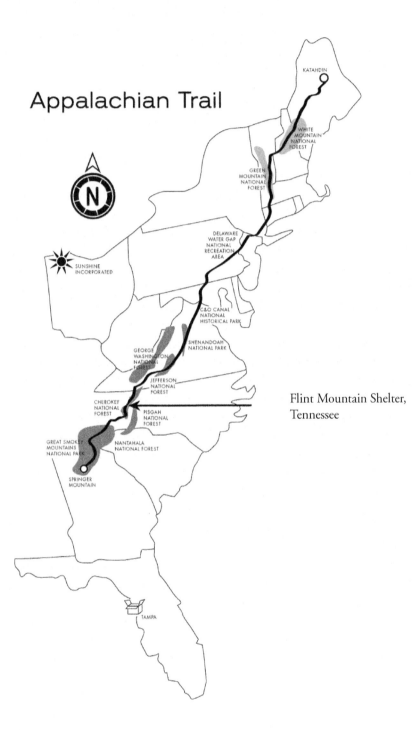

Appalachian Trail

Flint Mountain Shelter, Tennessee

Chapter 15

Leave the Stress Behind

Flint Mountain Shelter, Tennessee. March 23, 1998. 303 miles from Springer Mountain, Georgia.

The first few days out of Hot Springs were cold. Several inches of snow canvassed the mountains. Yet, over the next few days, the temperature began to rise and climbed into the 70s. Again, I was able to shed my coat, hat, and gloves.

Most of my physical ailments were gone. The blisters that plagued my feet from the first day on the trail were healed, although my feet still hurt from the daily pounding up and down mountains. My ankle and knee did not bother me at all.

Every day, before I strapped on my pack, I would pick a topic or issue to think about as I walked along, hoping to resolve that problem or at least come up with a possible solution. Throughout the course of my day, the beauty of valley overlook, the smell of forest pine, and the clean air always managed to jar my focus from the topic I was trying to ponder. But I always seemed to have an idea or answer to the problem when I recalled the original topic at the end of my day.

Most folks who escape into the woods with a sleeping bag, tent, and basic survival essentials are trying to get away from the daily stress of domestic life; however, stress still was present for me on the trail. Domestic stress of meeting project deadlines or paying bills transformed into the stress of fulfilling basic survival needs. Water availability was my No. 1 concern. I always tried to keep at least two full quarts with me. At the end of the day, cooking the evening meal always required water, so I would plan my camp near a water source. Injury had been in the back of my mind since I inherited my trail name, Wrongfoot. Weather had tormented me since the beginning, with bone-chilling temperatures and constant rain, and weather can make or break a hiker's day. Although I had discovered a simpler lifestyle, I also experienced stress, and if I didn't handle it properly, it could be just as debilitating in the woods as in the city.

Packrat and I were still together. But as usual, we walked with some distance between us, at our own paces, usually only catching each other during breaks and at camp.

During the course of my day, I took a break at a shelter called Jerry's Cabin. Like all of the shelters along the AT, Jerry's Cabin is maintained by trail volunteers. Volunteers check on the shelters frequently, packing out litter, making necessary repairs, and keeping a journal and register available for hikers. The volunteer of Jerry's Cabin had a sense of humor. While resting inside the shelter, eating a Cliff bar, my eyes were drawn to the sidewall. Above the fireplace, a mailbox, light fixture, and telephone were attached to the stone wall. None of these domestic amenities actually served a functional purpose other than reminding hikers of some of the luxuries that we were doing without.

Later that evening, I hiked to the next shelter. Packrat was already there. While I prepared dinner, I heard several voices approaching. A group of 15 college students appeared in front of the shelter. Thruhikers become dependent on the string of shelters along the trail. Three weeks on the trail had ingrained a sense of ownership for shelter space. Although they technically are for use by everyone, an unwritten rule on the AT is that thru-hikers get preference. Shelters along the trail were our footpath hotels from Georgia to Maine. They were a home for the night.

You don't need a degree in forestry to realize the damage a large group can cause. A group of more than ten hikers is bad for the trail. It's like cattle grazing in one spot of a pasture, not to mention the obvious factor of all those voices infiltrating the serenity. Needless to say, we were a bit apprehensive of our instant battalion of neighbors.

The shelter accommodated only eight, so several from the group pitched tents. Some of the students were quite friendly and curious about our expeditions. This co-ed group had escaped to the woods from a college in South Carolina. They stayed up talking into the wee hours of the night, not allowing us much sleep. To make matters worse, several coyotes closed in on the shelter, howling in the night. A coyote howl sounds like a hurt dog yelping. This created quite a stir with the college group.

I was not a pleasant person in the morning after several rude awakenings from laughing, yelling, and coyote howls throughout the night. I sat in my sleeping bag, sipping my coffee, hoping that the caffeine would supplement the lack of sleep. The group was miserable from several days of cold, sleet, and rain. The group leader mentioned that the group was hiking south and had planned on staying at Jerry's Cabin. They asked me about the trail south of here. I described the terrain and showed them a profile map. I explained all of the fine qualities of the Jerry's Cabin Shelter.

"Jerry's Cabin has a telephone, a night light, and a mailbox if you want to send a letter," I told them. To convince them, I showed them The Thru-Hikers Handbook, which makes mention of these amenities as well. The group mounted their packs, and the last thing I heard as they were walking off was, "I think I'll call my mom." A grin split my face. What will they think of Wrongfoot when they arrive at Jerry's Cabin?

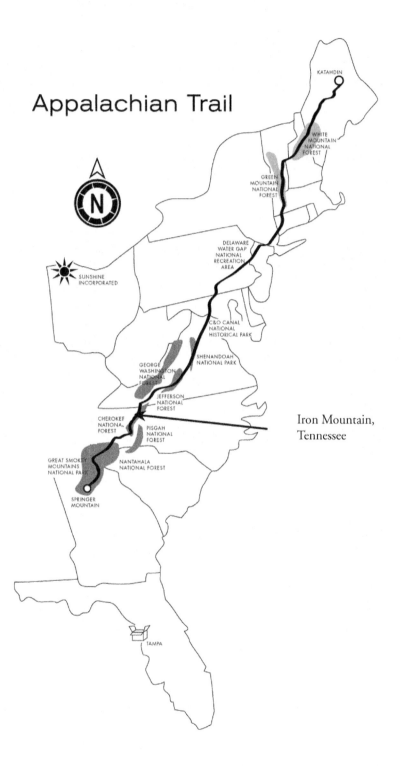

Appalachian Trail

KATAHDIN

WHITE
MOUNTAIN
NATIONAL
FOREST

GREEN
MOUNTAIN
NATIONAL
FOREST

DELAWARE
WATER GAP
NATIONAL
RECREATION
AREA

SUNSHINE
INCORPORATED

C&O CANAL
NATIONAL
HISTORICAL PARK

SHENANDOAH
NATIONAL PARK

GEORGE
WASHINGTON
NATIONAL
FOREST

JEFFERSON
NATIONAL
FOREST

CHEROKEE
NATIONAL
FOREST

PISGAH
NATIONAL
FOREST

Iron Mountain,
Tennessee

GREAT SMOKEY
MOUNTAINS
NATIONAL PARK

NANTAHALA
NATIONAL FOREST

SPRINGER
MOUNTAIN

TAMPA

Chapter 16

Psycho on the Trail

Iron Mountain, Tennessee. March 26, 1998. 360 miles from Springer Mountain, Georgia.

Most shelters along the trail have a notebook that hikers use as a register. The majority of thru-hikers leave notes as they pass through. Registers provide communication to everyone behind. Who knows how many hikers were behind me? The only way I would ever know would be to turn around and walk back the way I had come, and there's no way that would happen. After walking several hundred miles, the last thing I was about to do was go back. Only eight thru-hikers were ahead of Packrat and me, according to the registers. Zeb's entries were dated one day ahead of us since he had left Hot Springs.

Erwin, Tennessee, was my next supply town. My support team had been diligent in shipping provisions to preplanned locations along my route. A supply box awaited my arrival at a campground office that was 100 yards off the trail, just outside of town.

Erwin had been stigmatized for an incident that occurred in the early part of the century. Sometime in the 1920s, a circus came to town. One of the circus elephants had stomped a circus worker to death. The town held a trial and prosecuted the elephant for murder. The elephant was sentenced to death by hanging. A rail car was used to mobilize the huge animal as it hung to its death. Apparently, the lynch man was unsuccessful with his task. After several attempts, the poor animal was shot. It certainly was not an event I would want associated with my hometown.

Erwin also was the town where Packrat had bagged four previous thru-hike attempts. As the two of us approached town, we could see the Nolichucky River below us in the valley. Soon, we would begin a major descent into Erwin. Would Packrat hang up his pack for a fifth time in Erwin? Was he secretly trying to set a record for the most failed thru-hike attempts? The suspense was killing me. On the approach down the mountain, I decided to use a little reverse psychology.

"Hey, Packrat, can I have your pack and gear when you quit?"

"I'm not quitting."

I thought to myself, Why not? You quit here four times before. Still, Packrat kept heading north.

High up on the mountain ridge, I came to an outcrop overlooking the valley below. The Nolichucky River ran through the valley a half-mile straight down below my feet. If I were to jump off the ridge, I probably could guide the dive into the water but would meet certain death on the river's rock bottom.

Five days after leaving Hot Springs, we arrived at our next supply point. I still had several days of food left in my pack. The campground with my provisions was nestled along the Nolichucky River. Packrat also had a supply in Erwin. We picked up our boxes and paid for a night at the hiker hostel, which was adjacent to the campground office. A hot shower was my first intent after dropping my pack.

While we paid for our hostel, the campground manager mentioned that another hiker was checked in for a second night. We stepped inside the hostel and were shocked to find Zeb sitting on a bunk. I was puzzled as to why he was not further along the trail.

"Zeb, we didn't expect to catch up to you," I said.

"I spent the night with a freak two nights ago near Big Bald Mountain. I want this guy to get far ahead of me."

I asked him to explain.

"This guy shows up at Bald Mountain Shelter," Zeb explained, "He interrogated me, then took out a Rambo knife and began sharpening it on a stone. A little nervous, I packed up my gear and said I was heading to a lower elevation to keep warm. I hiked four miles down the mountain and set up my tent right on the trail. A half-hour later the creep shows up at my camp. No tent. The creep slept out in the snow. I lay awake all night wondering what was next. At first light, I hiked here and have been here since. The creep came in and left this morning. I'm staying here until he's way ahead."

He was pretty shaken up. Zeb was an Army veteran, and he was not the type that would get spooked easily. That guy must really be a creep.

Since the trail's inception, relatively few crimes have been reported compared to towns and cities. Because danger and crime on the trail are rare, when it does occur it is a big deal. In the spring of 1996, two women were murdered near the trail in the Shenandoah Mountains of Virginia. The killer was never caught. These murders caught the national spotlight and heightened the sense for security of hikers.

After getting the scoop from Zeb, Packrat and I caught a ride into town to do laundry and hit the grocery store. Packrat and I decided not to let fear of the creep keep us from heading onward. After listening to Zeb's story, Packrat and I decided that we would reverse the situation and spook this creep right back. We didn't know how, but we had plenty of time to come up with a plan.

The next morning after some coffee and granola bars, we donned our packs and continued north. The white blazes that mark the trail led us up a few thousand feet, cresting on a ridge. Soon after the trail leveled off, we stumbled across a shelter, so we stopped for a break. A Boy Scout troop had camped the previous night at the shelter and was still there. A stray black Labrador retriever was hanging around.

We asked the Scouts if they had seen another hiker pass through. One of the Scouts spoke up. "Some guy going by the trail name Sponge stayed here last night. He was not very friendly."

I flipped open the trail register. Sponge had made a bizarre entry: "I hate boys and dogs." Staying with a group and leaving a message of that nature is totally inappropriate. In the register, Sponge had listed all of the sections of the AT he had hiked over the years with dates written next to them. One date and place caught my eye: Shenandoah, 1996. Reading this passage sent a chill up my spine as I thought of the women who were murdered there. The Scouts said that Sponge had left the shelter two hours earlier. Since the killer had never been caught, any creep on the trail easily aroused suspicion. His leaving a register entry of a previous hike corresponding to the year and general location of the murders did not sit well with me.

Packrat and I devised a plan for when we met up with him. We were going to look at the guy with crazy looks on our faces. If we ran into him before we stopped for the night, we would keep hiking until we were sure that he wouldn't catch up to us. Although usually we each followed our own pace, we stayed close together on the trail all day.

Several hours passed. Packrat and I had lugged our resupplied packs up and down quite a few peaks. Packrat was 20 yards ahead of me. Above the crunching sound of my feet hitting the trail, I heard Packrat mutter, "There's a man sitting on a log just up the path." I looked ahead. There was a 100-foot dip on the trail in between two hills. A man fitting the creep's description was sitting on a log in the dip. We picked up our pace and ran down the hill. I looked at Sponge with a goofy face, said "Hello," and kept trotting right by, up the hill following Packrat. Sponge was sitting on a log holding a large branch, which was too short to serve as a walking stick. He seemed to be in a meditative trance. He had sunglasses on, but I still felt his eyes slice through me as I walked by. A cold chill crept up my spine. Breathing was difficult.

A mile later we reached the shelter, never once slowing our pace. Packrat said I looked like a Vietcong soldier running through the bush in a war movie. When we reached the shelter, it was late in the day. We hoped that the creep would stay there, so we would keep walking. Our plan was to fill our water and keep going until dark. Before we finished pumping water, Sponge showed up. He would have had to hike at a trot to arrive as quickly as he did. Panic swept over Packrat and me. Pumping water became difficult because my fingers were trembling with fear. Why would this creep run to catch up to us?

"Are ya staying here tonight?" Sponge asked.

Packrat responded, "No, we're going at least another 10 miles more."

"We never stop walking until we have put in at least 25 miles," I chimed in.

Sponge sat down on the shelter platform. He had red hair, and a deep bronze tan darker than your average beach bum. He sat and looked at us while clenching a log. I asked him what the log was for.

"To hit with," he replied.

That response was enough for me. "Let's go, Packrat!" I said. This guy gave me the feeling that at any moment he would go off in a murderous craze. We said good-bye and sped north into the night.

The sun set, and the trail became more and more difficult to see. We kept walking, hoping to find a decent campsite near water. After going a few miles, we gave up trying to find water. Just a flat spot would be nice. Eventually, we came across a flat ridge overlooking a farmhouse down in the valley. A dog on the farm acknowledged our presence by barking continuously. Even with Sponge miles back, we still felt insecure. Zeb had walked four miles down a mountain in the middle of the night, and Sponge had followed him. We expected him to show up.

In the morning, the sun peeked above the mountain ridge off in the distance. I unzipped my tent and lay there. The sunrise was spectacular. Down in the valley, streaks of shadow from the mountain still blocking the blaze were mixed with fingers of sunlight. If we had not run into the creep, we never would have stayed on this ridge, and we would not have witnessed such a beautiful sunrise. Sponge never did catch up to us. It was a bad encounter with a sunny ending.

Appalachian Trail

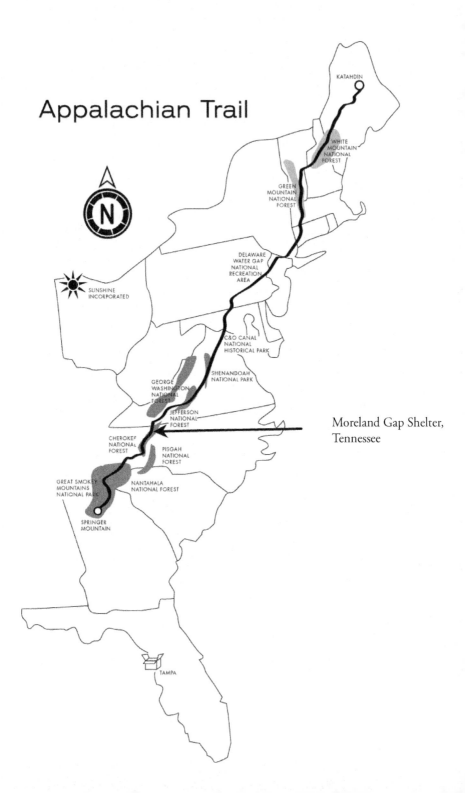

KATAHDIN

WHITE MOUNTAIN NATIONAL FOREST

GREEN MOUNTAIN NATIONAL FOREST

N

DELAWARE WATER GAP NATIONAL RECREATION AREA

SUNSHINE INCORPORATED

C&O CANAL NATIONAL HISTORICAL PARK

SHENANDOAH NATIONAL PARK

GEORGE WASHINGTON NATIONAL FOREST

JEFFERSON NATIONAL FOREST

Moreland Gap Shelter, Tennessee

CHEROKEE NATIONAL FOREST

PISGAH NATIONAL FOREST

GREAT SMOKEY MOUNTAINS NATIONAL PARK

NANTAHALA NATIONAL FOREST

SPRINGER MOUNTAIN

TAMPA

Chapter 17

Don't Drink the Water

Near Moreland Gap Shelter, Tennessee. March 28, 1998. 390 miles from Springer Mountain, Georgia.

The weather had improved significantly over the past week. I was comfortable wearing a T-shirt and shorts during the day. Snow persisted at the higher elevations but had melted away in the valleys and lower elevations.

I ascended above 6,000 feet for the last time in Tennessee to the top of Roan Mountain. Several feet of rapidly melting snow still covered the mountain. Beneath the snow blanket, Roan Mountain is littered with rhododendrons and mountain laurel. Off the trail, whole mountainsides are carpeted with rhododendrons and tall grass. Tourists come from all over when the rhododendrons bloom brilliant pink flowers. Unfortunately, it was too early in the season to witness the pink masterpiece.

A drastic descent off Roan Mountain opened up to Carvers Gap, which is a series of bald mountains. I could see for miles across the mountain peaks and down into valleys dotted with farms and cleared fields, surrounded by forest.

As usual, I walked alone for most of the day, sometimes running into day hikers and meeting up with Packrat at night in the shelters. Shelter trail journals contained notes written by the half-dozen thru-hikers ahead of me. I wondered how many thru-hikers were behind me.

My mind often drifted back home. I would think of someone close to me, look at my watch, and make a guess as to what that person was doing at that moment in time as I walked. I wondered if those who knew me were wondering what I was doing at given moments in time. Of course, a simple guess of "walking, eating, or sleeping" would sum up my typical day. My life was very simple. As I breathed a beautiful sunset in a valley or paused at a stream to drink in the tranquil sound of fast-moving water, I envisioned different people from home who would appreciate what I was seeing and experiencing. I wished that everyone could stop what they were doing and walk with me. I wished that Aaron could experience this adventure firsthand.

Not far from the Virginia border, the trail left the forest and led out onto a rural road for a half-mile. Old mobile homes and tiny one-room shanties lined the road. Between the homes were small farm plots. I could hear dogs barking as I crept along. A Rottweiler lept from a doghouse just off the right edge of the road, only to be stopped mid-air by a choker with a few feet of chain leash attached to the doghouse. A rusty mobile home slouched behind the doghouse. Posted all over the front of the trailer were signs saying "No Trespassing." A tractor sat in a field up ahead. A case of beer was perched on the tractor's engine cover in front of the driver seat. I waved at some folks sitting on the porch of a house, but they just stared, silent and still. This was definitely not Mr. Roger's neighborhood. I was wondering if I had walked into Deliverance.

A trail marker sent me back into the woods off the road. Thank goodness! My water supply was low. I always tried to carry two quarts of water. When one was empty, I would refill at the next available water source. I had not encountered water in some time, and I had only a half-quart left. It was hot, and I was afraid of running out. Just off the road, I stumbled upon a small stream that ran behind one of the farms. Without hesitation, I took my pack off, got my water filter out, and pumped my water bottles full. This water filter had served me well so far, filtering out possible Giardia bacteria. The Giardia lambilia bacterium, which causes Giardia, is a parasite that lives in animal feces. It is contracted by drinking water that has been contaminated when an animal relieves itself in a stream or brook. Symptoms of Giardia are fever, diarrhea, and stomach cramps, but several weeks may pass before the symptoms appear. The trail guides were pretty accurate about safe water sources to drink from, but it was recommended that all water be treated. I found out later that the stream that I filtered my water from was actually runoff from a pig and cow farm. Fortunately, I never got sick.

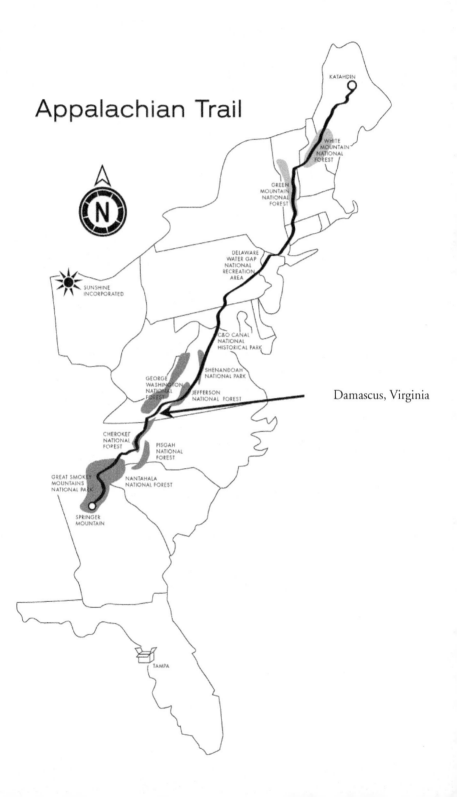

Appalachian Trail

KATAHDIN

WHITE MOUNTAIN NATIONAL FOREST

GREEN MOUNTAIN NATIONAL FOREST

N

DELAWARE WATER GAP NATIONAL RECREATION AREA

SUNSHINE INCORPORATED

C&O CANAL NATIONAL HISTORICAL PARK

SHENANDOAH NATIONAL PARK

GEORGE WASHINGTON NATIONAL FOREST

JEFFERSON NATIONAL FOREST

Damascus, Virginia

CHEROKEE NATIONAL FOREST

PISGAH NATIONAL FOREST

GREAT SMOKEY MOUNTAINS NATIONAL PARK

NANTAHALA NATIONAL FOREST

SPRINGER MOUNTAIN

TAMPA

Chapter 18

Over the Hump

Damascus, Virginia. March 31, 1998. 452 miles from Springer Mountain, Georgia.

Thirty days had passed since I left my family in Georgia to trek north. Crossing into Virginia signified my fourth state on the trail. It is said that a month on the trail refines the body to physically handle the entire length. Although I had constant aches and pains, I was now in the best shape of my life.

Journal entry: March 29, 1998. Watauga Lake Shelter. 16.2 miles hiked. Great weather 82° and sunny. I forded two streams today at Laurel Falls. Melting snow caused the streams to rise, washing out the footbridges. I have walked 142 miles in a week. Several section hikers are in the shelter with me. Just two days from Virginia. Yahoo!

Supposedly, the miles of leveled-off ridges in Virginia would be easier for hiking. Approaching Damascus gave me a preview of what was to come. The terrain leveled off after I climbed onto a ridge. Other than periodic ups and downs, the trail was much more forgiving than it had been in Georgia and North Carolina. Packrat, another thru-hiker named Hungry Bear, and I were so excited to make it to Virginia that we walked 30 miles into the night using headlamps. We wanted to get as close as we could to Damascus so that the next morning we would have a leisurely 10-mile stroll down the mountain into town.

As I walked along the ridge off to the west, I could see bumper-to-bumper traffic on every road converging on a town in the valley. I later learned that a Nascar racetrack was located in nearby Bristol, Tennessee. Thousands of spectators from all around were squeezing into the speedway to watch cars speed around a track. They say car racing is the fastest growing spectator sport in the country. As I descended the mountain into Damascus, I realized how I relied on these towns to re-supply, much as a Nascar driver relies on frequent pit stops to complete a race. In essence, my body was my car. While in town, I would replenish my fuel (food), wash my body (shower), repair any mechanical failures (torn straps, sprained ankles), and provide needed maintenance (pizza, beer, ice cream, and lots of motivational encouragement from my support team). When I pulled out of town, my car was ready for another 100 laps—well, miles. Of course, a racecar driver needs a competent pit crew. My support team was well qualified to take this car all the way to Maine.

The trail wound down the mountain, beneath an arch welcoming us to Damascus, and along Main Street. Damascus is well known among hikers as the friendliest town along the trail. Every year, Damascus holds a festival for hikers. Some hikers actually hitchhike to the festival from wherever they are on the trail at the time. One visit was good enough for me this year.

The trail follows the usual white blazes through town past Mount Rodgers Outfitter and on the way to the hostel. Even though we all looked forward to a hearty breakfast, we decided to stop at the store and get the thru-hiker news and gossip. Outfitters along the trail are well informed about who has passed through and of any upcoming issues with terrain, trail, or weather. The three of us dropped our packs against the outside of the building and went inside. Shopping for gear was the last thing on my mind. The gentleman behind the counter introduced himself.

"Hi, I'm Jeff." I liked his name.

"Jeff, where's a good place to get breakfast?"

"Dot's, just up the road a few blocks."

"Thanks!"

"Tell Betty to make you some of her special pancakes."

"Hmmm! That sounds pretty good."

"I'll see you after breakfast," Jeff said.

A hostel called The Place, run by the United Methodist Church, was another block on the way to Dot's. I checked in, picked a bunk, and left my gear. Packrat and Hungry Bear filed in and did the same. We continued our march to Dot's.

Dot's is a genuine greasy-spoon diner. We stepped inside and sat down at the bar. An aged woman came out of the kitchen and stood behind the bar. Her gray hair was pulled back in a ponytail, and she wore a knee-length summer dress and apron.

"Are you Betty?" I asked.

"Yeah!"

"Jeff down at the outfitter recommended your special pancakes."

"I don't make pancakes. I'm retired."

"Oh. Well, he must have told us that to rile you up. OK then, I'll take four eggs, toast, grits, bacon, hash-browns, and some coffee instead."

Packrat and Hungry Bear ordered huge breakfasts, too. Food consumption is how Hungry Bear earned his trail name. Betty set coffee cups in front of each of us and walked into the kitchen. She hollered back, "The coffee is behind the bar, get it yourself." So much for service with a smile.

Mail was my next order of business. The post office, just a block from the hostel, had three boxes addressed to me, along with a handful of letters. It took me two trips to get my mail back to the hostel. Sunshine employees and residents had sent a care package with cookies, candy, and many letters from staff, residents, and friends. The letters were awesome to read and inspired me to keep going. Read an example below, and you'll understand.

Dear Jeff,

Just a quick note to say hello. Hope your hike is going well! You should feel very good about yourself!!! You are hiking for a great cause!

I am very new to this field. I was hired in December and was not sure how I would do. I started with respite and am now at a group home. I love my job! Most of society views people with disabilities as not being normal. Each and every person should spend one day working with our residents. Most of them are nicer than the "normal" people we deal with on a daily basis.

Well, I will sign off for now, but I am working on a tape for you—don't know your musical preferences so I am making one with mine. The Grateful Dead, John Mull Band, and some others. As the boys in the Dead would say... "Let inspiration move you brightly."

Have a Greatful Day!

Love & Peace

M

P.S. Look for your tape in April. Good luck with your hike.

The Sunshine director of development, Douglas Siebenaler, sent a letter updating me with the success of my fundraiser. To date, we'd raised $9,500, with more commitments coming in daily. Apparently, the television interview that was broadcast the day that I began my journey had caught the eye of several folks who reached deep into their pockets to help out. Wow! I sat and read letters for a few hours. I was completely inspired with the support from everyone at home. Not only was I making progress toward Maine, but also my hike had created awareness for the needs of the people being served at Sunshine.

Finally, I unpacked my supply box. This was my fifth supply point. I was getting sick of eating trail mix and peanut butter. Since each box contained the same items, I decided to trade some of my food with other hikers in an effort to increase variety. Hostels have grab boxes to pick through and leave extra supplies. A jar of peanut butter was worth two days of beef jerky, and my trail mix bought me a cache of candy bars.

The next chore was laundry. As I waited for my clothes to cycle through, I read the local paper. Not much had changed in the news in the past 30 days. The United States had managed to avoid getting involved in war, and Clinton was still president. Coke and Mr. N's mouse competition back in the Smokies was definitely more interesting than the newspaper.

Back in the hostel, I noticed a scale in the dining area. Curiosity led me over. One foot up, and then the other. Wow! Fifteen pounds less than I weighed 30 days ago. Though my appetite had increased enormously, I could not seem to eat enough to replenish the calories. A thick, juicy steak had been on my mind for several days. There was no chophouse in town, so I ventured to the grocery store. My shopping cart filled with charcoal, two pounds of New York strip steak, potatoes, and two big aluminum throwaway baking pans. All the way back to the hostel, I practically danced a jig knowing that I was going to eat steak.

The aluminum baking pans became a grill. I punctured holes in the bottom of one pan to use as the grill surface. I poured the charcoal in the other pan and lit it. When the charcoal turned a gray and glowing red color, I put potatoes in with the briquettes, put the other pan over top, and slapped the two pounds of steak on it. Thirty minutes later, a meal fit for four was finished. And in less time than it took to prepare the meal, I ate every bit of it.

Easter was a week and a half away. Most of my family had planned to meet me along the trail for Easter. Coordinating where to meet was difficult. After several phone conversations with my stepfather, we agreed on a meeting place that was about 130 miles up the trail. He understood that plans might change as my walk unfolded. I spent the evening writing postcards.

By the end of the second day, I was ready to move northward. Packrat asked if I would wait another day and head out with him. He was waiting on a new pack to ship in to the outfitter. Packrat had bought several hundred dollars in new gear, which I did not understand because he had complained at various times about a shortage of funds. Although my family was planning to meet me, which put me on a strict time schedule, I agreed to wait for him. But I explained that I would have to maintain an aggressive pace to stay on schedule.

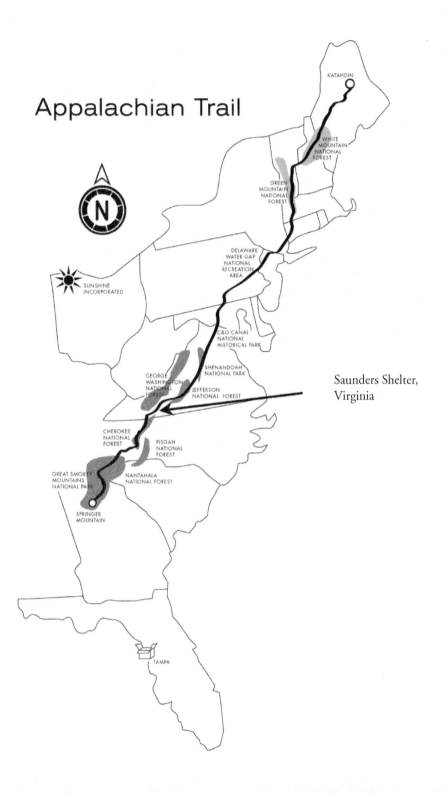

Appalachian Trail

KATAHDIN

WHITE MOUNTAIN NATIONAL FOREST

GREEN MOUNTAIN NATIONAL FOREST

DELAWARE WATER GAP NATIONAL RECREATION AREA

SUNSHINE INCORPORATED

C&O CANAL NATIONAL HISTORICAL PARK

GEORGE WASHINGTON NATIONAL FOREST

SHENANDOAH NATIONAL PARK

JEFFERSON NATIONAL FOREST

Saunders Shelter, Virginia

CHEROKEE NATIONAL FOREST

PISGAH NATIONAL FOREST

GREAT SMOKEY MOUNTAINS NATIONAL PARK

NANTAHALA NATIONAL FOREST

SPRINGER MOUNTAIN

TAMPA

Chapter 19

I Believe in You!

Saunders Shelter, Virginia. April 3, 1998. 462 miles from Springer Mountain, Georgia.

Finally, after three days in town, I was walking north again. Packrat had received the equipment that he had ordered. We had camped together for 28 of the last 31 days, so I felt that I could not just leave town without him.

After a hearty breakfast at Dot's, we marched north. The AT skirts the main highway going out of town north of Damascus. An hour or so north of town, Packrat complained about his backpack not fitting right. We were near the road. Packrat wanted to go back to town to fix his pack. I told him there was no way that I could waste another day waiting. Family came first. We arranged a ride for him back to town. In order to meet up with my family, I needed to cover 100 miles in the next few days. From the looks of things, I would be blazing trail on my own. Packrat said he would catch up to me in a few days. As I walked on, I pondered what he had said, wondering if he would ever catch up to me.

The day was half over when I left town, limiting my distance. Saunders Shelter was 10 miles north of town, so I planned to stay there. No one was in the shelter when I arrived. It was surrounded by hardwood oak and pine forest with a small grassy clearing to the right side of the shelter. I gathered up some firewood, retrieved water from the stream, and cooked some macaroni and cheese.

Thunderstorms had threatened all day with occasional growls and a light mist, but no real rain. As night fell, I could not see a star in the sky. I hoped that the rain would fall while I slept so that I would not have to walk through bad weather the next day. Rocks the size of bowling balls were assembled as a fire ring beneath the roof overhang, just a few feet in front of the bunk space. I piled some twigs in the fire ring, lit a match, and waved a shirt to create some artificial wind. In no time, I had a fire. I lay awake for a few hours gazing into the embers, lost in thought about my journey.

Journal entry: Hiked from Damascus to Saunders Shelter for the night. Just me here. I started a blazing fire. Looks like a lightning storm is rolling in. 9.5 miles hiked.

Gazing into the core of a fire usually puts me into a trance. In this case, it put me right to sleep.

Sometime around midnight, the wooden plank bunk I was sleeping on shook and a loud crash awakened me. I jolted up into a sitting position. The sleeping bag was zipped, so all that was sticking out was my head. A few seconds passed. I realized that I was fine and dry, under the protection of a shelter roof, in a warm sleeping bag, and that it was just a little thunderstorm. Buckets of rain pelted the ground hard enough to leave divots. Rain splattered and puddled. I ruffled my clothes into a makeshift pillow and began to lie back when a bright flash sliced down into the forest right before me, burning my eyes as I watched. A gust of wind smacked my face, sending cinders from my fire all through the shelter, followed by a thunderous bang. The ground shook as trees smacked the forest floor. Lightning struck less than 30 feet from the shelter.

I was covered in soot from the fire and spellbound by what had just occurred. The safety I had relished only minutes ago was stripped away. Oh, man, that lightning was dangerously close. A basic precaution to take during lightning storms is avoiding large metal objects, and here I was, huddled beneath a tin roof. Hello, Ben Franklin! I did not know whether I should stay beneath the dry shelter roof or seek cover away from it. A tent offers no protection from lightening, but at least it's not made of metal. Although they say lightning never strikes twice, I panicked, jumped out from my sleeping bag, and ran from beneath the shelter roof. I looked up at that sky and yelled, "I believe in you!"

What should I do? Sleep in the shelter or set up my tent? Slowly, a calm sensation gathered in my thoughts. I felt as if I was directed back to the shelter. Something told me everything would be OK. Could this be? Is God letting me know that He is walking with me on my journey? Am I safe beneath this tin roof?

I removed my T-shirt and shorts, which were saturated from me standing in the rain. Only moments ago, my heart was echoing in my ears. Now, I was as calm as I have ever been. I managed to clamber into my down sleeping bag and fall asleep.

I have never felt a stronger connection with the forest and God. In the morning, I lay in my sleeping bag and peered out at the rain still falling from the sky. During my college years, I explored various church services as I tried to find what suited me best. I have always believed in God, but I had never experienced a strong connection. Through the years leading up to my journey, I would escape to the mountains often. I felt at peace with the world when I was in the woods. My best thoughts seemed to occur while walking over mountains and taking in the fresh air. Four walls and a minister are not necessary for me to worship. God's house has no walls. I was immersed among all of God's natural creations, and He had let me know that the forest, weather, and everything that surrounded me was indeed His creation.

Processing what had happened was difficult. All day as I walked, I thought about my profound encounter. Sitting there helpless in the shelter made me realize how simple life is. Lightning striking close but not hitting the shelter roof was a reminder that I had very little control over the natural forces and beauty that surrounded me.

One thing was reaffirmed from this day forward: I was not on this journey alone. Yes, I was walking solo, but God was keeping me safe and watching over me.

Appalachian Trail

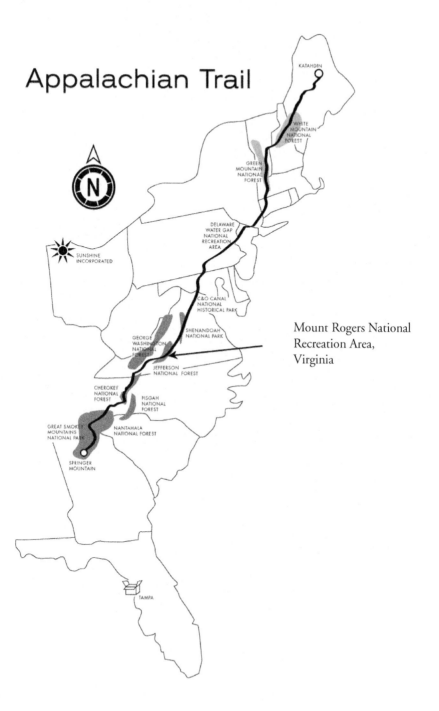

KATAHDIN

WHITE MOUNTAIN NATIONAL FOREST

GREEN MOUNTAIN NATIONAL FOREST

DELAWARE WATER GAP NATIONAL RECREATION AREA

SUNSHINE INCORPORATED

C&O CANAL NATIONAL HISTORICAL PARK

GEORGE WASHINGTON NATIONAL FOREST

SHENANDOAH NATIONAL PARK

Mount Rogers National Recreation Area, Virginia

JEFFERSON NATIONAL FOREST

CHEROKEE NATIONAL FOREST

PISGAH NATIONAL FOREST

GREAT SMOKEY MOUNTAINS NATIONAL PARK

NANTAHALA NATIONAL FOREST

SPRINGER MOUNTAIN

TAMPA

Chapter 20

Let's Go All the Way!

Mount Rogers National Recreation Area Headquarters, Virginia. April 6, 1998. 516 miles from Springer Mountain, Georgia.

Virginia is supposed to be the easiest state to walk through along the entire trail, but first I had to get north of Mount Rogers, the highest elevation in the state—5,792 feet, according to my *Appalachian Trail Guide*. Mount Rogers is located just south of the Grayson Highlands State Park. My trail guides and other hikers advised me to keep all cold weather gear until I got north of this mountain.

After some coffee and a Pop-Tart, I loaded my gear, fastened down the straps, and slipped my rain cover over my pack. A backpack rain cover is the silliest thing. The package claimed it's waterproof, but every time it rained, my pack was wet at the end of the day. By the way, backpacks are not waterproof, either. You can buy waterproof boots and clothing to keep your body dry, but you cannot buy a waterproof backpack.

My boots were protected with brand-new, knee-high gaiters, which I bought in Damascus. Gaiters wrap around your boot, calf, and shin. They keep debris and water from penetrating your socks and boots. Knee-high gaiters protect your shins from cuts and scrapes caused by briars or thorn bushes. Since most hikers wear shorts, walking through town in a pair of gaiters usually attracts a few stares. Gaiters look like a thick pair of socks that are pulled up too high. The only skin revealed is from the knee up to the mid-thigh—definitely a fashion statement.

In spite of all this high-tech rain gear, I was wet from head to toe within an hour of leaving the dry shelter. The temperature dropped to freezing by mid-afternoon, and the rain was now sleet. My lips were purple; my cheeks red; my body wet, and my mind was drifting—typical symptoms of hypothermia.

The trail opened up to a clearing and a parking lot as I left the protection of the tree canopy. As soon as I reached the grassy opening, I was smacked with sleet, which was carried by a strong, icy wind. The trail continued up a barren, grass-covered hill. I could see where the tree-line picked back up at the top of the hill, a little over a half-mile ahead. The same trees I feared crashing onto me the night before were now my only barrier to the brutal chill.

Keeping my winter gear was good advice. I turned around and walked back into the tree line. My body was quivering from the cold, and my teeth were chattering. I dropped the pack off my back. My fleece gloves were covered with ice. I pulled some waterproof wind pants and a thermal top from my pack and put them on. I was wearing a fleece hat, two layers of clothing beneath my waterproof jacket, wind pants, and gaiters. Only yesterday, I had walked in a T-shirt and shorts.

Marching up the wind-exposed hill was at least bearable with my new clothing layers. Finally, a shelter came into view. I had reached the Mount Rogers summit. A blue plastic tarp had been tied across the front of the shelter to break the wind. I pulled the tarp aside and stepped in.

Two young gentlemen wearing wool hats pulled over their ears were sitting on sleeping bags, leaning up against the back wall. I could smell some sort of beef. A boiling pot of water sat on a one-burner stove with ramen noodles flipping around in the water. Instantly, both hikers expressed concern at my purple lips, red cheeks, and chattering teeth.

"Are you OK?"

"I think so."

"Would you like some hot tea?"

One of the gentlemen handed me a piping hot cup of tea.

"Thanks."

"Want some cheese and crackers?"

"OK."

I did not feel like cooking. I was just glad to be out of the weather. Slowly, I began to warm up. I took off all my wet clothes and put on a set of polypropylene long underwear. I rolled out my sleeping bag on the floor and dug through my food pack for some candy.

The tarp blocking the sleet and wind tore open. Packrat stepped into the shelter. I had walked 23 miles since leaving him at the road yesterday. "Here you are, Wrongfoot. I wondered if I would catch up with you."

"How did you catch up?"

"I've been walking since 7:30 this morning. I have a new pack, tent, and stove."

Packrat is a gear freak. He knows more trivia about the latest hiking equipment than most sales people in outfitter stores. I could not rationalize why he bought all this new equipment. His old pack was top-of-the-line and in mint-condition; his stove worked fine—it just needed cleaning—and his tent was a top-of-the-line, lightweight model. His original equipment was of higher quality than that of many other hikers. Normally, I do not question other people's buying decisions, but for the last few weeks, Packrat had complained that he might not have enough money to make it to Maine. Yet he had just shelled out $600 in new equipment with three-fourths of the trail left to go.

"Packrat, are you going to have enough money to last?" I asked.

He put his hands on his hips. "Yeah, as long as I don't spend too much in town." Many hikers get sucked into towns along the trail, spending all their money on hotels, food, and beer.

In the morning, I did not want to get out of my sleeping bag. I sat up, pulled my arms out of the bag, and heated a pot of water for coffee. When the water was ready, I poured it over some coffee grounds into my mug and leaned up against the back wall of the shelter while still in my sleeping bag. Ahh! Each sip infused me with warmth as I gulped it down.

Today I was heading through the Grayson Highlands. I had been to this park with my stepfather on a previous hike. The AT follows grassy, bald mountaintop meadows where wild ponies roam freely along the trail. A park service sign near the AT on a side trail advises hikers not to "molest the horses," among other suggestions. I do not even want to know what actions motivated the rangers to post such a sign. My advice to everyone: Keep your pony to yourself in these parts!

As I walked along, I could see for miles in all directions. I heard the ponies' naying as I walked along the open ridge. A mile north of the shelter, a herd of ponies was grazing on frozen, knee-high grass several hundred yards off the trail. There wasn't a cloud in the sky, but the temperature remained below freezing. Throughout the mountain meadow, the sunlight glistened on the ice-coated branches of leafless bushes. Eventually, I covered 10 spectacular miles across mountain balds. Soon after, the trail turned back into the forest.

***

This would turn out to be the last night I spent with Packrat on the trail. We walked 19 miles and set up camp in a park dedicated to the destruction caused by Hurricane Hugo. The hurricane had swept inland several hundred miles, as far as the Appalachians, ripping whole trees from the ground. The next morning, we ate some breakfast, took down our tents, and slung on our packs, ready for another day in the woods. As usual, we spread out on the trail at our own pace. Packrat was ahead of me by about a half-mile. By mid-morning, a couple of people out for a day hike passed me going south. They stopped.

"Are you Wrongfoot?"

"Yes, that's me."

"This note is for you from another hiker up the trail."

That's strange, I thought. *Why would Packrat send a note back to me unless something was wrong?* I unfolded the note.

"Wrongfoot, I'm leaving the trail at the park headquarters. Here's my address. Send me updates of your trip. Packrat."

Packrat quitting the trail was no surprise. He had attempted this journey four times before and quit not too far from here every time. With his track record and lack of money, the odds were against him making it to Maine. I really wanted to see him make it, but finishing is up to the individual.

Mount Rogers National Park headquarters was located several miles north of where I received Packrat's note. I reached the headquarters by noon. The AT crosses the parking lot. A souvenir shop and information center was open to the public. I dropped my pack, leaned it up against the outside wall of the building, and stepped inside. A young, attractive female ranger with long, brown hair stood behind the information counter. I stepped up to the counter.

"Hi, I'm a thru-hiker. I was wondering if you met another thru-hiker that went by the name Packrat?"

"Yeah," the ranger responded. "He came in asking for information on the nearest town. He called a taxi from the pay phone. You missed him by 15 minutes. He was headed for Atkins."

I thanked the ranger for the information, bought some peanut M&M's and a Coke, and went back outside. Food always took precedence. After a short break sitting on the steps outside the park office, I donned my pack and walked on.

Walking hundreds of miles with a total stranger is quite a concept. I had become friends with Packrat during the last 500 miles, over the course of a month. We had shared the same shelter and hostels almost every night that I had been on the trail. Having someone to talk with at the end of the day was nice.

If Packrat and I had grown up in the same neighborhood, we probably would not have been friends because we have totally different lives. He was nearly 20 years older than me. He was a tool and die worker; I am a speech-language pathologist. He had spent most of his life in Connecticut and Missouri. Packrat was down on his luck financially and was surviving on very few funds. He had befriended a woman from Alabama who was an avid hiker. She had agreed to act as Packrat's support team for his thru-hike and was mailing Packrat his supplies along the way. She also was managing his budget. Packrat had explained that he had a tough time managing money. Other than this woman, he did not have anyone except an ex-wife and kids. Packrat's background was completely contrary to mine, but we both were hiking the AT. We had developed a trail bond. My walk had taken another turn. Just as when I started my trek, I was solo once again.

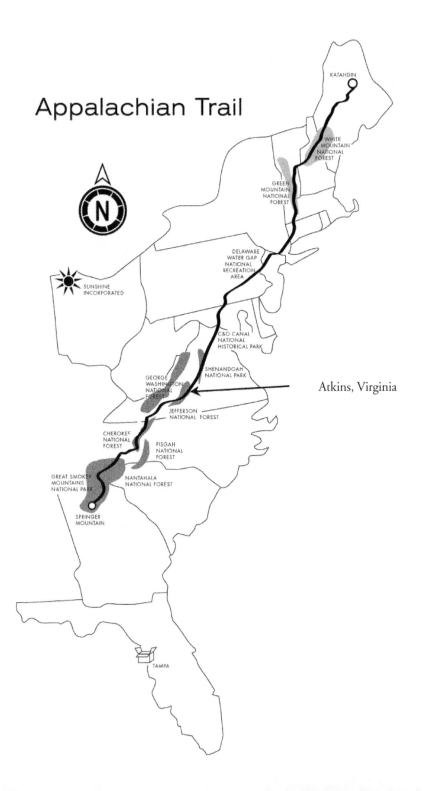

Appalachian Trail

KATAHDIN

WHITE MOUNTAIN NATIONAL FOREST

GREEN MOUNTAIN NATIONAL FOREST

N

DELAWARE WATER GAP NATIONAL RECREATION AREA

SUNSHINE INCORPORATED

C&O CANAL NATIONAL HISTORICAL PARK

SHENANDOAH NATIONAL PARK

GEORGE WASHINGTON NATIONAL FOREST

Atkins, Virginia

JEFFERSON NATIONAL FOREST

CHEROKEE NATIONAL FOREST

PISGAH NATIONAL FOREST

GREAT SMOKEY MOUNTAINS NATIONAL PARK

NANTAHALA NATIONAL FOREST

SPRINGER MOUNTAIN

TAMPA

Chapter 21

Yee Haa! The Gang's All Here

Atkins, Virginia. April 8, 1998. 529 miles from Springer Mountain, Georgia.

Having family meet me on the trail was exciting. I had not seen them since waving good-bye on Springer Mountain more than five weeks ago. I knew that they would lift my spirits. Losing my trail partner had taken a toll on my enthusiasm.

Meeting up with someone along the trail meant adhering to a schedule, which is stressful and difficult for a hiker. Walking the trail had been an unpredictable experience so far. With unexpected weather, extra days off in town, and injuries, I could never predict how long it would take to walk a certain number of miles.

Originally, I planned to have my family pick me up at a roadside hotel just off the AT in Bland, Virginia. But the extra day of R&R back in Damascus to wait for Packrat had thrown off my mileage. To get back on schedule, I would have to walk 75 miles in three days—not my idea of fun.

The day that Packrat quit, I walked 28 miles to the town of Atkins. Just off the trail was a country diner and hotel. My parents were planning on meeting me in two days about 50 miles farther north. My feet were throbbing from all the miles. The reality of logistics and pain forced me to adjust the location where my family would meet me. The balls of my feet felt as if I were stepping on marbles. Ouch! I could feel lumps beneath the skin. This is where my family would have to meet me. I checked into a room and called my parents in Florida. They understood and adjusted their plans.

Not having to cover so many miles for the next two days took off a load of stress. The next morning I would make arrangements with the hotel clerk to drive me 12 miles north to where the AT crosses a road. I would walk the trail south back to the hotel. After the Easter weekend, I would have 12 miles fewer to travel. My hike would resume back at the road. I'd have my parents drop me off there.

I emptied my pack in the hotel room and left just two quarts of water and snacks in it. Not carrying a pack is termed slack packing among thru-hikers. The weather was beautiful, sunny, and 65 degrees. The trail rollercoastered over small mountains, weaving in and out of a leafless hardwood forest and up over stiles, which are ladder structures used to cross over fences.

Toward the end of my slack-packing tour, I ran into another thru-hiker, Hungry Bear. He was sitting in a shelter two and a half miles from the hotel. I had spent a few nights in shelters with him back in North Carolina. He was a 20-something, blond, bushy-haired fellow who came out on the trail to be free. The closer I got to the shelter, the more I noticed a chalky pale color to his skin and sweat running down his face.

"Hungry Bear, how are ya?"

"Not so good. I think I've got the flu. I've had stomach cramps for two days."

"Hmmm. You might have Giardia."

Hikers usually treat all water using a filter or iodine unless a sign indicates that the water is safe to drink. Some hikers take the risk and drink the water along the trail without any preparation. I remembered a conversation with Hungry Bear a few weeks before. He said he doesn't treat water at high elevations or if it's coming out of a rock. I didn't understand his reasoning. As far as I've known, elevation is not a factor in regards to animal needs whether they are at 500 feet above sea level or 15,000 feet. I have seen scat in the dirt, on rocks, and near clear, bubbling streams. Determining water's safety based on appearance or location is quite foolish. The Giardia parasite is less than one micron, which can be seen only under a powerful microscope.

"You should head back to Atkins and see a doctor."

"I don't have health insurance."

"If you have Giardia, you need to get treated. It won't go away."

"I'll be OK."

"Alright, take care."

I never saw Hungry Bear again, although I read some of his journal entries in northern Virginia. He dropped off the trail somewhere along the route.

I continued my walk back to the hotel. After showering off the day's walk, I ordered dinner at the restaurant in front of my hotel. Afterward, I bought some beer and retreated to my hotel room. My family was planning to drive through the night to meet me. They would arrive in the wee hours of morning. I looked forward to being with my family, my support team.

A knock at my door awoke me at 2:00 a.m. My brother, sister-in-law, and nephew had arrived from Atlanta. They checked into the room next door. Another knock at 4:00 a.m. awoke me again. My stepfather, mom, sister, and brother-in-law had arrived. We all slept for a few hours until the sun peeked over the mountain.

Our plan was to drive north to the Shenandoah National Park and spend Easter together in a lodge. My stepfather intended on day-hiking a section of the Shenandoah in his quest to section-hike the entire AT. My aunt and uncle from Toledo, Ohio, planned to meet us in the Shenandoah.

In the morning, we gathered in the restaurant. Everyone was sizing me up. My mom was not shy about her thoughts.

"Jeff, you have lost a lot of weight."

My sister perked up. "You look different with a beard."

My brother chimed in. "Yeah, what's that scraggly stuff on your chin?"

Ahhh, to be with family again. My defense: "Hey! Let me see what you look like after walking 600 miles." I had grown my first beard and had lost 15 pounds since everyone had seen me.

After breakfast, we drove north for two hours, which I found uncomfortable after walking for 30 days. The longest I had been in a vehicle in the last month was 15 minutes going from a town to the trail. Going down the highway at 75 mph felt too fast. I had grown accustomed to my 2.5 mph pace.

We entered the Shenandoah National Park and drove up to the Skyland Lodge. This was weird for me. The AT follows the Shenandoah ridge right through the park. I was 400 miles further north on the trail than I had been earlier this morning. I would not reach this point on the trail for another five weeks.

Our car wound around several switchbacks. Leafless oaks, maples, and other hardwoods mingled with bold, green pine encompassing the road. Several miles and a few thousand feet in elevation later, we pulled up to a wood-framed lodge. My door to the vehicle was open before the car had come to a stop. Enough driving for me.

My stepfather immediately threw together his day-hiking gear and headed off onto the AT to secure another section toward his northward quest.

"Jeff, want to come along?"

"No, thanks. I'll hike this area soon enough."

Later in the day, my aunt and uncle arrived from Toledo. We all walked to a rock outcropping that overlooked the Shenandoah Valley, just off the AT. During the Civil War, military scouts rode horseback along this very ridge to observe enemy troop movements in the valleys below. You could see 20 miles of valley in every direction. The scouts would then descend to their own military units and report the findings.

I was less interested in walking and more into talking. I'd had no one but Packrat to talk to for the past four weeks. I had my standard questions every time I encountered civilization:

"Is Bill Clinton still president?"

"Is the United States at war?"

And I was always wondering about the Olympic-bombing suspect. "Did they catch Rudolph?"

Then there was the social aspect of getting the family scoop, all the little tidbits of information to which I had been oblivious. My weekly phone calls home were need-based, not social.

During one of many conversations that Easter weekend, I talked about the creep on the trail who had spooked us. My creep story was more authentic when I informed them that the guy had caught a shuttle to the Shenandoah from Damascus while I was in town. He left a note in the trail journal that he was going to the Shenandoah to complete an unfinished section of trail. "And he's somewhere in the Shenandoah park right now," I told them. My brother, who has an extensive law-enforcement background, recommended that I report this guy to the rangers. I hadn't considered reporting him because I didn't think that he'd committed a crime.

Larry convinced me that I should make a report in case something happened later. The whole family walked with me to the ranger station. I submitted a verbal report to a ranger describing the man and why hikers were afraid of him. After the report was complete, the ranger asked where I was staying and how long I would be in the park in case he had more questions.

Finally, dinnertime arrived. Food dominated my mind most of the day. If I wasn't eating, I was thinking about something I wanted to eat. We walked to the park restaurant. My family said they would treat and picked up the tab. Big mistake on their part! I had given up on quality 300 miles ago. It was all about quantity now. The waitress took everybody's order and then looked over to me.

"I'll have a crab cake appetizer, a bowl of soup, and the prime rib dinner special, baked potato, and salad with Thousand Island dressing."

The waitress grinned. "You're hungry, ain't ya?"

Little was mentioned about my food consumption during dinner. When everyone was through, my sister asked if anybody wanted her leftover salad and chicken. I sat silently for a moment. To my excitement, no one wanted her leftovers. I spoke up. "I'll take it, Steph!"

Later in the evening, we gathered into a room at the lodge. My sister, a nurse by trade, took me aside for a general physical assessment. Other than minor cuts, scrapes, dry skin, and marble-sized lumps on the balls of my feet, I was fine. My sister-in-law, the family physical therapist, offered to look at my feet. She found the lumps using her thumbs. For the next half-hour, I had a luxurious foot massage. She literally pushed the lumps forward off the balls of my feet. She said the lumps were a buildup of calcium. Walking was less painful after that treatment.

I spent the next day relaxing. I made a point of staying off my feet as much as possible. Everyone decided to grill out for dinner. We picked up groceries, charcoal, and a grill in a nearby grocery store.

Dinnertime arrived. Dan, my brother-in-law, and Larry, my brother, assembled the grill on the balcony of our room, completely oblivious to the sign bolted to the wall: "No grilling on patio." In no time, an assembly line of buns, lettuce, tomato, and beans awaited our char-broiled burgers.

A knock at the door startled everyone. An undercover government agent presented his badge to my sister at the door. Oh, no! Someone had turned us in for grilling! But the agent asked to speak with me.

He was following up on the report I had made regarding the creepy hiker. Everyone sighed in relief when they realized that we weren't being busted for illegal cooking.

The agent and I stepped into the adjoining bedroom and shut the door. I figured this would only last a few minutes. An hour later, he finally concluded the interview. Ever since the two women hikers were murdered not far from our lodge, every suspicious-person report is pursued, in hopes of finding a break in the case.

At first, the agent asked me to repeat the report that I had made to the ranger a day earlier. Then he asked specific questions about the suspect—height, weight, hair color, and complexion. Finally, he concluded and left me a business card. If I was curious about the outcome of my report, he suggested that I call him when I hiked back into the area in a few weeks. I never did call when I hiked through. I figured he had all the information I could provide. To this day, I wonder if anything ever came of the information I provided. Did the authorities catch up to the creep?

After the agent left, I sat down for a cold hamburger. I was gone for so long that everyone had gone ahead with dinner. I couldn't blame them; I would have done the same.

What's Easter without an egg hunt? My two-year-old nephew was along, so we hid Easter eggs outside around the lodge grounds. While Austin looked for eggs, several deer grazed near us. Deer in the Shenandoah are practically domesticated because thousands of tourists feed them each year. Deer hunters must have a field day in these parts.

Three days off the trail with family had lifted my spirits and helped me refocus on my journey. Even though Packrat had left the trail, I knew many hikers were not far behind me. If I wanted to hike with anyone, I knew I could slow down and link up with someone.

My pack dropped a few pounds in weight. I was north of Mount Rodgers, the last of the high peaks until New Hampshire. According to my trail guides, the weather would be milder until the White Mountains. My parents from Florida had brought me a two-pound, 20-degree-rated sleeping bag, which was two pounds lighter than the zero-rated bag that I had been carrying. Some of the cold-weather gear I had would be unnecessary until New Hampshire as well. I gave my parents a set of thermal underwear and a pair of gloves. They would mail these items to me when I was farther north.

My brother, Larry, volunteered to drop me off on the trail where I had left it four days ago. It was an hour out of the way, and my parents had a longer drive back to Florida. Several hours went by before my brother's big Chevy truck pulled off on the berm of a rural country road at an Appalachian Trail marker.

He felt awkward leaving me there. "Jeff, I do not know too many people that are appreciative for being driven to the middle of nowhere."

I grinned. We opened the cab hatch of the truck and pulled out my backpack. Austin, my two-year-old nephew, and my sister-in-law just kind of stared at me like I was nuts. I expected this reaction from the two-year-old but not from his mom. After a few minutes of small talk, I slipped into my pack straps, posed for a picture with Austin, waved good-bye, and trekked off.

Appalachian Trail

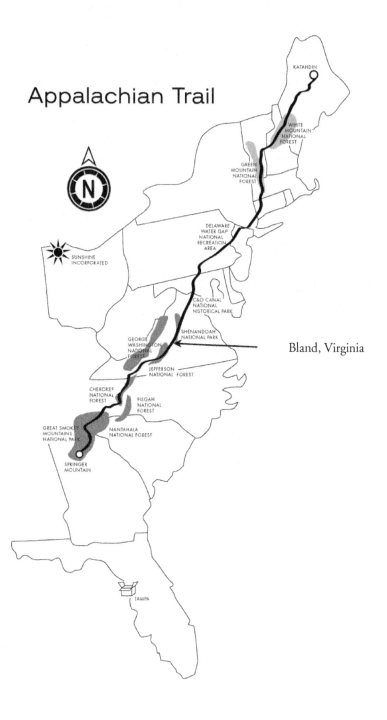

KATAHDIN

WHITE
MOUNTAIN
NATIONAL
FOREST

GREEN
MOUNTAIN
NATIONAL
FOREST

DELAWARE
WATER GAP
NATIONAL
RECREATION
AREA

SUNSHINE
INCORPORATED

C&O CANAL
NATIONAL
HISTORICAL PARK

SHENANDOAH
NATIONAL PARK

GEORGE
WASHINGTON
NATIONAL
FOREST

Bland, Virginia

JEFFERSON
NATIONAL FOREST

CHEROKEE
NATIONAL
FOREST

PISGAH
NATIONAL
FOREST

GREAT SMOKEY
MOUNTAINS
NATIONAL PARK

NANTAHALA
NATIONAL FOREST

SPRINGER
MOUNTAIN

TAMPA

Chapter 22

Woof, Woof!

Bland, Virginia. April 8, 1998. 575 miles from Springer Mountain, Georgia.

Watching me walk away from a perfectly good vehicle into the woods unnerved my brother. Even after I assured Larry that I would be fine, he did not drive off until I was out of visual range walking up the trail. I would rather have stayed with the family for a few more days, but I had to stay focused on my goal: Maine. After several days of family bonding, I was ready to walk again.

With a rejuvenated spirit from my support team, I was fired up for more miles. Over the last few days, we had laughed together, eaten together, and caught up with each other. For a few moments during our weekend, I actually forgot that I was walking to Maine.

Thru-hikers have coined the phrase, "No Pain, No Rain, No Maine." Pain had become a daily factor on the trail. The foot massage that I received from my sister-in-law; however, gave me the sensation of walking barefoot through soft sand. I hoped I could avoid some foot pain for a while.

Carrying 50 pounds for 500 miles gave me an appreciation for every ounce in my pack. The load I was carrying was a few pounds lighter, so each step I took seemed to hit the trail a little easier than before. I had become fine-tuned to notice subtle differences, such as losing a few pounds in the pack.

The weather was beautiful with plenty of sun—the temperature was 70 degrees. The AT weaved up and over small hills, roaming out of leafless forest into open meadows. Buds were beginning to form on the trees. Of course, I was climbing in elevation. A rule of thumb: When nearing civilization, the trail descends; when leaving civilization, the trail climbs.

I had planned on meeting a friend 35 miles from the road where my family dropped me off. It was noon when I began walking. That was stressful because Brian and I planned to meet at a road crossing at mid-afternoon the next day. This necessitated a faster pace.

I spent very few moments resting. As soon as one foot hit the ground, the other foot was right behind. I stopped for water and snacks but only for a few moments. On top of one of the ridges, I came across a middle-aged couple that had walked up the mountain to enjoy an Easter dinner over an open fire. They had carried an entire Easter feast up the mountain to a four-walled shelter called Chestnut Knob. The valleys and distant mountains were in view from the fire pit where the couple was sitting. It was apparent that I had interrupted a romantic moment, and the food had already been consumed, leaving little reason for a hungry hiker to hang around. We chatted for a few moments, and I continued north.

Nightfall set in, and I still was walking. Unless I covered at least 20 miles, I would not make it to the planned meeting place on schedule. With my headlamp beam shining light down the trail, I walked on. Somehow, I missed the campsite where I had planned to stay. Walking at night is an entirely different experience than walking in the woods during the day. During the day, I would notice the brilliant colors of leaves, the sun, and the sky. At night, my feet shuffled and tripped over roots. I had to focus to keep my balance. The forest was completely dark unless the moon was out. Frequently, my headlamp caught the glowing eyes of nocturnal animals—skunks, raccoons, mice. Step after step, I cut through the darkness. Finally, around 9:30 p.m., a shelter came into view.

After eating out for three days, I was not enthused about firing up the stove, but hunger overcame my laziness. In no time, I had a steaming feast of beef jerky, refried beans, and rehydrated tomatoes, onions, and green peppers. After dinner, I cleaned my pot, pan, and body at a nearby spring. Sleep was next on the agenda. I lay down and took out my maps. Only 12 more miles until I met up with Brian.

I had known Brian for more than a decade. He and I had hiked together many times through the years. If not for his career, he would be thru-hiking right along with me. We both had learned to associate hiking with problem-solving. Every major decision we had made over the past 10 years was reached after a walk in the woods. Over the years, we shared story after story with each other as we walked up and down mountains. Brian is the type of guy you could tell anything to, and he would ponder your problem and offer a rational, constructive, optimistic, and future-oriented opinion.

Not only would I soon be united with a friend of 12 years, but I also would get the opportunity to hike with a dog. Ever since I dreamed of walking the AT, I contemplated bringing a dog. However, most of the trail literature discourages walking with a dog. Having a four-legged companion would help with the lonely moments, but a dog also means extra responsibility. A few of the parks along the route do not allow canines, which means arranging for a dog shuttle around the park. Many of the hostels and lodges also do not allow dogs. After serious consideration, I ruled out taking a dog.

Brian's dog is not the ordinary domestic stock one rescues from the pound. His dog is a full-bred German shepherd. Her name is Enya, and she was bred for show in Germany with papers to prove it. This pup had X-rays verifying her hip joint qualities. Her fur coat is mostly light brown with black woven in. Not only is the dog authentic, but she was also professionally trained in obedience, tracking, and protection. Brian personally took part in the training. My friend and his dog are more than companions—they are a team. I looked forward to walking with them.

At sunrise, I assembled my gear, downed a cup of coffee and a granola bar, and hurried down the trail. Twelve miles to Route 52, the road where Brian and I agreed we would meet. Several miles down the trail, I came to a sign warning of high water. Apparently, there were several streams that did not have bridges. It had been raining for several days, causing the streams to rise to dangerous levels. It was another good example of obstacles that unexpectedly impede a hiker's progress. Luckily, a high-water trail offered safe passage around the series of stream crossings, but I had to back-track, adding a few extra miles to my day.

Around 2:00 p.m., I saw the highway. I was two hours late for my rendezvous with Brian, but he understood that I might be delayed. As I descended toward the highway crossing, I could see Brian's maroon Ford pickup. When I got to within a hundred yards of his truck, I could see Brian standing next to Enya. She sprang to a run right for me. She ran between my legs and circled me a few times as I continued walking toward the truck.

"Hey, Brian. Sorry I'm late."

"I figured you would be. I didn't recognize you at first. I've never seen ya with a beard."

"Yeah, but Enya knew who I was right away. Are you ready to hike?"

"Yep, the pack's in the back of the truck ready to go. Are you sure my truck is safe here?"

"It's fine."

"How far do you want to go?"

"Well, I've walked 35 miles since yesterday to get here, so I'm pooped. We could hike up to the shelter three miles away and get an early start in the morning?"

"I'm flexible, but we have plenty of day left if you want to go farther."

"The problem is water. My data book doesn't show another water source for 12 miles."

Brian and I had hiked many trails together over the years. Usually, we collaborated on the trip planning. This time, Brian was jumping on board the trail I had been blazing for the last 575 miles. He was the first person to hike with me other than thru-hikers. After looking at some maps, we agreed to stay at the shelter a few miles north.

Sometime that evening, another thru-hiker, Squanto, caught up to us. We talked for a while. Squanto, a graduate student from Virginia Tech, had been a day or two behind me for a few weeks. He knew of me from trail registers and from hearing about me from hostel keepers along the way.

In the morning, Brian, Enya, and I got an early start on the trail. Less than a mile down the path, we encountered another thru-hiker, Crash. Apparently, the few days off with family allowed enough time for some of the thru-hikers behind me to catch up.

Crash was a self-made millionaire from New Hampshire. He seemed to enjoy walking and talking with us. Brian and Crash talked about the stock market all morning. Soon, Crash pulled ahead and was gone. Enya would also walk or run ahead of us in pursuit of an animal and reappear on the trail moments later. She never really walked at a steady pace.

Enya was wearing a blue doggy saddlebag filled with dog food, biscuits, and a dog dish. She looked like a miniature packhorse. It was evident that she did not enjoy wearing the pack. She would stop and rub against trees trying to scrape it off her back. Finally she succeeded, but Brian stopped and fastened the saddlebag back. In no time, Enya successfully popped the saddlebag off her back by running between two trees. Brian fastened the pack on again. German shepherds are considered to be among the most intelligent canine breeds. This time, Enya displayed her superior canine intelligence by running into the forest until she was out of sight. Moments later she came back without the saddlebag. It took us twenty minutes to find the damn thing. Again, Brian fastened the bag onto the dog. This time, he added an additional rope to prevent her from knocking it off. The saddlebag remained on for the rest of the afternoon.

As the day wore on, my pace remained constant, but Brian had slowed down. Prior to my journey, we hiked at a comparable pace. Now I realized the endurance that I had gained from walking every day. Our conversations rambled all morning. At one point, I was so engulfed in conversation that I walked into the dog, which was stopped on the trail in front of me. We covered all of our favorite topics: marriage, early retirement, and the perfect job. After lunch, our paces left some distance between us. Enya led the way, never leaving my sight for more than a few minutes. Brian had fallen back, enjoying this stroll down the trail.

Up ahead, I could hear water flowing. A river at least 30 yards wide lay ahead. The trail crossed the river over a wooden footbridge with railings on both sides. I figured that as soon as I crossed the bridge, I would take a break and wait for Brian. Enya did not follow me across. She remained on the other side at the edge of the river watching me. I hollered back, "Come on, Enya."

Splash! She jumped in the river and was swimming across. When I yelled for her, I assumed she would cross over using the bridge. One of her basic commands Brian had taught me was "Enya, come." This command must mean take the most direct route. As she paddled, the current pulled her downstream. Oh, no! I didn't realize how strong the current was.

"Come on, Enya. You can do it!" I yelled. *Oh, man, if she drowns, Brian will be devastated,* I thought.

Finally, she neared the riverbank, but she couldn't spring her paws up out of the water to grip land. The current pulled her farther downstream as I followed along. I realized her saddlebags had filled with water, weighing her down. There was no way she could get out of the river. She needed my help. I had dropped my pack back by the bridge after I crossed over. OK, I thought, when the right moment comes, I will reach out and grab Enya. She struggled with her paws to grip the bank, but the current and the water-filled saddlebags kept breaking her grip. She had drifted about 30 yards down river. I was running out of opportunities to pull her out. My heart was pulsating in my ears. Everything seemed to be in slow motion. Subconsciously, I dropped down to one knee and reached my hands out, grabbing onto Enya's neck. My foot squashed into the muddy riverbank as I levered back away from the river, pulling Enya from the water. As soon as her four paws hit land, I let go and fell backward. She shook off, completely saturating me. Then she walked up and licked my face, thanking me for saving her.

Water remained in the saddlebags as she ran around with a joyful dance of being on land. I hoped she had learned not to attempt swimming with saddlebags, but I didn't want to chance it. I took the bags off her while we waited for Brian. Moments later, Enya's master crossed the bridge. After hearing the story, he decided to keep the saddlebags off and carry her food in his backpack. She won!

A few miles later, we decided to pitch camp along a stream. Both of us were exhausted. Brian's first full day on the AT consisted of 17 miles. The terrain was not as difficult as what I had been walking, but 17 miles with a full pack is a good day. It was a nice treat to share stories with my best friend. He was the one person besides my family who understood what I was experiencing out here.

"Brian, I'm glad I didn't bring a dog along with me."

"This is her first hike with saddlebags. Usually she's not a nuisance."

"Maybe she just needs more experience with hiking."

We collected firewood and got a little blaze started. One of our favorite fireside chats was reflecting on relationships with previous girlfriends, deciding what went wrong. Somehow, we always ended up dwelling on old relationships. Not to say that this is wrong, but ending the night thinking of beautiful women when you're all alone in the woods is, frankly, frustrating!

As the fire died down, we retreated to our tents. After we were nestled into our own nylon bedrooms, our conversation continued. The pauses between responses grew longer as we both fell asleep.

Enya was asleep underneath Brian's vestibule-canopy outside the door of his tent. The vestibule was zipped closed, serving as a tent without a floor. Sometime during the wee hours of night, I was awakened to the sound of a nylon tent ripping away at the seams. Then I heard the sound of Enya's paws galloping off into the woods, along with the sounds of another small animal running. Twigs snapped and dried leaves crackled as Enya's paws hit the ground in a full run as she chased the unknown creature further into the woods. As I lay there wondering what was going on, Brian hollered, "Enya, come."

"What's going on?"

"Enya took off after an animal."

By now I was awake and had unzipped my tent to look around. Brian's tent had partially collapsed. When Enya thrust out of the vestibule, she pulled up the front stakes of the tent. The only thing that kept Enya from dragging the tent along with her was Brian's weight.

The sound of snapping twigs and crackling leaves grew louder. Enya was responding to her master's command and returning to camp in the same full trot she chased after the animal. Enya burst out of the dark tree line. Her silhouette was visible in the moonlight. Then a horrible smell of garlic and dead animal smacked the olfactory glands. Oh, yuck. Enya reeked of skunk. Quickly, I zipped my tent door shut preventing her from getting near me.

"Brian, your dog got sprayed by a skunk."

"Enya, you idiot."

Brian zipped his door shut so the dog could not get near him. She had lost her privilege of sleeping under his tent vestibule. She did not particularly like the odor, either. As I lay in my sleeping bag, I could hear her pacing around outside, trying to avoid her own smell.

In the morning, I was wary to step out of the tent for fear of Enya rubbing her newly acquired scent on me. "Hey, Brian, where's your dog?"

"Outside somewhere."

"I don't want her coming near me."

I could hear Brian's tent unzip. "She doesn't smell as bad as last night."

"Are you sure?"

"Yeah, the skunk must have sprayed the area and Enya ran through it. I don't think it was a direct hit." With this assurance, I unzipped my tent and clambered out. Enya approached me. Her smell was very unpleasant but not nearly as strong as the previous night.

After some coffee and cereal, we broke camp, slung on our packs, and headed north. Brian's legs were stiff from our 17-mile day. My legs were stiff, too, but I had grown numb to this physical pain. Shortly, north of camp, I pulled ahead. Enya led the way. Occasionally, we would come upon a deer, and Enya would bolt after it in pursuit. This made me nervous. There were sheer cliffs fifty yards away on either side of the trail. With everything that had happened, I was concerned that Enya would follow a deer off one of these cliffs, but she always returned minutes later.

Three days had passed since Brian had met up with me. Spending a few days on the trail with Brian and his dog was definitely an adventure. Our trek together came to an end in Pearisburg. Brian had arranged for a car shuttle back to his truck. Of course, I would continue northward. Enya had demonstrated her professional training and intellect skills in the past three days. She had also confirmed my decision to not walk to Maine with a dog. In my mind, the responsibilities far outweighed the benefits.

The beginning.
Springer Mountain,
Georgia 3.1.98

Only 2,159 more miles to go!

A view of the snow capped
Great Smoky Mountains
3.11.98

Did someone say dinner?

Family and Mountains. What
more could you ask for?

Back row, left: Uncle Brian,
Jeff, & mom.
Front row, left: Aunt Ellen,
Austin, Steph, & Dan

Jeff, Packrat, & Zeb at a hostel in
Erwin Tennessee. 3.25.98

The first annual Walk with Sunshine. Toledo, Ohio 5.9.98

sunshine

Beth, Jeff & Brian at
Humpback Rocks, Virginia
4.25.98

*Almost half way to maine.
Just another 1000 miles!*

Jeff and Piasa.
Harpers Ferry, West Virginia

The day after
the skunk
encounter. Brian
w/ his infamous
dog Enya
4.14.98

Jeff. Harpers Ferry, West Virginia. 5.9.98

2,000 mile Feet

Jeff's dogs are still holding up. Caratunk, Maine 7.13.98

A walk in the park

A view of Katahdin, Maine 7.22.98

The simple life.

Kubiac and Jeff on Moxie Bald, Maine 7.14.98

Trail Angel

On top of Mt. Katahdin. Ron, Jeff, & Dan 7.25.98

The End!

Say Cheese!

Daicy Pond with Katahdin in the background. Baxter Park, Maine Back: Jeff, stepmom-Sue, stepdad-Ron, mom-rose, brother in law Dan, Front row: brother-Larry and father Mike

Naked Hiker Day

Aaron and Jeff celebrating back in Toledo, Ohio, after the hike.

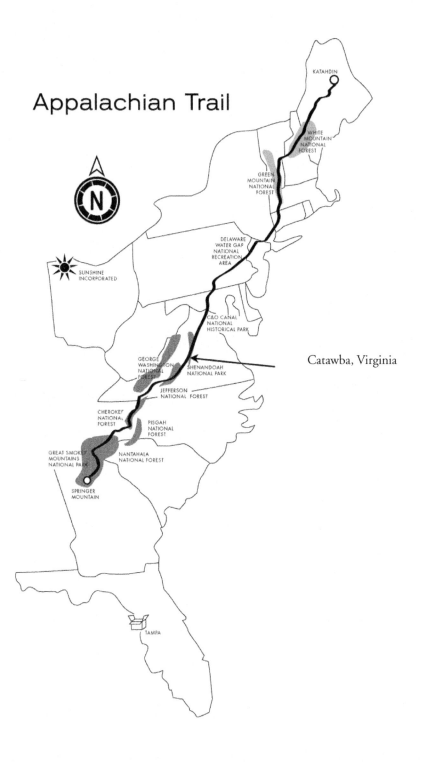

Appalachian Trail

KATAHDIN

WHITE
MOUNTAIN
NATIONAL
FOREST

N

GREEN
MOUNTAIN
NATIONAL
FOREST

DELAWARE
WATER GAP
NATIONAL
RECREATION
AREA

SUNSHINE
INCORPORATED

C&O CANAL
NATIONAL
HISTORICAL PARK

GEORGE
WASHINGTON
NATIONAL
FOREST

SHENANDOAH
NATIONAL PARK

Catawba, Virginia

JEFFERSON
NATIONAL FOREST

CHEROKEE
NATIONAL
FOREST

PISGAH
NATIONAL
FOREST

GREAT SMOKEY
MOUNTAINS
NATIONAL PARK

NANTAHALA
NATIONAL FOREST

SPRINGER
MOUNTAIN

TAMPA

Chapter 23

Only Forty-Eight Miles to Dinner

Catawba, Virginia. April 19, 1998. 684 miles from Springer Mountain, Georgia.

Virginia is the longest state on the trail. Of the estimated five million steps it takes to get to Maine, 1.25 million steps traverse Virginia's ridges, rolling hills, and small towns. Basically, you're in Virginia for a long time. Many hikers get what is known as the "Virginia Blues" from the endless miles of hiking without crossing state lines. Many of the thru-hikers give up in Virginia and go home, leaving the remaining hikers spread out and alone. On the other hand, the AT in Virginia blazes through a lot of historical battle sites, which offers a new variety of sites to see.

The recent attention of family and friends meeting up with me had helped to alleviate the feeling of loneliness that plagues many a thru-hiker at some point in the journey. Lately, I did not have time to get lonely. As soon as my family dropped me off on the trail, I raced against time to meet up with Brian. Now, Brian was leaving me after several days of hiking. A friend from college was expecting to meet me further up the trail but not for another week and a half, which focused my thoughts again on getting farther north. In spite of the stress of logistics, having friends meet me along the way was inspiring. Brian caught the shuttle back to his truck, and I headed for the Pearisburg post office to pick up my supply box.

The Sunshine home was receiving letters from people who had heard of my journey from the newspaper, TV, and radio broadcasts that had been reporting on my walk. Several folks from the Sunshine team were closely monitoring my progress. They would forward all the letters to my supply points along the way. It was motivating to read letters from people back home. Many of the letters that I received were from complete strangers. Some of the letters were from Sunshine residents and staff expressing thanks and encouragement for the money I was raising to benefit the home. Every letter I read sent warm vibes through my body. All of these people were encouraging me to keep going and were donating money to the Sunshine cause.

Getting my mail had become the highlight of every town visit. As I approached the post office, I was surprised to see Zeb sitting outside with his gear in disarray all over the sidewalk. I knew from Zeb's register entries that he had passed me while I was with family for Easter. He was a couple of days ahead, so I had not expected to catch up to him.

"Hey, Zeb," I said approaching him.

"Wrongfoot! How's the hike going?" he asked with a smile.

"Good. I took some time off with family, and I have been hiking with a friend from home for a few days," I replied.

"Too bad about Packrat," he said with sadness in his voice. Zeb knew from my register entries that Packrat had quit the trail.

"Yeah, I didn't know he was going to quit when he did." I told Zeb the story about Packrat quitting.

With a serious look on his face, Zeb asked, "Did ya run into the creep?"

With a voice of authority I responded, "Not only did I run into the slime dog, but I reported him to the authorities."

"Good," Zeb said with satisfaction. "And you were right. Brenda finally complained about my stinky socks," he said, referring back to Hot Springs when I razzed him about mailing home his dirty laundry. "But I have a solution," he said, pulling his resupply box closer.

"What's that?" I replied, figuring Zeb finally had realized how bad his clothes smelled and was doing his own laundry during town stops.

Zeb opened a box he had packed with his dirty laundry to mail home to Brenda, his girlfriend. Imagine getting a smelly box of hikers clothes in the mail! He pulled a pine branch from the box, held it up to my nose, and said, "I'm using nature's natural scent to take the sock odor away."

"Zeb," I said, "she's going to smell fresh pine and dirty socks when she gets this box. That won't take the smell away. She's going to associate your dirty laundry smell with you and pine trees." No more real

Christmas trees for Zeb and his lady. She would have flashbacks of Zeb's hiker boxes. "You can have some of my laundry detergent if you want to do your laundry. I get a baggie full at every supply point."

"No, thanks," he said. "I don't want to spend anymore time than I have to in town."

With a smirk on my face, I turned to step inside the post office. "I'll see you up the trail."

"Yep, I'm sure we'll cross paths again soon. See ya," Zeb said.

Zeb was determined to avoid doing his own laundry, and based on the stink, it was potentially at the expense of his relationship.

Several items awaited my arrival at the post office: a supply box, several letters, and a care package from Sunshine. The Catholic church in town offers a hostel for hikers, which I figured would be a great place to open my mail and resupply before hiking on. After picking up my package, I walked a mile through town to the hostel. Another hiker, Briggs, showed up. Early on, he had hiked with Zeb, but the two of them had separated at some point. We decided to walk to the laundromat, start a load of wash, and grab some food at the local Pizza Hut. It was lunchtime when Briggs and I stepped into the restaurant. Half of the Pearisburg workforce seemed to be eating at the same place. Our outlandish appetites from the calories we were burning had given us thru-hikers the eye for a good buffet. Both of us ordered the all-you-can-eat pizza lunch buffet. For the next hour and a half, as soon as a pizza was placed under the heat lamps, Briggs and I would grab the majority of it, leaving most of the customers without. The manager must have been a nervous wreck watching us wipe out his well-furnished food supply. The cooks struggled to keep up with demand. Between Briggs and me, three large pizzas, several pounds of lettuce, salad dressing, and several other consumable products disappeared from the buffet.

After stuffing ourselves, we wobbled across the street to the laundromat to wait on our clothes. When the laundry was done, I put my clothes in a sack, threw it over my shoulder and walked back to the hostel. Briggs planned on heading back to the trail when his laundry was dry, so I left him at the laundromat.

Slowly, I began loading up my gear, stopping every so often to write a postcard. By mid-afternoon, I was ready to continue heading north. The hostel keeper was concerned that something was wrong because I was not staying the night. While explaining that I had to keep going, another gentleman walked into the hostel. He introduced himself as Sunny Daze. He hiked the AT in 1996, and now he was traveling along the trail, helping out hikers as a trail angel. The hostel was a mile off the trail. Sunny Daze offered to drive me back through town and drop me off near the AT. Before I left his vehicle, Sunny Daze handed me a token good for a drink at a pub in Port Clinton, Pennsylvania, another 600 miles north. I thanked him and kept walking north.

Shortly after leaving town, I ran across Crash again. "Hey, Crash," I said.

He answered, "Wrongfoot, where's your friend Brian?"

"He got off the trail in Pearisburg and headed home," I answered.

With a chuckle in his voice, Crash asked, "Did you run him to the ground?"

"No, he only had a few days off and had to get back to work," I explained.

Crash was walking south when I ran into him. He was staying in a hotel in Pearisburg and slack-packing—walking with just a daypack. He had arranged for someone to shuttle him north of town so he could walk back and stay in domesticated comfort for a couple of days while still getting in miles on the trail.

Rain had been smacking me since leaving town. By the time I reached a shelter eight miles north of town, every stitch of my newly laundered clothing was bone-chillingly wet. As soon as I got beneath the shelter roof, I removed my wet clothes and put on a dry set. Zeb, Briggs, and another hiker were already in the shelter when I arrived. Everyone had heavy packs from their fresh supplies in town. Briggs shared some homemade cookies that were mailed to him. I pulled out some of the treats mailed to me and passed them around.

By morning, rain continued to fall. I left the shelter and walked through open mountaintop meadows. Cows grazed in the clearings. Walking through cow pastures had become commonplace. Two step-ladders were nailed together in an A shape. The A-shaped ladder was placed over the barbed wire fences, keeping the cows penned in while allowing hikers to cross in and out of pastures without having to worry about leaving gates open. The sour-smelling manure always alerted me of upcoming pastures. The cows were accustomed to hikers and would just stare as I passed. I always felt uneasy as I passed through, wondering if these big, four-legged T-bones knew that I consumed red meat on a regular basis.

***

My stepfather had been doing an excellent job of providing logistics of upcoming terrain. He had hiked the AT through all of the areas that I had walked thus far, so he would include lists in my supply boxes of things to look for, places to stay, and restaurants worth visiting. Ron had boasted about a restaurant up ahead called The Home Place in Catawba, Virginia. He claimed that the food was the best he had ever eaten—huge portions served home-style at reasonable prices. He was speaking my language. Food occupied my thoughts for the bulk of the day. Since I learned of The Home Place, I had intended to stop there for dinner. It was only a mile off the trail; however, it has limited hours of business. The place is open only Thursdays through Sundays, closing at 6:00 p.m. on Sunday evenings. The next few days brought continuous rain, which dampened my spirit. Eating at The Home Place became an obsession, which helped overcome the depressing wet weather.

On Friday, April 17, I stopped for the night in the same shelter as Zeb and Briggs. The next morning, I looked at my data books and maps. Catawba was another 48 miles north. No one really has an accurate weather report on the trail. It wouldn't matter anyway because you walk despite the weather. But when it's really nasty out, I became a point-A-to-point-B hiker. As soon as I left the comfort of a dry, warm place, I set my sights on the next dry, warm place. Rain had continued nonstop since I left Pearisburg a day and half ago. Hmmm. Forty-eight miles in two days? For a big, hot, all-you-can-eat dinner? Why not? My mind was made up. Next stop, The Home Place. If I did not make it by Sunday at 6:00 p.m., I would miss the opportunity to eat a great meal. The restaurant would not be open again until Thursday. I wouldn't be able to wait half a week to eat there if I were to meet my friend Beth farther up the trail. So this became the challenge of the week.

Rain continued to soak my boots, pack, and body for the next two days. When it rained, I took very few pictures in order to protect my camera from moisture. Unfortunately, my camera had managed to take on water anyway. Somehow, rain penetrated the plastic baggie in which I kept it. During a stop on a ridge outcrop overlooking the valley, I stood looking at the magnificent view. As I stood enjoying the bird's-eye view of the valley below, my fingers fumbled with my hip belt pouch digging out my camera. I held the 35-millimeter wonder to my eye pushed the button, and nothing happened. Looking it over, I noticed that it was all wet.

Later that day, I stopped at a rapidly flowing river to replenish my water supply. After taking off my pack, assembling my water filter, and opening my water jugs, I could not pump water through my filter. Ahhhhh! Mother Nature was lashing cold rain on me, and all of my equipment was breaking down. Luckily, I had some iodine tablets for water purification as a backup.

After 26 miles, I reached the Niday Shelter. I'd passed most of the day walking in dense fog and rain. Crash and several weekend hikers occupied the shelter. There was plenty of space for another sleeping bag, so I settled in. My skin was pruned from my all-day shower. As soon as I stopped, I put on some dry clothes, wrung out the wet ones, and hung them on a clothesline strung underneath the shelter roof. Only 20 miles to The Home Place. If I got an early start, I should reach the restaurant before closing time at 6:00 p.m. After dinner, I zipped myself into my sleeping bag and pulled out my pen and paper to write my daily journal.

4/19/98. 26 miles, rainy & cold. Everything is wet. My camera and my water filter broke. As I wrote, the light from headlamp dimmed to a faded yellow glow and fizzled out. *And my flashlight batteries are dead. I hope I have better days!*

The sound of rain pinging off the metal shelter roof put me right to sleep. The days had been growing longer as summer approached. The next morning, while waiting for water to boil, I slipped back into my wet, cold, musty T-shirt and shorts. I was on the trail by 7 a.m. Rain continued to fall for a third day. Crash still was at the shelter when I left, so I did not know if I would see him again.

All day, I clambered up and down the mountains. As I neared Catawba, I began an ascent up a very steep, rocky ridge known as the Dragon's Tooth. In dry weather, this area is supposed to offer gorgeous views of the countryside. But in wet weather, the steep rocky footpath becomes slippery and dangerous. Many hikers have injured themselves there. The ascent and descent are nearly vertical in some spots. Steps have been assembled with rocks to offer footing. Every step I took was a cautious one. On the way up and over, I envisioned myself finally reaching the restaurant and sitting down to dinner.

At last, I could hear the sound of cars whizzing by. A road was just ahead down the mountain. When I finally reached the road, I took a left and walked along the shoulder for a mile into town. A cluster of three or four buildings sat behind a sign declaring Catawba, Virginia. On the left side of the road was a sign in front of a Victorian-style farmhouse: The Home Place. The restaurant was set back from the road about 50 yards. Cars were parked everywhere, in the lawn and on the gravel driveway. Forty-eight miles in two days, and I made it with time to spare as I glanced at my watch. It was only 5 p.m.

Three dozen folks, dressed in khakis, ties, and dresses, sat about the covered porch waiting for their name to be called for dinner. My wardrobe didn't even come close to fitting in. Everyone pretended not to notice me, but I could feel their eyes upon me as I staggered onto the porch, finally out of the rain for the first time all day. Water dripped off my body smacking the wooden porch as I unfastened my pack straps, releasing it from my back. I gently leaned my pack up against the wall, on the porch. Inside the door, a host took my name and said it would be a few minutes. The aroma of fresh-baked corn bread, smoked roast beef, and chicken stoked my food fascination.

Ten minutes later, I was called to supper. A hostess led me to a table smack dab in the middle of the main dining room. All eyes were on the hungry, wet hiker. A few minutes later, a waitress approached me.

"Can I get you a drink?" she said, as she poured a glass of lemonade and water into cups already on my table. "Yes, coffee, please." She explained my dinner options: "We are serving roast beef as the main entrée tonight. It comes home-style with coleslaw, baked beans, potatoes, corn, green beans, rolls, and dessert."

My tongue was hanging out as I listened to every morsel mentioned. "Sounds good to me," I replied.

A few minutes later, three servers approached my table, each placing several bowls and plates of food down. The entire table was covered. Even though I had ordered roast beef, half of a fried chicken came with the meal. It was quite a switch from the ramen noodles and dehydrated veggies I had as the last night's dinner. At first, I was unsure where to start, but my fork guided by hunger probed into the coleslaw, then the roast beef, potatoes, beans, all around the table. Amazingly, I ate all eight slices of roast beef! The waitress grabbed my empty plates and brought them back full again. Within minutes I had consumed another plate of roast beef. The waitress approached me, "How much more do you think you will eat?" Lifting my thumb and finger with an inch gap in-between, I answered, "About that much." Roast beef stacked two inches high arrived at my table. If it weren't for my stomach filling up, I would have kept on eating. Finally, I asked for a box. "Sure," the waitress replied as she set an ice-cream sundae on my table with hot fudge slipping down the sides of the overfilled cup.

With a total focus on making it here for dinner, I had not thought about where I would spend the night. While waiting for the box to wrap up my food, a gentleman who had been dining a few tables away approached me. "Son, do ya have a place to stay?" Wow, this guy is thinking ahead of me.

"No, sir," I answered with curiosity.

"I'm Bill," he said.

"Hey, Bill, I'm Wrongfoot," I said, shaking his offered hand.

"Wrongfoot, I own the grocery store across the street. You're more than welcome to stay in our feed barn. It's warm and dry."

I had not planned beyond this meal where I was going to stay or whether I was going to continue up the trail. The rain had not let up, and I really wanted to get out of these wet clothes. "Well, thank you. I think I'll take you up on the offer," I said eagerly with a smile. Bill left the restaurant and went back to his store across the street.

With my doggy bag in one hand, my hiking poles in the other, and my soggy pack on my back, I trudged across the street in pursuit of a dry place to stay the night. Bill saw me coming from the store window and came outside to greet me. "Follow me," Bill said walking toward a white, metal barn. He opened a door and walked in with me right behind. As soon as he flipped the light switch, I could see pallets of animal feed in hundred pound burlap sacks stacked all around. "You can spread your stuff out on that plastic sheet," he said as he pointed down on the ground at a 10-by-10-foot plastic sheet. "If you stack some of the feed bags evenly, they make a pretty good mattress." I thanked him for his hospitality. "We open the store at 6:00 a.m.," he told me. "We have hot coffee and some breakfast foods." Wow! Trail magic at its best. If I hadn't pushed myself, I probably would be in a shelter several miles back, wondering what a meal at The Home Place was like.

In the morning, I packed up my gear and stepped into the country store. Several of the area farmers were standing around talking. The smell of fresh coffee caught my attention as I peered around looking for the pot. Everyone greeted me with kindness. Bill's wife introduced herself and asked me where I was from. We chatted a bit and she said, "There is another hiker down the road at the bed and breakfast. My friend keeps me updated on her guests." Nothing beats small-town America; everyone knows each other. If you want to know about other hikers, the town folks will tell you. I figured Crash was the hiker at the bed and breakfast. He's the only thru-hiker I've met able to swing the expense of staying in luxury on a continual basis.

Nothing felt better than hot coffee and good conversation after a good night's rest. It appeared as if the rain had stopped and the sun was trying to come out. Bill's wife offered to deliver my gear to the next town 20 miles north. "Wow, that would be great!" I said, taking her up on the offer. I went back to the barn and dumped out my pack, keeping my rain gear, some snacks, and water containers. Everything else I put into a box and carried back to the store to give to Bill's wife. What an awesome gesture! All day, I would walk without the weight of a pack. As I headed up the highway back toward the trail, I noticed a bounce in my step as if I was on the moon with no gravity. Just when my spirit was wearing thin, a magical act of kindness rekindled me for another leg of my journey.

Appalachian Trail

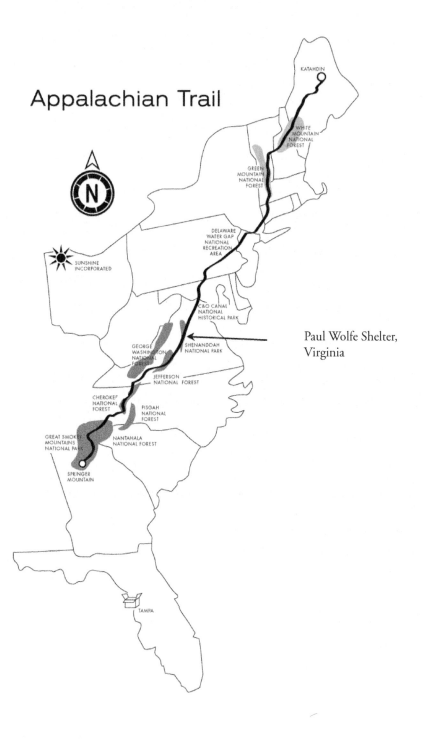

KATAHDIN

WHITE MOUNTAIN NATIONAL FOREST

GREEN MOUNTAIN NATIONAL FOREST

N

DELAWARE WATER GAP NATIONAL RECREATION AREA

SUNSHINE INCORPORATED

C&O CANAL NATIONAL HISTORICAL PARK

GEORGE WASHINGTON NATIONAL FOREST

SHENANDOAH NATIONAL PARK

Paul Wolfe Shelter, Virginia

JEFFERSON NATIONAL FOREST

CHEROKEE NATIONAL FOREST

PISGAH NATIONAL FOREST

GREAT SMOKEY MOUNTAINS NATIONAL PARK

NANTAHALA NATIONAL FOREST

SPRINGER MOUNTAIN

TAMPA

Chapter 24

All For a Woman

Paul Wolfe Shelter, Virginia. April 23, 1998. 756 miles from Springer Mountain, Georgia.

Again, I was off on another race against time to meet up with a good friend. Actually, Beth was more than a good friend. Ever since I had set eyes on her in graduate school two years before, I had hoped to become more than friends. Our relationship had grown, but my goal was not complete. Just before departing on my journey, Beth had driven to Florida with me to help pack my supply boxes. All week, I had hoped that our friendship would develop into something more.

I guess all work and very little beach play did not help much. Getting all of my supply boxes prepared for the journey was my focus. At one point during the week, Beth demanded a day at the beach. She had spent endless hours bagging up pasta and dried vegetables and sorting items into the many boxes that I would receive on the trail. All week, she wondered when we would stop and enjoy the fact that we were in sunny Florida. After all, we had come from the snowy north. Realizing the possible mutinous situation, I put aside packing operations, and we spent the day at the beach. Of course, in January, it was too cold for bathing suits. We sat on beach chairs wearing long pants and jackets, shielding our faces from sand being blown at us. We were still just friends at the end of the week.

Here was another opportunity to take our relationship to a new level. All of our friends and family assumed something was going on between the two of us. We talked on the phone and went everywhere together—out on the town, and running. We studied together and sat next to each other in class. Nothing was going on, though. We were just friends.

Beth had made arrangements to fly into Richmond, Virginia, with her brother. He had attended law school at the University of Virginia in Charlottesville. Our plan was to meet up in Waynesboro, just off the AT. From there, we would head to Charlottesville for the weekend. Beth's brother would get the chance to enjoy his alma mater, and I would have another shot at developing my relationship with his sister. And, of course, a few days would give my feet a rest.

Again, I had overestimated where I would be on the trail when we made arrangements to meet. In order to walk to the meeting point—Waynesboro, Virginia, to meet Beth—I would have had to cover 150 miles in three days. Impossible! When my family came to meet me, I simply called them and changed where we would meet. But Beth was flying to a state that she had never visited. Her brother had gone to school in Virginia, and, like most college residents, he was oblivious to the exact whereabouts of the Appalachian Trail and was more concerned with academics and social life. Asking Beth and her brother to pick me up on some rural interstate in the middle of the woods was out of the question.

Crash came to the rescue. Crash is the only person I had ever met who could turn a rugged 2,000-mile walk through the mountains into a posh, five-star affair. This guy stayed at bed and breakfasts for more nights than he slept in a tent. Of course, most hikers I knew didn't have the money to stay in bed and breakfasts as a regular venue. Crash did not see money as an obstacle. He had been very successful with the stock market in recent years. He had mastered the art of slack- packing—walking without a full pack by getting shuttles to pick him up and drop him off at the trail. He suggested that I catch a bus north to skip ahead a hundred miles and walk the last 50 miles to Waynesboro. Then I could come back to complete the section that I had skipped. What a concept: catch a bus in the middle of the woods.

Sure enough, I was able to catch a taxi from a hotel near the trail to the bus station. A Greyhound bus dropped me off in Lexington, Virginia, a picturesque college town 50 miles south of Waynesboro. From there, I caught a taxi to the trail 10 miles outside of town. The plan was to hike the rest of the way to Waynesboro. After a weekend of fun, I would catch the bus back to walk the section I skipped, and then take the bus ahead to Waynesboro again. Going through all of this was stressful, but Beth was worth it.

Even with skipping 100 miles, I had spent so much time planning logistics and catching buses, I was only able to achieve 13 miles after all the shuttling around. At 7:00 p.m., I reached a shelter filled beyond capacity with Girl Scouts. They offered me some leftover food for dinner. At first I had intended on stumbling on into the night, tripping over tree roots, following the path by headlamp. After sitting down for some food and conversation, however, I rationalized that I could keep a faster pace walking in the daylight and decided to stay for the night. Thirty-seven miles remained between Waynesboro and me with a day and a half left to get there. At first light, I would break camp. Around 5:00 a.m., the sound of the spring-hinged privy door slammed shut, startling me from sleep. That probably was the first of all 20 girls who would slam that door in the next hour, preventing me from getting any more sleep. I decided to break camp even though it was still dark.

Being the first person on the trail in the morning is a tranquil, pure feeling. Dew weighs down the leaves. Deer frolic about, not yet frightened away by humans. A good measure for telling if I was the first hiker on the trail was the abundance of cobwebs strung through the night by ambitious spiders. Often, one would smack across my face and catch me in the mouth, a feeling that I despised.

All day, I sliced along the trail. Occasionally I would stop to enjoy a view, but I did not drop the pack and lollygag around like I had in earlier days. My biggest obstacle of the day was the second highest peak in Virginia, The Priest. For all the hype the literature gave this mountain, it really was not all that difficult to ascend. Or maybe I was just in better shape than when I climbed previous difficult peaks? I clambered over Spy Rock, legendary in local historical literature for providing Confederate spies an elite hideout. With terrain so rugged, Union soldiers never were able to overrun the position during the war. Thinking about the rich history of the area inspired me. As I rambled along I wondered if the Civil War armies marched to a drum as they climbed up and over the mountains. In my mind, I could almost hear the beat with each step.

Soon, the moon replaced the sun, leaving the landscape in darkness. Again, my headlamp served as guidance down the trail. I wondered why I continually put myself in these forced-march predicaments. Finally, around 9:30 p.m., I saw a flashlight beam up ahead. Walking into a shelter in the dark can startle people already there. So I always announced myself to put everyone at ease. As I approached the shelter, I raised my voice and shouted, "Hello, I'm a thru-hiker looking for the Paul Wolfe Shelter. Is this it?" A voice from behind the flashlight beam shining at my face answered affirmatively. Two teenage boys, their father, and their schoolteacher, all from Maine, occupied the shelter with plenty of room to spare. This shelter was one of the nicest I had seen. It had a loft, a porch, and picnic tables, and it was nestled along a fast-moving spring with a waterfall.

As I cooked a very late dinner, the two boys drilled me with questions. "Where did ya hike from today?"

"Seeley-Woodsworth Shelter," I replied.

"Wow! It took us three days to get here from there."

This was the longest day I had hiked since beginning the trail: 34 miles. As a matter of fact, it turned out to be the longest day of my entire journey. A marathon and an additional 13k with a 50-pound pack is enough to wear down even the most energetic. I said to the boys with my most macho voice, "It's amazing what a man will do for a woman."

In the morning, I had only a five-mile walk to the road into Waynesboro. The group at the shelter had a van at the road and offered to drive me the five miles into town, but I declined. There was an outfitter shop just off the trail where I wanted to stop to repair a broken walking pole. The father of the boys gave me his address in Maine, explaining that they have a cabin in Monson, the last trail town. He offered to let me stay there when I got to Monson. Although Maine was another 1,300 miles north, I filed his address away to refer back to when the time came.

Beth and her brother were planning to meet me at 2:00 p.m. at the YMCA in town. The YMCA allows hikers to shower and put tents behind the facility. When I asked if I could use the weight gym, the woman behind the counter said, "Sure!" Then with a puzzled look on her face, she went on to say, "You mean you want to lift weights after all that walking? I mean, that's the last thing most of the hikers coming through here want to do."

She had a good point, but I was curious about my weight-lifting routine. Prior to my journey, I lifted weights three days a week. Now it had been two months since I had been to a gym. Amazingly, I was able to go through my entire routine, although I was very sore the next day.

After working out, I walked to the post office. I had been mailing a box of clothes and repair kits, called a bounce box, along the trail to myself. I kept a pair of jeans, a shirt, and shorts for occasions in town. When Beth arrived, I wanted to look my best.

Appearance was an issue that I had not worried about since Springer Mountain, Georgia. My razor went home with my dad when he left me in Georgia almost two months ago. Not knowing when I would see a barber again, I had a haircut and beard trim in Damascus, Virginia, although it was more for comfort than appearance. Other than other grungy hikers, there was really no one to impress in the woods. A hot shower had become a weekly occurrence, only when I was in town. I managed to clean up on the trail by washing in streams and using throwaway towelettes. Trail clean and domestic clean are two different standards. Soap and deodorant were applied to my body only when I was in town. In addition to the beard, I had lost 20 pounds since Georgia. I wondered how Beth would react to my new appearance.

Two o'clock rolled around as I eagerly sat in the YMCA lobby waiting for Beth and her brother Brian (not to be confused with my friend Brian and his dog). Beth's brother had never met me. He only had seen pictures. Beth cautiously peered into the lobby. Her brother stood next to her. A handful of other people milled around the lobby. Beth stood less than three feet away but looked everywhere except at me. She didn't recognize me. Her brother tapped her on the shoulder and pointed to me. He had only seen my picture, but he recognized me before his sister did. Beth and I hugged, and she introduced me to Brian.

In a teasing manner, I said to Beth, "I'm hurt that you couldn't pick me out of a crowd of five people."

She answered defensively, "Jeff, you're thin as a rail, and you have a beard." I guess the trail had changed my appearance. Even with a clean set of clothes, shower, and the same smile, I looked much different.

Beth and Brian helped me pile my gear into their rental car. They wanted to see the Appalachian Trail before we drove back into Charlottesville for the weekend. Neither of them had ever been hiking. They'd grown up in suburban Chicago. As kids, they had traveled and stayed in a pop-up camper that they'd taken on vacations but had never roughed it on an overnight hike. When we were planning this trip, I suggested that they hike with me for a few days. I figured because Beth and Brian are avid runners that they could handle the physical aspect. Their reply was, "Unless there are flush toilets and a shower, we're not interested." Yet when we all got in the car, they asked where the trail was. So I took them to the AT for a stroll.

We drove back up to where I had left the trail earlier that morning. A tourist information center is across the road from where the AT emerges at Rockfish Gap. This is where the Blue Ridge Parkway ends and Skyline Drive begins. We parked the car.

"Follow me!" I yelled, as I scurried across the road avoiding oncoming traffic. The AT follows the road with a guardrail separating the walkers from cars. After about 100 yards, the trail dips back into the forest.

Fewer than 20 yards onto the AT, Brian hollered, "Hey, Jeff, what's this from?" I stopped and turned around. He was pointing at some dung laying on the trail. Now, Brian was expecting some explanation from me like a bear, a mountain lion, or another exotic species, but the sad truth was that he was pointing at human feces.

In a disturbed voice, I explained: "Brian, that's from a ferocious human too damn inconsiderate and lazy to hold themselves until they found a restroom." On the trail, I always knew when I was getting close to a road. Litter and disgusting human things always became more abundant.

We walked down the trail into the forest. Beth spoke up. "Jeff, I thought the trail was paved. I figured it would be as wide as a sidewalk."

I replied, "This is it, Beth. This is how it's been for 700 miles."

"Jeff, some of my friends back home have never even heard of the Appalachian Trail," she answered.

Now that amazed me. Everyone I know is familiar with the AT. Of course, most of my friends hike. After about a mile, we turned around and walked back to the car. All of us were careful not to step in the dung. Beth and Brian had a better perspective of the AT, but unfortunately, their first trail experience involved human feces. They had flown all the way from Chicago, and I was determined to show them a section of trail they would remember in a positive light. As we were walking back to the car, I brought up the idea of taking another day hike to a scenic spot on the AT before the weekend was over. They agreed.

Brian was eager to get to Charlottesville. He had spent three years in law school at UVA. He had our activities planned for the whole weekend, which was fine by me. Just so it didn't involve walking. We drove the short distance to town and checked into our hotel.

Brian had reservations for us at his favorite law school restaurant, the

C&O. On the drive to dinner, Brian explained how nice the restaurant was. "They have a chef; the food is top-notch, and the atmosphere is classy." As he was describing the place, I was translating his explanation to hiker terms: "They have a chef" = expensive: "the food is top-notch, and the atmosphere is classy" = quality, not quantity. Two things I had grown to appreciate with food choices on the trail were how expensive and how large the portions were. Luckily, I had eaten a large pizza for lunch. Brian had his heart set on this restaurant, so I was not about to offer my savage trail-dining input.

We sat down for dinner, and a waitress took our drink order. She described the chef's specials for the evening, which sounded very good. We each ordered an entrée. The waitress placed a basket of bread on the table, and I quickly snatched up a roll smearing on several chunks of butter before biting in. Soon, our meals arrived, and the waitress set my plate before me. It had an attractive presentation of kale and green leaf garnishes surrounding the entrée. A piece of pork sat in the center, surrounded by brown rice. The plate was the size of a Frisbee with a two-inch rim around the edge. It appeared quite large in contrast to the food portion, which was about the size of a McDonald's cheeseburger. In less than two minutes, I had consumed my very delicious dinner. Brian and Beth continued to eat as we talked. My eyes now focused on Beth's chicken, and I felt pathetic. Here was my opportunity to look into Beth's eyes and win her over with romantic and polite conversation, but instead I sat gazing at her chicken breast. Every slice of her knife into the poultry appealed to me. She must have caught on that I was still hungry. She offered the rest of her meal to me.

"No, you eat your food, Beth," I replied. "I'm sorry. My appetite is enormous."

She said she was full and scraped a chicken breast and some rice onto my plate. I inhaled every scrap. Beth insisted on paying the bill, claiming that her parents wanted to buy us dinner.

After dinner, we strolled through town as Brian described the history and significance of each building we passed. An ice cream parlor caught my eye in the charming cobblestone district. All of us went in and ordered. Looking at all the choices confused me. I wanted to jump over the counter and eat some of every flavor in the freezer case. Instead, I ordered two scoops of chocolate peanut butter swirl. We sat outside at a table on the sidewalk. The street was closed to traffic and was filled with people. As we ate our ice cream, we listened to a guitarist, sitting in the middle of the mall, playing folk music.

Beth and Brian were still eating their scoop of ice cream after I had finished my two scoops. I returned to the parlor and ordered two more scoops. In the time it took them to eat their one scoop, I had gobbled down four. Beth and Brian were quietly stunned at the amount of food I was consuming. Brian teasingly asked me if I wanted any more ice cream before we moved on.

"No, I think I'm full for a while," I replied with a sincere tone in my voice.

In the morning, Beth and Brian donned their running shoes for a jog. I declined the offer to join them. While they were gone, I hobbled across the street, still in pain from my 34-mile blaze against time and a session of weight lifting, to the popular donut chain Krispy Kreme. A neon sign posted in the front window said "Hot and Fresh." As I waited in line, I watched the donuts emerge from an oven onto a conveyer belt. They remained on the belt, coasting under a mist of sugar glazing. I ordered a dozen glazed donuts and brought them back to the hotel. When Brian and Beth returned from their run, I offered them some doughnuts. Brian ate one and Beth tore a half piece off. Brian wanted to take us to a bagel shop for breakfast. While everyone showered, I ate the other ten and a half donuts. We all went to the bagel shop and ordered bagel sandwiches.

That weekend, we toured Monticello. We went to a popular annual horse race, Foxfield. Brian showed us around the UVA campus, which was quite nice with large, green lawns encased in courtyards and surrounded by Georgian-style red brick dormitories with white columns and dark shutters. It was truly a beautiful campus and town. Living here would be easy.

The weekend was drawing to a close. I boxed up my civilian clothes to send ahead to another post office further up the trail. After organizing my hiking gear, I called my parents to give them updates on my plans and to verify where my next supply box should be.

Sunday morning, we headed for Skyline Drive, which skirts the AT. A scenic view called Humpback Rocks, which I had encountered on my way to meet Beth and Brian, was not far. As it turns out, Brian had hiked to Humpback Rocks several times during law school without realizing that he was on the Appalachian Trail. I hoped that they would get a better perspective of why I was enjoying this journey while sitting on a rock with a bird's-eye view of the valley and mountains. We parked at the trailhead and trekked into the forest. Two miles later, we emerged from the trees onto a cliff-hanging boulder. The weather was gorgeous, blue skies with few clouds. The wind whistled in our ears and blew Beth's hair all over. We could see Waynesboro down in the valley. It consisted of little dots far off in the distance.

After sitting for a moment, I perked up. "This is what it's all about."

Our moment of serenity ended abruptly, however, with the reality of schedules. Beth and Brian had a flight leaving Richmond in the afternoon. They drove me to the Greyhound bus station in Charlottesville, where I would catch a bus back to the section of trail that I had skipped. All weekend I had hoped that something significant would spark between Beth and me, but nothing had. This would be the last time that I would see her until the end of my journey. After shaking Brian's hand and thanking him for the tour, I reached out to hug Beth goodbye. My instincts told me, "This is it: kiss her." I puckered my lips and moved my mouth toward hers, but she turned away, leaving me to kiss her on the cheek.

On the bus ride back to the trail, I came to the realization that she wanted to be nothing more than friends. For the next few days, I was in a mental fog with the realization that I would never develop my relationship with Beth beyond where it was. But what a better place to get over someone than the trail? Thinking of the 1,000 miles of hiking that lay ahead kept me occupied. Beth and I wrote to each other a few times after our weekend in Charlottesville, but just as friends.

For the next thousand miles, I learned to accept where our relationship stopped. Who would have thought that we would get married the next year?

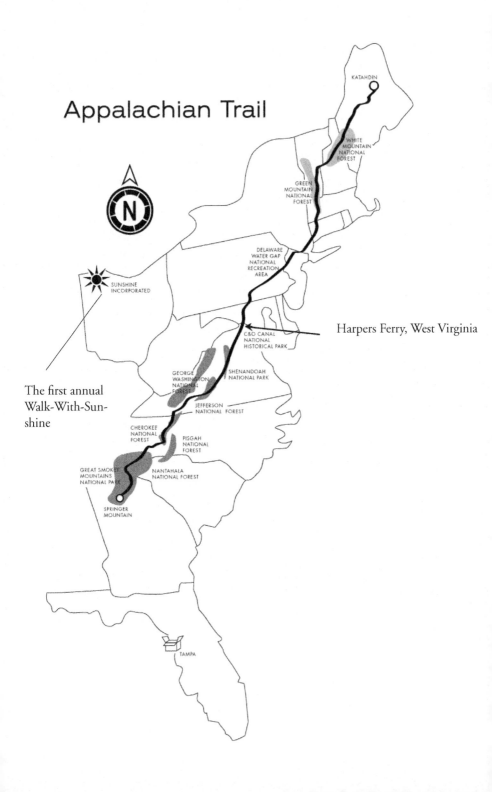

Appalachian Trail

KATAHDIN

WHITE MOUNTAIN NATIONAL FOREST

GREEN MOUNTAIN NATIONAL FOREST

DELAWARE WATER GAP NATIONAL RECREATION AREA

SUNSHINE INCORPORATED

C&O CANAL NATIONAL HISTORICAL PARK

Harpers Ferry, West Virginia

GEORGE WASHINGTON NATIONAL FOREST

SHENANDOAH NATIONAL PARK

The first annual Walk-With-Sunshine

JEFFERSON NATIONAL FOREST

CHEROKEE NATIONAL FOREST

PISGAH NATIONAL FOREST

GREAT SMOKEY MOUNTAINS NATIONAL PARK

NANTAHALA NATIONAL FOREST

SPRINGER MOUNTAIN

TAMPA

Chapter 25

Let's Walk Together

Harper's Ferry, West Virginia. May 9, 1998. 997 miles from Springer Mountain, Georgia.

Leaving friends and family who had visited me and going back to the trail community was like reading two good books at the same time. I looked forward to both continuing on the trail and also visiting with friends and family from home. My friends and family kept me going. Each time someone from home left after meeting me on the trail, I would re-enter the hiking community with a new sense of spirit, ready to trek on.

Going back to cover the areas I had skipped on the trail had its perks. I was able to meet several hikers that had been behind me since Georgia. I rode the Greyhound bus back to Roanoke, Virginia, and caught a cab to Cloverdale, a town along the trail.

When I returned to the trail, I met up with Hopper. On the third night of my journey, I had shared my whiskey flask with him in a cabin back in Georgia. He had lost weight, and his beard gave him a wild look, unlike the clean-cut, stockbroker lifestyle he had left two months prior. He was hiking with two others, a married couple from Holland—Dharma Bum and Yoon.

We caught up on trail talk. They told me about hikers who had quit, about who was behind them, and about who was in front of them. They informed me that Magaroni was a day ahead of us. He had hiked with Packrat and me during the first few weeks of my journey. We shared personal stories of trail life. I explained how I had skipped this section and was filling it in before shuttling ahead.

They were curious about my fundraiser. Anytime my mission for Sunshine came up in conversation, I pulled out a newspaper clipping from The Toledo Blade newspaper about my hike and fundraiser. I had been sharing my fundraiser journey for the Sunshine charity mostly with town folks along the way because I had not met too many other thru-hikers. The townspeople in turn were relaying my story to hikers behind me, so almost everyone who knew of me on the trail had heard about my fundraiser. My intent was not to raise money on the trail but to share the spirit for which I was walking.

We all headed on together. A relentless rainstorm pelted us, but it cleared after several hours. We came upon a shelter occupied by a homeless woman. She had a warm fire going and kept the shelter very tidy. Not a bad way to be homeless, from a hiker's perspective. Most hikers left her with some food when they stayed at her shelter.

All day we splashed through the rain, up and down mountains, over stiles, and onto mountain ridges. The trail crossed the Blue Ridge Parkway twice before we called it a 19-mile day and stopped at Bobblets Gap Shelter. Not long after the four of us rolled out our sleeping bags, another hiker named Rob wandered in. He pitched his tent in front of the shelter. Everyone went about their own business of cooking dinner and writing in journals, but we all gathered around the picnic table for mealtime as if we were a family. As I ate my couscous, I realized that this was the largest group of thru-hikers I had been with at one time since the first few days on the trail.

In the morning, I was up and ready to go before Hopper, Dharma Bum, and Yoon had climbed out of their sleeping bags. Rob had already left. This would probably be the last I would see them because I would be skipping ahead the 50 miles that I had previously hiked, so I said my good-byes and good lucks. I followed the trail all day through tunnels of rhododendron, which were beginning to bloom. The flowers were a peach color and would eventually turn a brilliant pink. I completed the day with a respectable 20 miles. A large school group from Maine was set up at Thunder Hill Shelter, where I intended to stay. I inquired about the attraction of Virginia to school groups from Maine.

"The weather," the teacher explained. "Many of the schools have outdoor programs, but the weather is still unpleasant for hiking this time of year."

As I dropped the pack off my back for the evening, I noticed a dark-haired bearded man wearing aqua blue hospital scrubs. Magaroni was the only hiker I knew wearing hospital scrubs. I hollered his name. His head turned. Sure enough, beneath his thick, two-month beard was the same hiker with whom I had trekked a hearty 80 miles farther south. He had dropped quite a bit of weight since I last saw him. Although only six weeks had passed, it seemed like a lot longer. Again, I found myself explaining how I had skipped this section to meet a friend and would soon skip ahead. He asked about Packrat and why he had quit the trail. Conversation flowed well into the evening, until we both drifted off to sleep.

Magaroni and I headed north together in the morning. The next night we hitchhiked off the trail a few miles to a campground. Another thru-hiker, Viking, was already there. Viking was another participant in my John Wayne whiskey night back in Georgia. We all pitched in a few dollars and bunked in a small camper used by hunters during deer season. Viking made a living as a corporate jet pilot, but he also was an Appalachian Trail volunteer. He had spent many hours working on the trail. Viking was a middle-aged man enjoying the freedom of the trail. He was a good storyteller, so we sat up listening to tales all night.

The next day, the three of us tackled 20 miles over a few mountains. We passed a serene shelter, which is nestled along a small pond in the middle of the forest and once had been featured in a National Geographic article. At one point while fording a stream, Magaroni dropped his water bottle into the water. Watching him running downstream with his pack on, reaching into the water, and trying to pull his jug out was the funniest sight since Bugs Bunny. Viking and I were laughing too hard to give a helping hand. After 20 miles, we plunked ourselves in a shelter only a few miles from the point where I would take a prearranged taxi ride 50 miles north to put me back on course.

Being able to mix with some of the hikers that were several days behind me added substance to my journey. Now I had an understanding of who was following me. Hearing their adventures and sharing mine created a closer bond. Now when I left notes in shelter registers, I knew who would read them. If I left extra food in a hostel grab box from my re-supply, I knew who would benefit. We were neighbors in a close-knit trail community.

Since beginning my trek, I had not encountered as many thru-hikers as this. Walking with other hikers who shared the same goal was nice, but I had also grown accustomed to walking alone. Even when Packrat walked with me, we usually only saw each other at camp at the end of the day. Now, if I got lonely and needed companionship, I knew I could slow down for a few days and several hikers would catch up to me.

In the morning, I said goodbye to Magaroni and Viking and walked up the trail to the road. In the short stroll to the road, I saw knee-high, mountain-stone foundations of cabins on either side of the trail, with the chimneys still erect—a reminder of a simpler life. A short while later, a taxi arrived and took me to Lexington, Virginia. From there, I waited for a bus to Waynesboro.

While waiting for the bus, I noticed a horse stable across the parking lot from the bus stop. Inside the entrance, I could see several employees grooming big Clydesdale-size horses. It was raining, and this looked like a great place to stay dry while waiting for the bus. Assuming the bus would stop when it got to Lexington, I walked into the stable and began chatting with a local female college student while she brushed down a horse. In the meantime, the Greyhound bus pulled through town. It slowed down, never stopping. Seeing no one at the bus stop, the driver stepped on it and proceeded on. I could hear the grinding sound of a bus engine over my conversation.

"Oh, no!" I yelled, as panic surged through my body. I grabbed my pack throwing it on my shoulders, and in the same motion began to run after the bus. My feet had taken me almost 1,000 miles, but there was no way I could outrun a bus. I thought for sure the bus was gone. I ran up the street and down an alley, hoping to head the bus off at a traffic light. Luckily, it was stopped at a red light.

"Hey!" I yelled as I pounded on the door.

The driver opened the door and in a monotone, authoritative voice said, "Ya got a ticket?" I flashed him my ticket stub. "Hurry up, sit down. I'm behind schedule," he replied.

Well, that's obvious, I thought as I tried to catch my breath and wipe the sweat from my forehead. The driver didn't stop to let me load my pack in the luggage compartment. Every seat but the one behind the driver was taken. For the next 50 miles, I sat on the bus with my backpack sitting upright in my lap, blocking my view and making my trip quite uncomfortable. I guess I should have waited patiently at the bus stop.

The next hundred miles or so would include the Shenandoah National Park and the parallel Skyline Drive, a north-to-south scenic road along the Appalachian ridgeline.

Earlier in the season, a winter ice storm glazed the trees with ice, weighing them down and causing some to topple over. Those trees are known as blow-downs. Trees that fall on the AT require maneuvering over, under, or around. Just one blow-down can slow a hiker tremendously as he contemplates the best route. There were so many blow-downs earlier in the season that the trail was allegedly impassable. Early hikers going south had to reroute onto the Skyline Drive. Situations like this demonstrate the commitment of the all-volunteer force that maintains the trail. Hundreds of determined trail maintainers armed with chainsaws and axes worked feverishly to clear the blow-downs before the surge of thru-hikers began traversing the Shenandoah. By the time I reached the southern terminus of the park boundary, the trail had been cleared for uninterrupted foot travel. Thank you, volunteers!

Before trekking on, I resupplied in Waynesboro and took lodging for the night. As I registered at the hotel, I recognized the clerk. She was one of the passengers in the car that drove me off the mountain into Gatlinburg back in Tennessee. She had insisted that I stay at the hotel she worked at when I passed through the area.

She recognized me despite my smaller frame and scraggly beard. "I wondered when you'd make it through here," she said with a smile as she stood up from behind the counter. She gave me a reduced price on my room, more evidence of trail magic. In the morning, I went to the hotel restaurant for breakfast. After eating four eggs, toast, bacon, grits, and some coffee, the waiter pointed to a man at another table and said that the gentleman had paid for my meal.

The man who paid for my meal came over and offered me a ride around town to run errands. "Thank you very much, sir," I said. "If you wouldn't mind, could you drive me to the post office?"

We hopped in his car and headed to the post office. He then drove me to the AT where it enters the park. Before parting ways, the man asked a tourist to take our picture. He jotted down my home address and mailed the picture to my parents with a kind note that explained our encounter in Waynesboro. As I moved along the trail, my steps had quite a bit of pep from the trail magic in Waynesboro.

A waterproof parka shielded my upper body from the rain, which had been falling since the day before, but the temperatures remained in the 60s. Shorts and a T-shirt had become my daily outfit. Just inside the tree line, not far from the road, I came across a cabin-sized ranger's office with a posted sign that read "Back Country Registration." All hikers were required to register with the park before entering. While filling out the permit, a car pulled up. A younger gentleman with long, black hair handed the driver some money and pulled his backpack out of the back seat. He looked too clean-shaven to be a thru-hiker.

He looked at me and in an excited voice asked, "Would you mind if I walked with you through the Shenandoah?"

"Not a problem. I'm going north, and I'm averaging some high miles," I replied.

He asked with doubt in his voice, "What are high miles to you?"

"Twenty or so."

"I can swing that." So we were off.

The Shenandoah is the second and last national park that I would trot through in my northward expedition. The Shenandoah is another heavily visited park, hosting millions of tourists every year. The park offers lodging, restaurants, and the scenic Skyline Drive, not to mention easy access to the Appalachian Trail.

The Shenandoah is well known for its abundance of deer. These Bambis are so accustomed to humans that they will eat out of your hand. Black bear heavily populate the park, but my luck would not allow me the opportunity to see one.

All day we walked in the rain, but the weather did not deter anyone from hiking. Midday, I stopped on the trail for lunch. While resting, a father and two college-age women stumbled upon me heading in the opposite direction. They noticed my ball cap with my alma mater in bold red letters: Miami. As it turned out, the girls were students at the University of Dayton in Ohio, not far from Miami University. A small world even on the Appalachian Trail.

Moving onward, I realized that just a month earlier, I spent Easter weekend with my family in this park. Now I was finally blazing through it. John, the hiker who had asked to tag along, was keeping pace—a surprise, considering that I had been walking for almost 1,000 miles and had established a rigorous pace. The terrain was not as difficult as most sections of the trail that I had walked. Several times, we crossed Skyline Drive, which was built where the original trail once followed. The trail was relocated into the trees along the road. Most of the views and outlooks through the Shenandoah also were accessible by car. Almost every lookout is located in a parking lot off Skyline Drive. The

AT intersects the road at the lookouts. It was easy to see why the road had bumper-to-bumper traffic in autumn with people eager to see the fall foliage. It can be compared to driving the AT for a 100 miles. It's beautiful.

We stumbled into our shelter by early evening. Several hikers—a family of three and a solo section hiker—already occupied some of the bunks. As John and I rolled out our sleeping bags, we learned that the family was hiking the trail southward. They just started a few weeks ago in Harper's Ferry, West Virginia. They planned to walk to Georgia and then catch a bus up to Maine and walk south again to Harper's Ferry. They hoped to avoid running into the huge surge of thru-hikers by attacking the trail with this strategy.

The more I talked with this family, the more intrigued I became. They were from Texas. The parents were older than most couples with an 8-year-old boy. While walking the trail, they were home-schooling the child, whose trail name was Sam. One of Sam's projects was to write in the trail registers along the way. What a neat way to learn and experience new things! Imagine the insights this 8-year-old boy would have from this experience, of course assuming that he enjoys life in the woods.

In the morning, I exchanged addresses with the family. They were inspired by my walk for a charity. I promised to send them a newsletter when I finished. John headed on with me, apparently ready for another 20-mile day.

Not long after leaving the shelter, the AT crossed Skyline Drive near a parking lot and headed back into the forest. John had fallen behind. As the trail began an ascent, I rounded a bend in the trail and discovered a young couple getting amorous. The woman's top was removed, and they didn't hear me coming. Obviously, they thought they were all alone on a primitive trail in the woods, and with that thought, they decided to play Tarzan and Jane. What they didn't consider was the fact that they were on the most popular trail in the world, with thousands of hikers eager to step where they had decided to get romantic.

I yelled as I approached. "Top of the morning to ya!" The women grabbed her shirt and covered herself as I passed. Chuckling to myself as I forged on, I forgot to advise the couple that John would also pass by shortly. Sure enough, later in the day, John and I sat along the trail sharing stories as we ate lunch. He said he ran into a couple making out on the trail with their tops off.

Rain relentlessly soaked every part of my gear and body for three days without letting up. Although I had traveled through horrible weather since beginning my journey, I still found it difficult to trek through rain and cold and keep my spirits up at the same time. But the Shenandoah National Park had snack bars and restaurants called Waysides all along Skyline Drive. Since the trail was always in close proximity to the road, these added luxuries were accessible and helped keep me motivated. As I slushed along the muddy trail, wet branches smacked my body as I passed. Every day of my walk through the Shenandoah, I treated myself to a blueberry shake, a hot sandwich, and a cold beverage.

John and I also partook of full-course dinners and drinks at the two lodges that the AT passes. The Shenandoah National Park offered the most domesticated amenities for hikers than any other section of trail that I had encountered thus far.

Deer and bear were overwhelmingly abundant in the park due to strict laws against hunting. So far, I had not seen a bear, but the deer had become so used to humans and would get so close that you could almost touch them. One night as I lay in my sleeping bag in Pass Mountain Shelter, the sound of grass being torn from the ground just outside the shelter startled me. The culprit was disguised in the complete darkness of the evening forest. As my imagination ran wild, I quietly snatched up my headlamp, aimed, and turned it on. I saw several deer eating the grass where I had relieved myself earlier. Yuck! Apparently human urine is abundant with nutrients, and the deer were taking advantage of this.

Six days of soggy walking brought me almost 100 miles to the Tom Floyd Shelter. It was the last shelter before the end of the northern terminus of the national park on the way to Harper's Ferry, West Virginia. John had managed to keep up with my rigorous pace. If he had a beard, I would have sworn he was thru-hiking. He planned to exit the trail just north of the Shenandoah near Front Royal, where he had left his car and caught a taxi to the beginning of his hike.

Several hikers were at the shelter when we arrived. After rolling out my sleeping bag, I grabbed my water containers and cellular telephone and trotted down a steep, rocky side trail to a small stream. At the last town, I received notice from Sunshine that a reporter would like to contact me by phone for an interview about my progress. She was preparing an article to feature my hike along with the first annual walk back in Toledo, in conjunction with my hike.

Before I hit the trail, some volunteers were so inspired by my hike for Sunshine that they committed themselves to organizing a local walk in conjunction with my journey with hopes of making it a yearly event. The idea was fabulous because my walk to raise funds was just a one-time event.

Before I left on my hike, a date of May 9 had been set for the local walk. Determining where I would be on the trail that day was impossible to forecast. But I agreed that I would make sure to have access to a phone. The Sunshine director of development planned to relay a message from me on the trail to everyone participating in the walk.

While sitting on a rock pumping water out of the stream through my filter, I was startled by the phone ringing. I never knew if I would have reception or not, so when the phone rang, I was always surprised. How often do you get a phone call in the middle of the woods? Sure enough, the reporter from the newspaper back in Toledo proved her reliability and called right on schedule. She was as surprised as I that I was talking to her from the middle of the forest on the side of a mountain several states away.

She asked a lot of questions. How was my journey going? Have I had any problems? What were some of the highlights? The weather, my weight loss, my huge appetite, and daily mileage were the primary points I discussed. A story ran later in the week that told about my walk and promoted the homegrown Walk With Sunshine.

Knowing I had inspired a local walk back home was keeping my spirits up. The rain had been continuous for five days. Once again, I was sloshing alone northward. The opportunity to drop off for a hot meal and milkshake had kept me motivated through the Shenandoah. I was now north of the convenient trailside restaurants that the Shenandoah offered, but knowing that volunteers and residents from Sunshine were planning to walk along with me helped to renew my spirits.

Whenever I came across one of the various shelters, I would duck in for a few moments to read the register and have a moment without getting pelted with rain. The last entry in the shelter register was a note from Piasa, dated that same day. Hmm! Piasa had just been here. Ever since beginning my journey, a half-dozen hikers including Piasa had remained several days ahead. For the first time, I was close enough to catch up to one of them. For more than two months, I had read their register entries and met others who had met them. Even though I had never met these hikers, I felt as if I knew them.

All day, I hiked at a gallop, wondering what Piasa looked like. From reading his entries, I had a picture in my head. Now I felt like a bounty hunter, wondering when I would confront him. Of course, bounty hunters don't have the luxury of following the same well-marked footpath of the person they are pursuing.

The next shelter I came to had no register entry or sign of Piasa. After refilling my water and eating a candy bar, I pressed on. Four miles later, I ducked into the next shelter. No Piasa. The next shelter was another eight miles away. It was late afternoon with several hours of daylight left, so I kept moving.

Eventually, night fell, and I was still walking. Again, I found myself tripping over roots and rocks as my headlamp bounced light down the trail. Around 8:00 p.m., I came to the trailhead leading to Rod Hollow Shelter. If Piasa was not there, I would have to catch him another day.

As I neared the shelter, I shouted, "Hello, anybody there?"

"Yeah," a voice replied from beneath the dry comforts of a shelter roof. Sure enough, I had found Piasa.

He did not look anything like the image I had in my mind. He was from Colombia and spoke with a strong accent. Of course, he had a scraggly beard in the manner of most thru-hikers after several months on the trail. Piasa explained that he had taken a few days off the trail to spend time with his sister and her friend. He fell behind the group he had been with for almost 1,000 miles.

Piasa worked as a chef in the Washington, D.C., area. As I cooked dinner, I asked him to share some trail culinary creations he had come up with. He said he really didn't get creative with his trail menu. But then he melted a Snickers bar into his hot cocoa. Mmmm! That looked good. They say good chefs are nonchalant about their creativity. I added that idea to my list of trail desserts.

Together, we headed toward Harper's Ferry, West Virginia. This town is considered the psychological halfway point of the entire AT. The Appalachian Trail Conference is located there. Even though the true halfway point was a few hundred miles north, Harper's Ferry is like the AT check-in station. The AT Conference has a tradition of taking a Polaroid of every thru-hiker who makes it this far. This is about as official as a thru-hike gets.

As it turns out, Harper's Ferry became historically significant to my Sunshine expedition. The day I marched into town, I spoke with Douglas back in Toledo by phone from the Bears Den Hostel. Seventy-five volunteers and residents had gathered for a six-mile Sunshine walk along a Rails-to-Trails path in Toledo. A state senator was present for the inaugural walk as well. Douglas repeated my brief statement over a microphone to the waiting walkers as he spoke to me on his cellular telephone. Shortly after ending our conversation, the walkers executed a six-mile walk, contributing an additional $4,000 to my fundraiser.

All of my efforts for Sunshine seemed to have struck a note in many people. One of the difficulties of performing a charity hike is getting people involved. The Appalachian Trail is separated from Toledo by hundreds of miles and several state boundaries. Not only were volunteers rallying around this tremendous cause, but also the Sunshine residents themselves were walking and rolling in step with me.

This day was by far one of the most inspiring of my hike. As I had ambled up and down mountains for the previous 68 days, I often had thought about ways to involve more people in this great cause. On May 9, tears of happiness streamed from my eyes as a feeling of solidarity set in. We were walking to Maine.

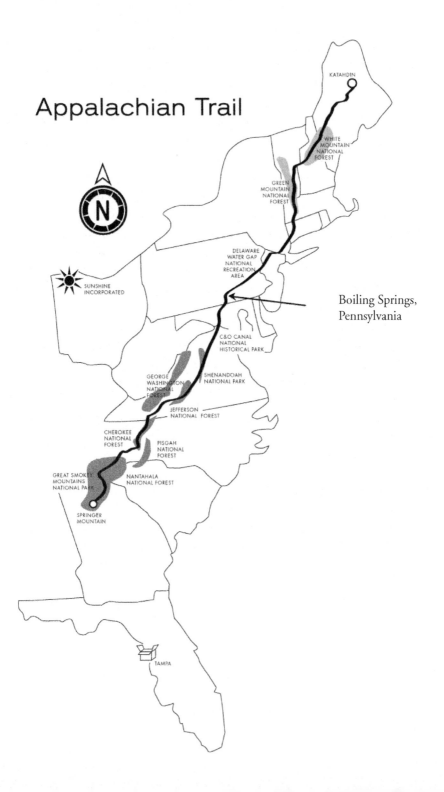

Appalachian Trail

KATAHDIN

WHITE
MOUNTAIN
NATIONAL
FOREST

GREEN
MOUNTAIN
NATIONAL
FOREST

DELAWARE
WATER GAP
NATIONAL
RECREATION
AREA

SUNSHINE
INCORPORATED

Boiling Springs,
Pennsylvania

C&O CANAL
NATIONAL
HISTORICAL PARK

GEORGE
WASHINGTON
NATIONAL
FOREST

SHENANDOAH
NATIONAL PARK

JEFFERSON
NATIONAL FOREST

CHEROKEE
NATIONAL
FOREST

PISGAH
NATIONAL
FOREST

GREAT SMOKEY
MOUNTAINS
NATIONAL PARK

NANTAHALA
NATIONAL FOREST

SPRINGER
MOUNTAIN

TAMPA

N

Chapter 26

Your Beer Will Be OK!

Boiling Springs, Pennsylvania. May 17, 1998. 1,065 miles from Springer Mountain, Georgia.

After speaking over the phone to the Sunshine walkers, I was in very high spirits. Piasa and I cruised through the hillside leading into Harper's Ferry. With the momentum of 75 Sunshine volunteers walking and rolling along at the same time, I cranked out a 21-mile day all the way into town—despite the rain that continued for the ninth straight day.

Piasa was fun to walk with. He was the same age as me, so we both had similar generational experiences. In contrast to the ski-like hiking poles that I was using, he walked carrying a big stick for balance, which gave him a native appearance. He told me stories of the group of eight ahead of us with whom he had walked.

The forest was in a full, springtime bloom. As I strolled, I could smell the sweet pink azaleas, honeysuckles, the pine, and the musty smell of moss and decaying fallen trees. Every tree had fully developed leaves, which concealed distant roads. Yet occasional sounds of trucks and cars whooshing by could be heard, reminding me how close I was to civilization at times.

When I got to Harper's Ferry, I planned to take a few days off the trail. I checked into the Hilltop Hotel, which had some low-priced rooms for hikers. The post office was a block away, so I switched into my tennis shoes and went to pick up my mail. When the postmaster stacked three boxes on the counter, I realized that I would have to make two trips, but Piasa saw me as he was hiking into town. He grabbed a box and walked with me back to the hotel, as he had a girlfriend meeting him in town at the same hotel. We planned to meet up and continue north in a few days.

Harper's Ferry is a historical town. The uptown district is actually a national park and has been preserved in its original Civil War state. Buildings of weathered red brick and gray mountain stone line the streets. Tourist shops and restaurants occupy the old structures. The town is the tri-state point of Virginia, West Virginia, and Maryland. The Potomac River splits the states as it wraps around Harper's Ferry in a half-circle fashion. According to historical markers, Harper's Ferry changed hands between the north and the south several times during the Civil War. Apparently, the town was a strategic position because of its close proximity to Washington, D.C. Historical markers located all throughout the town explain various battles and buildings.

After getting my mail back to the room, I ventured out for a tour. Flower gardens enhanced the AT on its way into town. President Clinton and Vice President Gore had recently planted some of the flowers along the trail during a dedication to Earth Day. A chair-sized boulder named Jefferson Rock was perched along the trail right behind the uptown district. Apparently, Thomas Jefferson had stood atop this rock and given a campaign speech. After climbing onto the rock, I enjoyed the view that Thomas Jefferson had seen as he preached politics nearly 200 years before. Yet as I stood on the rock, I had a much different experience. The smell of greasy food emanating from nearby restaurants caught my attention, pushing political thoughts from my mind. My mouth would better serve me by inhaling a hamburger and fries. With this thought, I brought my scenic tour to an end.

Back in the hotel lobby, I noticed a sign advertising an all-you-can-eat buffet. When the buffet opened, I was one of the first seated, and I made several trips to the food bar. Each time, I returned with a plate loaded with prime rib, shrimp, green beans, and assorted casseroles. Three couples were seated at a round table next to mine. They were whispering comments back and forth about the quantity of food I was consuming. The waitress had not cleared the four empty dinner plates stacked in front of my current plate, which by normal diet standards was an enormous amount of food.

Finally, one of the ladies spoke up in a joking fashion: "You must be very hungry." After they learned of my AT adventures and the fact that

I had been walking from Georgia, they were a bit more appreciative of my appetite. It is estimated that a hiker burns more calories each day than a marathon runner does on race day.

When I returned to the table with a hot fudge sundae stacked three times higher than the bowl in one hand and a fudge brownie in the other, one of the ladies exclaimed, "That's it! I'm going to walk that Appalachian Trail so I can eat like that!"

The next day was Sunday, May 10. It was Mother's Day. After talking with Mom by phone, I picked a scenic spot out of the rain, under the porch roof of the hotel overlooking the Potomac, and wrote my second newsletter. Before departing on my journey, I had written the first newsletter, which my Aunt Ellen had professionally printed and mailed to all of my sponsors. Now I was writing the second of three newsletters, updating my sponsors on my progress. The Sunshine home planned to add pictures to the newsletter of the equipment that had been purchased with the funds raised, and all sponsors giving more than $100 were recognized in the newsletter. As I wrote, I reflected on my progress over the last two and a half months. It was hard to believe that I had walked 1,000 miles already. After completing my newsletter update, I dropped it and a disposable camera with pictures into an envelope and mailed it to my aunt for publishing.

On Monday morning, the Appalachian Trail Conference Center (ATC) opened for business. I checked out of the hotel and strolled over to the ATC to register. The first person I met was Lori Potteiger, an ATC employee with whom I had spoken by phone several times prior to my journey. Finally, I was able to combine her friendly voice with the actual friendly person. She snapped a Polaroid photo of me and added it to the class of '98 thru-hikers. Pictured in the class of '98 book of Polaroids were the eight hikers that were ahead. Now I had a picture to visualize as I read the trail register entries of these hikers.

Piasa was still enjoying the time with his girlfriend, so I ventured northward alone. The AT passes through the uptown historic district and onto an old railroad bridge that has been converted into a footbridge to cross the wide Potomac River. As soon as my foot hit land on the other side of the river, I was in Maryland, the sixth of fourteen states I would eventually journey through. Yahoo! Another mental and physical celebration.

The first few miles follow an old canal boat towpath, which was as flat as any trail back in Toledo, Ohio. But the easy strides ended when the trail darted up toward the mountains. As I began my ascent, I looked back from atop a rock perched on the mountainside and took in a picturesque view of Harper's Ferry and the Potomac River. The old, tree-surrounded brick buildings sat on an outcropping, which was encased by the river. Although boundary lines were invisible, I was sitting in Maryland looking at both West Virginia and Virginia.

Piasa caught up to me the next morning as I sat drinking my coffee out of the rain. Beads of sweat already speckled his forehead at 7:30 in the morning. He had been moving at a fast clip since 4:30 a.m. to catch up to me. By the time I was packed and ready to saddle up, the sun was breaking out from the clouds. Finally, after 15 days, the rain stopped.

The weather was gorgeous for the first time in more than two weeks. All day, we relished the sun. Around lunchtime, we came to Washington Monument, the first structure erected in recognition of the country's first president. The monument was round, about the size of a grain silo. It was made from gray stone. Inside a doorway was a set of steps that took us to the top. We sat up there and ate lunch. All around, I could see farm fields cut in various shapes, crops of different colors growing in each field. Supposedly, a bomb bunker for the president sat beneath the mountain that we had just traversed. We ended our day at a shelter that was not quite of the same quality of the shelters back in Virginia.

In the morning, we got an early start. The weather was motivating. The sun warmed my body along with the rigorous exercise of hiking. By mid-afternoon, we crossed into Pennsylvania. Not only did we cross another state line, but we also crossed the Mason-Dixon Line, which divides the South from the North. *No more grits or Southern hospitality,* I thought as I passed the sign.

Even in the secluded forest, I heard about the final episode of the very popular TV sitcom *Seinfeld.* For almost 10 years, I had watched *Seinfeld* every Thursday. The final episode was set to air that day. Piasa and I both wanted to see the finale. For a year, advertisement had hyped up the finale. Even in the woods, we were victims of advertisement. If we had been out for just a few days in the woods to get away from it all, and I craved to watch a TV show, it would be pathetic. But I had been in the woods for 75 days. A 60-minute sitcom wasn't going to affect my overall experience. We studied the map, looking for a nearby town. There was nothing on the map for the next 30 miles. However, *The Thru-Hikers Handbook* mentioned South Mountain, a little community of 2,000 residents, which was located a few miles down a side trail. We hoped we could find a bar or restaurant with a TV. This was our only practical solution to see *Seinfeld*.

Not more than 100 yards down the path leading to the town of South Mountain, two bicyclists out for a ride stopped and asked us the usual questions.

"Are you thru-hiking? How long have you been on the trail? Where are you going?"

Piasa and I looked at each other and we both replied in stereo, "We are walking to South Mountain to find a place to see the finale of *Seinfeld*."

One of the cyclists offered to come back in his truck and take us back to his house to watch the finale. Without hesitation, we both said yes to the trail magic that was offered.

A short while later, a blue Chevy truck pulled up along the AT. An older man hopped out of the cab with the cyclist whom we had seen earlier. As it turned out, the cyclist's father is a trail maintainer in the area. They loaded us and our packs into the truck bed.

In a matter of minutes, we pulled into a driveway of a modern ranch home in a well-kept, middle-class neighborhood. The gentlemen helped us out of the truck bed and led us around back to a patio. We removed our muddy boots and let ourselves inside. Our hosts handed us towels and led us to the showers. As the dirt ran off my body and down the drain, I felt excited that I was actually going to see *Seinfeld*. The whole family assembled with us in the living room. Our host left to answer a knock at the door and returned with a hot pizza. Not a bad setup considering that less than an hour ago we were in the middle of the woods. Like the majority of Americans, Piasa and I were glued to a TV set on May 14 for the final episode of *Seinfeld*.

Our hosts invited us to stay the night, offering to drop us back at the trail on the way to work in the morning. At 6:00 a.m., we rolled up the sleeping bags, downed a cup of coffee, grabbed a donut, and piled into the back of the pickup truck. A few minutes later, we were standing on the AT where a road intersects the trail, waving goodbye to our host as the blue truck got smaller and smaller down the road.

Four miles up the trail, we came to an interstate road. Piasa had a mail resupply in Fayetteville, Pennsylvania, a few miles west down the road. Shortly after hanging our thumbs out, a truck pulled over and shuttled us into town, dropping us at the post office. Piasa went inside to get his package. While I sat outside, a car pulled up and a middle-aged couple hopped out. The man asked me if I needed a lift anywhere.

I responded, "Could you drop my friend and me at the laundromat?" The man happily agreed.

More trail magic. We were whisked away in a vehicle. But instead of dropping us at the laundromat, the man's wife insisted that we come back to their house and do our laundry for free. Again, we found ourselves in the home of people who had met us not even a half-hour earlier. Repeatedly, I tried to count the number of times my own family had taken in strangers and opened up our house to them. Every time, I arrived at zero.

Not only did we do our laundry in the comforts of their house, but our hostess offered to cook us breakfast. She soon learned of Piasa's culinary talents as he explained that he is a chef. She yielded her kitchen to Piasa, who dazzled us with culinary professionalism. As Piasa went to work in the kitchen, I offered to make the toast. Before Piasa could respond that he had it covered, the spring of the toaster ejected the first batch of crisp bread. Piasa had the kitchen under complete control, commandeering multiple appliances and living up to the expectations. In no time at all, he had produced a full-course feast of 13 scrambled eggs, a half loaf of toast, and a pound of crisp bacon. On top of this, we had bananas, donuts, coffee, orange juice, and bagels.

While Piasa was cooking the meal, I was able to view my webpage on the Internet. The man of the house ran his own business out of the basement and had an elaborate computer setup. Seeing all of the updates on my website for the first time since Hot Springs, North Carolina, put the distance that I had covered into perspective. The couple was impressed as I shared my charity mission with them.

By noon, our laundry was clean, our stomachs were full, and our hearts were blessed with trail magic. The couple helped us load our gear back into the car and drove us up to where the AT intersects the road. We thanked them and waved as they drove off. Wow! With trail magic like this, you would never believe the news headlines reporting on all of the terrible sides of our society. These instances of trail magic were more than one-time occurrences. Trail magic was what our country was founded on—goodwill to all.

***

For the first time on the trail, I began to notice the presence of mosquitoes and knats. The knats would hover around your head and make kamikaze dives into your eyes and ears. My ball cap brim kept the knats from my eyes as I walked, but they were relentlessly diving into my ears. Every few steps, I drilled my finger into an ear, overcome by the itching of a knat stuck in earwax.

Not far from where we were on the AT is the famous Gettysburg battle site. At one point in history, thousands of soldiers crossed our path on the way to battle. Many never returned home.

A popular hostel was our intended goal of the day, 23 miles from our start. Despite our late start, the terrain was not too difficult. Most of the climbs were short in duration, which allowed us a quicker pace than usual. Trees shielded us from the direct sunlight. We managed to blaze many miles without strenuous effort.

Near the end of the day, we were a few miles from the hostel when we approached two shelters built one in front of the other. From a distance, we noticed a clothesline tied between two trees with a pair of women's panties hanging up to dry. Women had been a rarity on the trail so our adrenaline perked up along with our curiosity. We saw two people inside one of the shelters. With smiles from ear to ear, we both said hello. Two women were sitting side by side, conversing. As it turns out, both were on their own and coincidentally stopped for the night at the same camp. One of the ladies, the owner of the panties, was strikingly gorgeous. Not that the other woman wasn't attractive, but this woman looked like Disney's Pocahontas, with long black hair flowing down her back. She had defined cheekbones and a deep bronze complexion. Her perfect hourglass figure was visibly defined from beneath the skintight black polypro long underwear that she wore.

Piasa and I tried to conceal our panting. Both women were out for a few days heading south. Dusk was setting in, so we had to make a decision about staying here or pressing on to the Iron Mansion hostel just another 30 minutes away. The hostel offered a hot tub, shower, kitchen amenities, and beds with clean sheets. Without ever openly conversing, both of us silently debated staying with the ladies or hiking on. The knats and mosquitoes were ferociously attacking as we sat, still pondering our lodging options. Instead of staying in the woods with the ladies, I invited them along with us to the hostel, but they were more interested in the wilderness experience. So we saddled up for the last stretch of trail.

All the way to the hostel, Piasa insisted that Pocahontas was interested in me. He claimed that every time I looked away she would stare at me.

"Why didn't you tell me this when we were there?" I asked.

Piasa explained with his Spanish accent, "Wrongfoot, I couldn't get your attention. You were talking to her the whole time."

"Oh, well, there's probably more women at the hostel."

"I don't know, Wrongfoot. Pocahontas had it for you, man."

Soon we saw a big, red brick mansion along the trail. It was an old hotel that dated back to the revolution and now served as an American Youth Hostel (AYH). During the Revolutionary War, iron casters lived in the hotel and used the iron furnace nearby to produce musket balls and cannonballs for the colonists fighting against the British. For a mere eighteen bucks, anyone could check in for the night and stay within the same walls as our forefathers.

Several youth groups and church groups were already checked in when Piasa and I arrived. Rob, another thru-hiker, was already nestled in. Rob thought trail names were silly and refused to take one. What he had not considered was the possibility of being named by other hikers, which usually occurs if you don't already have a trail name. It's a thru-hiker thing.

Rob was quite boisterous with his hiking philosophy. He claimed to be a purist, which in the thru-hiking culture means passing all the white trail markers, not skipping any sections of trail. I had met many purists along the route, and I considered myself a purist in all practical senses. I had covered every mile of trail with the exception of a high-water route and a few miles of road walking where the trail was impassable. But Rob had taken his view of purism to a bizarre level. He refused to hitch into towns for supplies, even if it meant walking an extra five miles off the trail. He felt purism was walking from Georgia to Maine without help from anyone—contradictory to my own idea of hiking as a team effort. But everybody hikes his or her own hike, and I was not about to invoke my opinion.

Rob, on the other hand, continued to voice his opinion of hiking to Piasa and me, and frankly it had become quite annoying. We were simply trying to enjoy a soak in the hot tub in the basement of the hostel. He continued to tell Piasa and I that when he supplied, he loaded his pack down with 80 pounds of provisions. Now, if he was leaving on an expedition without an opportunity to supply for 10 days or more, then he was packed correctly, but the AT zips by modern amenities (grocery stores and convenience stores) about every 80 miles or so, giving no reason to haul 10 days of food over mountains. In addition, Rob claimed to have had several hernias, which summed up in my mind that carrying 80 pounds was just plain idiotic. After listening to him and learning that he was an offshore clam fisherman, we arrived at his newfound trail name: Captain Clammy.

The aroma of eggs and bacon woke me the next morning. When I shuffled into the kitchen, the entire church group was assembled, preparing a morning feast. They offered Piasa and I breakfast, which we eagerly accepted. Rob came into the kitchen moments later with no interest in any free food handouts.

Not long afterward, Piasa and I saddled up and moved on. A few miles north, we came to the official AT halfway sign with an arrow pointing south indicating the same number of miles as an arrow pointing north. Not only was this a significant photo opportunity, but it has also become an AT tradition to eat a half-gallon of ice cream to celebrate. As soon as I hit the next town, I planned to do just that. I wondered as I treaded further north: Does this mean that thru-hikers should eat a whole gallon of ice cream when they reach Katahdin, Maine? Sounded good to me.

***

Piasa seemed to walk at an unusually slower rate than he had before. In no time, I was quite a distance ahead. I walked alone all day. The terrain remained relatively easy, with the exception of occasional rock formations and some short-lived ascents. Again, the weather was picture perfect. May has always been my favorite month of the year. It's not too hot or cold, and the fresh smell of spring leaves and flowers fill the air.

The next stop for the night was Boiling Springs. As I stepped from the forest canopy into an open field, I could see two people walking south toward me. From across the field, I could see they were carrying big, suitcase-size containers in their hands and were wearing uniforms. As the distance between us narrowed, I could tell one was a man and one was a woman, and they were emergency medical personnel. When they caught up to me, they were breathing heavy from their fast-paced walk up the trail.

The man asked me between breaths, "Have you seen an injured woman on the trail?"

"No, and I have been walking all day for the past 15 miles," I responded. "Where is she supposed to be located?" The man pointed on a local topographical map to a circled spot.

"Sir, you're going the wrong way. That is north of here a few miles, according to my trail map."

He replied in an authoritative fashion. "The trail is not headed in a northward direction. She has to be somewhere in this direction." Without waiting for me to explain that the AT rarely extends in a perfect north-south direction, the two of them ran off continuing south.

A few minutes later, I began to hear diesel engines idling and muffled voices. The trail crossed a dirt forest road. Up and down the road were several fire trucks, an ambulance, and a few police cars. The entire volunteer Boiling Springs Fire Department was sitting there.

Another paramedic approached me and asked the same questions as the other two. "Have you seen an injured woman?"

I replied, "No. If she is where you say she is, then she is another two miles north of here." I explained briefly that the AT does not travel in a straight grid of due north. I offered to lead the paramedics to her.

Two paramedics grabbed some medical cases and followed me. They struggled along with their bulky cases. After a few minutes of watching them struggle, I stopped and offered to strap their equipment to my backpack. Within minutes, my backpack resembled a Sherpa's load of supplies as we continued north. The paramedics explained that they got a call about a woman who had fallen down a rock formation and couldn't move her leg.

We passed a group of Boy Scouts that had placed the emergency call. The Scoutmaster pointed north up the trail. "She's just a little farther."

In a few minutes, we stumbled across a woman lying on the ground near a tent with a young girl sitting next to her. She had tears of pain in her eyes and began to describe her leg injury to the paramedics. Her shin was all cut up, swollen, and bruised.

The paramedics went to work on her. One of them radioed for a fire truck to drive up one of the forest roads to get closer. In a few minutes, we could hear a diesel engine struggling up a narrow, dirt road. Soon, two more volunteer firemen arrived at the site with a stretcher board to carry the injured woman out of the forest.

Everything seemed to be going smoothly with the lady getting medical attention, but her daughter was crying. No one had comforted the little girl. I dropped my pack and went to sit by her on a log. Her mom saw me and told me that the girl was deaf. Here I was in the middle of the forest, and an opportunity to use my sign language skills had arisen! I had spent the last four years studying to be a speech language pathologist. One of the many requirements was to take two sign language courses, which were introductory-level. Many more courses and experience are necessary to become fluent with sign.

As I struggled to recall some sign language appropriate for the situation, I decided to become useful and disassemble their tent. They obviously would not be hiking back into the woods. The little girl helped me. Together, we pulled the stakes and poles out of the hoop attachments and rolled the poles up into the nylon house. We bundled up all their camping equipment as best we could and followed the paramedics carrying the woman strapped to a stretcher to a nearby forest road where several trucks and an ambulance awaited her arrival.

All of their camping gear was loaded into the ambulance. The little girl and I stood along the edge of the road. She had a frightened look on her face and tears in her eyes. I turned to her and waited for her eyes to focus on me, getting her full attention.

When she looked at me I extended my hand to sign "Your."

I then held my hand to my cheek to sign "Mom."

I sliced my hand like a knife forward to sign "Will."

I brought my thumb to my index finger making an "O" shape and then brought my thumb to my middle finger making a "K," signing the phrase "Your mom will be OK."

The little girl gave me a hug and signed "Thank you." She climbed up into the ambulance with her mother and the procession of emergency vehicles descended back down the dirt road, toward town.

Still several miles from town, I continued walking north. I felt like a Good Samaritan for being able to help out the paramedics. Even better, I felt that my education had paid off, being able to comfort a deaf girl with my rustic sign language.

Several months later after completing the trail, I shared this story with some colleagues who I thought would appreciate my opportunity to use sign language in a real-life situation. When I signed, "Your mom will be OK" to my colleagues, demonstrating what I signed to the little girl, they burst out in laughter.

"What's so funny?" I demanded.

After catching her breath, one of my colleagues replied, "You told the girl, 'Your beer will be OK.' "

For a thousand miles, I thought I had comforted the girl with my basic signing skills when in fact I may have confused her. I hope not. No wonder she gave me a hug!

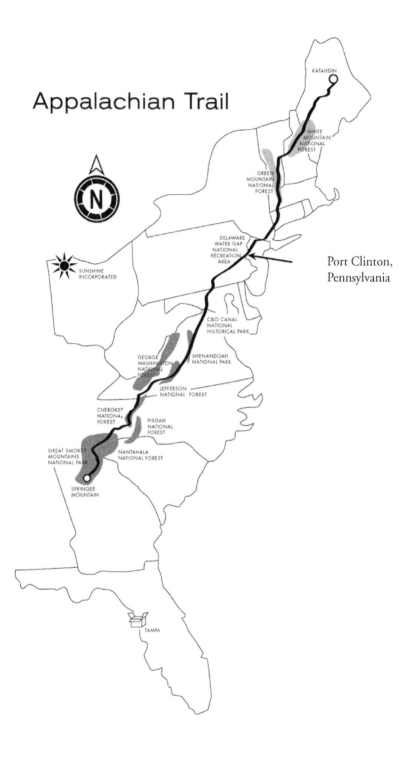

Appalachian Trail

KATAHDIN

WHITE MOUNTAIN NATIONAL FOREST

GREEN MOUNTAIN NATIONAL FOREST

DELAWARE WATER GAP NATIONAL RECREATION AREA

Port Clinton, Pennsylvania

SUNSHINE INCORPORATED

C&O CANAL NATIONAL HISTORICAL PARK

GEORGE WASHINGTON NATIONAL FOREST

SHENANDOAH NATIONAL PARK

JEFFERSON NATIONAL FOREST

CHEROKEE NATIONAL FOREST

PISGAH NATIONAL FOREST

GREAT SMOKEY MOUNTAINS NATIONAL PARK

NANTAHALA NATIONAL FOREST

SPRINGER MOUNTAIN

TAMPA

Chapter 27

A Rocky Birthday

Port Clinton, Pennsylvania. May 22, 1998. 1,188 miles from Springer Mountain, Georgia.

Pennsylvania has been ridiculed in hiking circles for the abun dance of rocks that rip, knaw, and tear apart hikers' feet. Due to geologic occurrences during the formation of mountains, the type of exposed rock in Pennsylvania was broken into jagged pieces. I heard that walking all day on these relentless rocks results in a feeling similar to running barefoot on a stone driveway. Yet, so far the Pennsylvania terrain had not been that bad. The infamous rocks were yet to come.

Boiling Springs is a peaceful little town in the Cumberland Valley that is known for the bubbling natural springs that emit from beneath the soil. The AT winds down off the mountain ridge onto some of the richest soil in the world. A few miles before reaching town, the trail blazes across acres of farmland, occasionally crossing rural roads. Sod trucks whiz by, loaded with green grass grown on the fertile soil.

When I reached town, I needed to find a place to stay. Several B&Bs offered hospitality at premium prices. One of the B&B owners agreed to let me pitch my tent in the backyard for a dollar, but I couldn't use the amenities inside.

Piasa trudged into town an hour or so later looking weary and moving very slowly. It had been a long day on the trail. He said that if I hadn't left a note for him under a rock telling him that I was heading into town, he would have stopped a few miles back at a shelter.

We made our way to a German tavern in the center of town to down a few beers and eat a hearty meal. I shared my emergency paramedic experience with Piasa. He had been only a few miles behind me but was oblivious that any of this had even occurred. In the morning, we both used a pay phone outside of an outfitter shop to call home before pressing on. Piasa used the phone first. As he talked, his smile changed to a worried look as he hung up the phone. He looked at me and said his nephew had just been diagnosed with leukemia. He wanted to go home to be with his family.

Just then, a taxi pulled into the outfitter parking lot and let out a person with a backpack, apparently to hike this section of the AT. Piasa asked the driver if he could take him to the nearest bus station. Whoosh! Without hesitation, Piasa had left the trail to be with his family in a time of crisis. My thoughts and prayers were with him and his nephew.

Sluggishly, I shouldered my pack and continued northward. The trail scurried through the flat Cumberland Valley. All day, the walking was easy, in and out of wet marshes. Twice, I crossed major roadways: the turnpike and Interstate 81.

To combat the gnats torpedoing into my ears, I picked up a trick from a section hiker. My handkerchief was draped over my head, secured in place by my ball cap. The handkerchief hung over my ears and prevented the little pests from entering the ear canal. From a distance, I looked like I was wearing a French foreign-legion hat, but it worked.

At the end of the valley, I entered a wooded tree line. The trail weaved along a stream. As I rounded a bend in the trail, I encountered a man holding a shotgun. He explained that he thought he heard a turkey, so he dropped his fish line and picked up the gun. Apparently, it was turkey season. Thank God I wasn't gobbling as I walked. Not long after passing the trigger-happy hunter, a turkey walked across the trail. I grinned knowing that it would not fall victim.

After 15 miles of flat valley terrain, I began climbing a mountain, leaving the Cumberland Valley behind. As I peered back, many new housing developments were visible throughout the valley. Urban sprawl has become a national epidemic in recent years. Throughout America, thousands of acres of forest and fields that once yielded corn, wheat, beans, and other agriculture varieties have been canvassed with new housing and strip malls. As I witnessed from the ridge, even some of the most fertile soil in the United States was losing ground to urban sprawl.

By dusk, I'd had enough hiking for the day. The Darlington Shelter situated on the ridge of the mountain became my home for the evening. Even though I began my journey alone, I had spent most of the nights in shelters with other people. When I did get a shelter to myself, my senses were more fine-tuned to the surrounding area. With no one to talk to, I would internally reflect instead of sharing my thoughts with another hiker. With the silence, I felt an enhanced presence of nature. The little critters seemed to move loudly, checking my gear for possible food, and the wind was more noticeable as it swayed the trees, causing a sound similar to a rocking chair as the tall stems flexed back and forth.

Whether I walked 10 or 30 miles, when I stopped at the end of the day, my legs cramped up. After removing my pack, my steps became short little shuffles, and I was hunched forward from carrying a pack all day. If someone filmed me walking around camp and played the film to a group of physicians who didn't know that I was hiking 20 miles a day, they might suspect Parkinson's and scoliosis.

In the morning, I broke camp at first light and trekked on. The infamous rocks were present in every step. At first, I tried to avoid stepping on the rocks, but there seemed to be more rocks than trail. I stopped at Hawk Mountain Overlook, from which I could see the Susquehanna River meandering in the valley. Supposedly, many Indian wars were fought in this area as the settlers moved west.

Port Clinton, Pennsylvania, where I wanted to be for my 31st birthday, was 70 miles north. Despite the treacherous rocks, I blazed 29 miles to Rausch Gap Shelter. By the end of the day, my feet hurt, and after removing my boots and socks, I noticed that my heels were bruised from banging on the rocks. The tips of my toes had blood blisters from countless scrapes and stubs on jagged rocks.

As the sun nestled behind the mountain, I sat along a man-made trough in front of the shelter, soaking my feet with the cool mountain spring water running into the metal bin. Morning came fast, bringing more great weather. The pain in my feet had subsided.

No, not again! Now I was deep in the heart of rock country. This trail was not a footpath in some places but rather a continuous path of rocks of all sizes and shapes piled up just perfectly so that every step crushed down on a jagged point, toes scraped the edge of a block slab, or my heel bounced off a boulder. At one point I became so frustrated from these seemingly endless miles of boulder fields that I dropped my pack and began tossing rocks off the trail. I worked for half an hour, clearing a measly 6-foot stretch of trail. At least the next hiker that walked by would get a few steps of relief. At the next shelter, I left a note in the register declaring a "Clear Pennsylvania of Rocks" campaign. I figured if every hiker cleared a 6-foot stretch of trail each day while traveling through, eventually the AT would be rock-free. Maybe I could convince the governor to send prison chain gangs out to help clear rocks.

During my noon meal, I dropped my pack on the trail and chose a flat-surfaced rock on which to slice some cheese and sausage. Supposedly, some old phone lines used to run up the mountain directly in line with where I was perched. The trees still remained clear in a narrow line down the mountain, offering a limited view beyond the tree cover. Sunlight warmed the rocky area as I leaned back onto my elbows with my feet elevated on a rock to reduce some of the swelling. As I rested in the sun, a subtle movement to my right caught my attention. A rattlesnake was coiled on a rock less than 3 feet from where I sat! It must have been there the entire time. Slowly, I crawled off the rock on the opposite side, crammed my equipment back in my pack, flung it on my back, and continued my rock hop. This time, my eyes were watching for snakes in addition to rocks.

Over the next two days, I covered 40 aggravating miles to arrive in Port Clinton, Pennsylvania, a small village on the AT. I planned to take a day off the trail—a zero-mile day—in celebration of my birthday. A roofed pavilion in the town park is offered to all hikers passing through as a free shelter, and the Port Clinton Hotel offers rooms at reduced rates. Back in Duncannon, Pennsylvania, I had phoned the hotel and reserved a room as a birthday treat to myself.

Since Pearisburg, Virginia, 600 miles south, I had carried a token good for one beer at the Port Clinton Hotel Pub. Sunny Daze, a man that drove me back to the trail, had given me the token as a gift. Finally, I would redeem its value of a cold draft. The hotel had the only bar in town. Neon beer signs glowed in the front window.

It was 4:30 in the afternoon when I stepped into the lobby, which actually was the bar. With my pack still on, I asked the bartender where I should check in. He told me I could check in right there.

"Are you the birthday hiker?"

"Yep."

The bartender pulled a six-pack of Yuengling Stout—a Pennsylvania brew—from the cooler behind the bar and handed it across the counter to me.

"Happy birthday."

"Well, thank you!"

Several patrons seated at the bar ordered drafts for me. I thanked everyone and asked if I could drop my pack in my room first. The bartender handed me a key and gave me directions up the stairs to my room.

The hotel was old but had been renovated and was fairly clean. Inside my room sat an antique, cast-iron bed and an antique dresser. Down the hall was a community bathroom for all guests to use. I splashed some water on my face, washed my hands, and headed back down to the bar.

In no time at all, several tokens for free drinks were assembled in front of me.

"My birthday isn't until tomorrow," I pleaded after downing my third free beer.

The bartender replied, "Tomorrow will be shots on the house."

Everyone was very friendly. The local clientele joked and shared stories all night long. Life in these small rural towns seemed more at ease than the city life I was used to.

A few thru-hikers arrived in the midst of my celebration, Foxtrot and Rob, a.k.a. Captain Clammy. Foxtrot had just gotten on the trail back in southern Pennsylvania. His parents live just down the road from the AT near Gettysburg. He literally hopped over his backyard fence and onto the trail. He thru-hiked the trail the previous year and was back to do it again. He planned to hike north to Maine from his parents' house and then shuttle back down to Pennsylvania, visit with his family, and continue south to Georgia. Now how do you fit two thru-hikes into your life in two consecutive years? I wondered. Then Foxtrot explained his occupation. He is a fisherman like Captain Clammy. He works on a ship off the coast of Alaska only three months of the year, making enough money to subsidize nine months of hiking and travel.

In the morning, I didn't want to see another Yuengling beer. I walked down the street to a diner for breakfast. A local newspaper lay on the counter in front of my seat. As I gobbled down some chipped beef and toast, I read the paper. The headlines weren't much different than they were two months ago, as far as big politics and world affairs. Clinton was still the president, and our nation had avoided getting involved in a war. Again, I realized how simple my life on the trail had become while civilization continued on without me.

All day, I kicked back and enjoyed my birthday off the trail. The owner of the hotel drove me into an adjacent town for a haircut and a grocery trip. Then I spent time writing postcards to everyone.

Since I had dedicated my hike to my brother Aaron, I tried to involve him with my journey as much as possible. At every town stop, I had made a point of dropping him a postcard. His rehabilitation aides had assembled a bulletin board to follow my hike using a trail map. They were attaching each postcard to the bulletin board and talking to Aaron about my journey. Aaron can't speak or read and does not have a way of formally communicating. No one really knows if he understands, but in my heart I felt that he knew what was going on.

Later in the afternoon, I spoke to my mom and stepfather in Florida and to a friend back in Toledo. They all were planning to meet me another 80 miles up the trail at Delaware Water Gap, New Jersey. This time, I made sure everyone understood that I might not be on schedule.

By late afternoon, the hotel pub filled up with the same group with whom I had rubbed elbows the night before. The bartender was not kidding when he said tonight I would get free shots. Again tokens began appearing before me, but the bartender said I could only cash them in for shots. Knowing that I had quite a distance to hike the next day kept me from drinking liberally. A few beers would be adequate. So I thanked everyone but declined the offer to drink shots of liquor.

At one point in the evening, the bartender placed a shot before me with whipped cream swirled over the top, capped off with a cherry. She explained that I would not get served any more beer until I drank the shot. The locals wanted to see a hiker all washed up with liquor. The music stopped, and everyone began chanting "Go, go, go, go!" Knowing this group would persist until I cooperated with their silly demands, I gave in to peer pressure and drank the shot. It was a birthday I would not soon forget.

Appalachian Trail

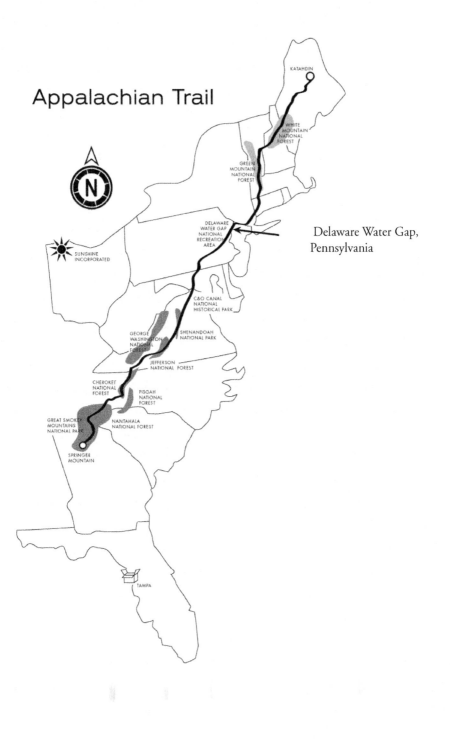

Delaware Water Gap,
Pennsylvania

Chapter 28

Bootless in New Jersey

Delaware Water Gap, Pennsylvania. May 26, 1998. 1,273 miles from Springer Mountain, Georgia.

Saturday morning, I dropped some postcards at the post office, ate a hot breakfast at the local diner, and continued north. Not long after climbing out of Port Clinton, I ran into a Boy Scout troop full of questions about my journey. A short while later, I came across a thru-hiker from 1997. He blessed me with some trail magic by offering some candy bars.

By lunchtime, I came to the Pinnacle Overlook. With another clear, sunny day, I could see far into the valley below. Nothing but rolling green farmland lay below, speckled with occasional farmhouses, barns, and silos. It was true Amish and Pennsylvania Dutch country. Overhead, hawks hovered in search of food. Tourists were everywhere—sitting on rock outcroppings, enjoying the views, and watching the hawks. This is considered the prettiest view in all of Pennsylvania. Not far from this area was a sanctuary for hawks.

Shortly north of the Pinnacle, I came across a pile of rocks as wide as a truck and taller than I. A sign posted above the rocks stated: "Please put a rock on the pile to eliminate them from the trail." It was signed by the local trail maintenance club. Apparently, they get so much grief from hikers about the rocks that they decided to instill some humor on the trail. Rest assured, I tossed several rocks onto the pile before moving along.

A day-hiker introduced himself as a trail maintainer in Pennsylvania, then he grinned and pointed to the rocks: "Are they sharp enough for ya? I file 'em down to points and then place them on the trail." Not my idea of funny.

At the end of my day, I had traversed 16 miles of rocks. The Eckville Shelter was my planned stopover. As I descended the mountain, I could see two people along the road ahead. As I got closer, I recognized Sunny Daze, the trail angel that had given me a beer token. He handed me a cold beer. With him was Comfortably Numb, one of the eight thru-hikers who had been ahead of me since Georgia. Finally, I had met one of the eight trail ghosts that I had only read and heard of for more than 1,000 miles.

Comfortably Numb ironically acquired his trail name by describing the physical state of his feet from a day of hiking as he lay in agony in one of the shelters. He was hiking the trail to raise money for Habitat for Humanity. It was nice to meet another fund-raiser out here.

Sunny Daze had picked up another thru-hiker, Bluegrass, from a point several days south of where we were and had brought him to the Eckville Shelter. Bluegrass wanted to meet some of the thru-hikers ahead of him. It was a unique opportunity to meet a hiker whom I would otherwise never have met.

The Eckville Shelter is actually a garage with wooden bunks positioned behind a small bungalow home. The Appalachian Trail Conference purchased the house as an outpost. A short distance off in the yard, a bathroom with a solar-heated shower had been built for hikers. Showers are a rarity on the trail, so I took advantage of this modern amenity.

In the morning, I said goodbye to Sunny Daze and Bluegrass as they drove off to drop Bluegrass back on the AT where he had left it. Comfortably Numb and I climbed out of the valley back up onto the ridge, continuing north. To take my mind off the rocks, I had a stereo cassette headset mailed to me in Port Clinton. A few friends had made tapes for me to listen to as I trudged up and down the spine of the Appalachians. The Pennsylvania rocks forced me to resort to music to distract me from the pain. Twenty miles later, we stopped for the night at Bake Oven Knob Shelter.

The next day, Comfortably Numb and I cranked out some fast miles. By noon, we had walked 15 miles. Up ahead, the map showed a huge descent known as Lehigh Gap, with a 1,000-foot drop in elevation. As we approached the descent, I could see a road down in the valley. On the other side of the road was another mountain with a steep, angled rock face that looked impossible to climb. No way is that part of the AT, I thought. It's too steep to be a trail. For a mile and a half, we descended drastically into the valley. Sure enough, the AT crossed the road and meandered toward the steep rock face.

The trail was almost vertical. As we began climbing, I realized that this was the steepest part I had ever hiked on the AT. It was so steep that my hiking poles were useless. They hung from the arm straps sliding up and down my wrists as I grabbed rocks with my hands for support. Occasionally, I would peer over my shoulder, realizing that with one slip of the hand, I could lose my balance and fall, bouncing off jagged rocks on a long plummet to the road. Yikes! Fortunately, I would not have another climb like this until New Hampshire.

At the summit, the trail leveled off onto a flat clearing with nothing but dead, gray, weathered trees. It was as if napalm had been dropped on the mountain. The only living plants were occasional weeds and shrubs. Minerals had been mined from the earth, depleting nutrients necessary for plant life. The AT did not always blaze through the most desirable places on earth.

Comfortably Numb and I ran into Foxtrot at a shelter. All three of us decided to blaze another four miles to a road crossing, Wind Gap, and share the cost of a hotel room listed in The Thru-Hiker's Handbook. By day's end, we had conquered 30 miles.

The hotel was far from a five-star resort. At one point in time, it may have been a pleasant roadside inn, but now paint was peeling off the building. Inside, the walls were stained yellow with cigarette tar. The decorations dated the room to the 1970s. Nonetheless, it had a shower, television, and telephone. Besides, I had been living in unfurnished shelters and tents for three months.

The next day, I would hike another 20 miles to Delaware Water Gap. There I planned to meet a friend from Toledo as well as my mom and stepfather from Florida. We all planned to do some hiking and relaxing for a few days.

Reaching Delaware Water Gap also meant crossing into another state, leaving the rocks behind. It was a sobering moment when I realized that I had journeyed more than 1,200 miles through eight states, more than half the distance to Katahdin, Maine.

In the early morning hours, I quietly slipped out of the hotel, allowing the other two to sleep in. The sun was just rising over the mountain. The previous night, I gave Foxtrot and Comfortably Numb some of my food, reducing my supply pack to a few snacks so that I could travel lighter and faster into Delaware Water Gap. My Florida parents planned on hand-delivering my supply box.

By mid-afternoon, I had covered the 20 miles into town and continued up the street to a Presbyterian church where I planned to meet my friend Amy from Toledo. Sure enough, she had been waiting most of the day for my arrival. As a matter of fact, she was unsure of the exact day we were to meet, so she had arrived a day early. My parents planned to meet us at a hotel in town. Amy and I drove to the hotel parking lot, where I noticed my parents' Blazer. Right on schedule.

Originally, I had planned to slack-pack the AT with Ron and Amy. But Amy was wearing a leg brace to protect her knee from a recent surgery. Needless to say, she would not be able to hike. Amy and my mom agreed to go shopping in town while Ron and I blazed some trail. Ron, who had been hiking the AT in sections for several years, looked forward to completing some miles with me to add to his list of sections hiked.

Ron and I filled up some water bottles, grabbed a few snacks, and drove north to where the trail intersects a forest road. We planned to walk south back to Delaware Water Gap. The terrain was still rocky but not as relentless as some areas in Pennsylvania had been.

A few miles into the forest, we ran into several large groups of eighth-grade students from Newark, New Jersey, who were experiencing hiking for the first time. Each group was divided into ten boys, which impressed me. They had read up on good trail etiquette, which recommends limiting your party to 10 or fewer. The weather was beautiful, with sunny skies and 75 degrees. We zipped along without the weight of full backpacks, passing long strings of the young adventurers.

Soon after encountering the youth groups, several of the young adventurers came running down the trail yelling "Bear, bear!" as they zipped by us. Sure enough, a large black bear was perched on a rock off to the right as Ron and I approached cautiously, armed with cameras. A torn backpack lay on the trail. A group leader explained what had happened. Apparently, the group of students had stopped at McDonald's for breakfast on their drive from the city to the woods. One of the young guys decided to load his backpack with a few extra Egg McMuffins. Who would know? Shortly after the students hit the trail, the bear caught the scent of the McMuffins and began following the group. One of the teachers in the group noticed the bear. Panicked, the boy with the Egg McMuffins confessed. The teacher made him take the pack off and leave it on the trail. Good thing, because the bear wasted no time tearing open the pack with his teeth.

Of all the states I had hiked through, my first bear sighting was in New Jersey. Prior to my trip, I viewed New Jersey as being a barren, treeless, industrial land. As a matter of fact, I wondered why the wilderness trail was routed through this state. All the stories of big city life had given me the mental picture of an urban parking lot. In fact, the trail in New Jersey was dense forest with an abundance of wildlife.

During the two days I spent with Amy and my family, we drove around the Delaware Water Gap region, sightseeing and eating in several restaurants. Ron and I blazed 29 miles of trail.

Before my parents departed, they handed me my supply box and a pair of hiking boots. I had asked them to bring my spare pair of boots so that I could give my current pair a rest after 1,200 miles. When I had asked my parents for the boots, I was on a pay phone in between the rocky sections of Pennsylvania. As it turned out, the rocks in Pennsylvania had scuffed them up, but all in all they still were in good condition. But I figured wearing a spare set of boots for a few hundred miles would preserve my original pair for the last stretch of trail. In case I developed boot problems, I mailed my original boots ahead 400 miles to Dalton, Massachusetts. Amy drove me to the post office and then back to the trail. We said goodbye, and I headed back into the forest.

With a triumphant feeling of crossing into another state and relishing the past few days spent with family and a friend, I flew down the trail. The mosquitoes had become noticeably annoying. At one of my frequent breaks, I saturated my clothing with the powerful bug repellent DEET.

Toward the end of the day, I stopped at a creek to resupply my water. A hiker I had not met before stopped, and he introduced himself as Gingerbread Man. We chatted for a few minutes. This young man had recently graduated from high school and started his thru-hike on April 1, a month later than me. This guy caught up to me even though he was 30 days behind me from the get-go. He had been averaging 38-mile days. Geez! Those are some miles!

After topping off my water, I tried to catch up with Gingerbread Man but realized that I did not have that kind of endurance. We both were planning on stopping at the same place for the night, so I looked forward to getting the trail gossip because he had passed everyone that followed us.

By dusk, I had torn through 23 miles of New Jersey terrain into Unionville, New York. The AT weaves in and out of New York and New Jersey before finally leaving New Jersey once and for all. A small bunkhouse attached to a tavern offered basic accommodations for hikers. Foxtrot and Gingerbread Man were already claiming bunks when I arrived.

As we socialized, Foxtrot and I learned that Gingerbread Man got his trail name from some hikers who thought he looked like a gingerbread cookie cutout. His head was bald and round. He explained that he had no body hair due to a childhood illness. He was wearing a small daypack. His primary food intake had been cans of cake frosting, graham crackers, and fruit. He carried a plastic tarp for shelter. At night on the trail, he would roll up in the tarp like a burrito. He had not taken any days off since beginning the hike, in contrast to my many days off with friends and family. He did not really have too much information about hikers behind us, probably because he was traveling at such a high speed that no one really connected with him. Foxtrot and I said goodbye to Gingerbread Man in the morning, not even trying to keep his pace.

The trail passed through farm fields and wound in and out of swampy marshes. Volunteer trail maintenance crews had built bog bridges through the swamp so that hikers would not have to wade through muck. Two wooden boards were nailed down to large four-by-four blocks, elevating the boards above the water. One foot used the left board, and one foot used the right. Green ferns peeked out of the swamp water between the trees, making up a dense, green, wooded canopy. If not for the relentless mosquitoes, the swamps would have been a tranquil section of trail. The mosquitoes were so thick that if I stopped for even a second, a swarm of them would drill me. Repellent didn't help because it was so hot that I would sweat it off. Running became the only option. By running along the bog bridges, I created a wind strong enough to keep the darn things off of me. Eventually, the trail left the swamplands, allowing me to slow my pace without getting eaten alive. Temperatures had topped 90 degrees. Sweat dripped so heavy that I could have wrung out my shirt to fill my water jug. Yuck! That day, May 31, marked my third month on the trail. To celebrate, I lit citronella candles to keep the mosquitoes away. The water source for the shelter was a spigot attached to a park ranger office a short distance up the trail. While we unrolled our sleeping bags and made camp, a warning siren began to blare. A short while later, we walked up to the ranger's office to fill our water jugs. A ranger noticed us and told us that a tornado had been spotted nearby. The ranger said that the shelter was the safest place to be if the tornado touched down. Luckily, it never did.

***

Beavers can be a real nuisance. They dam up rivers and streams, causing floods. These little critters had successfully flooded a mile of AT. What once was a stream on the map was now a flooded marsh. Splash, splash, I plunged along. Toward the end of the flooded area, I noticed the original stream with neatly piled sticks, branches, and trees molded into a beaver dam. It's amazing what a little animal with a sharp set of teeth can do.

We had ascended a ridge and stopped to enjoy the view. My left foot suddenly felt bootless. Every time the wind blew, my foot felt the air just the same as the skin on my exposed arm. Looking down, I noticed that my left boot leather had separated from the sole all the way from toe to heel along the inner arch seam, leaving my foot without arch support and exposed to the elements. Great. I'm 40 miles north of a town with another 80 miles until the next town. Now I was kicking myself for parting with my original boots. Then I noticed that the right boot also was beginning to tear along the seam. Damn, these things had only a few hundred miles on them! My other pair, Danner Mountain Light II, had taken me 1,200 miles and still was in good shape. But they were useless to me sitting in a box at a post office.

Duct tape to the rescue. Entire books have been written about the many uses of duct tape. Yes, even hikers have found the benefits of this magnificent adhesive. Before I moved on, I unraveled several feet of duct tape that I had wrapped around my water bottle for situations like this.

I wrapped the tape around my boots, hoping they would hold together. If the boots tore any more, I would have to revert to my camp shoes, a lightweight pair of track shoes that I wore around camp. By the end of the day, the boots had not torn any more. But friction had worn away the duct tape, and my feet hurt from walking without arch support and from the sticks and rocks that kept getting stuck in the tear.

On the road, motorists can call AAA to get a flat tire replaced, but getting boots replaced in the middle of the woods is not so easy. Until the next town, the best I could do would be to manage with what I had: a torn pair of boots, a pair of tennis shoes, and a few feet of duct tape. As it turned out, I was not able to change my flat tires until Kent, Connecticut, 87 miles north.

Appalachian Trail

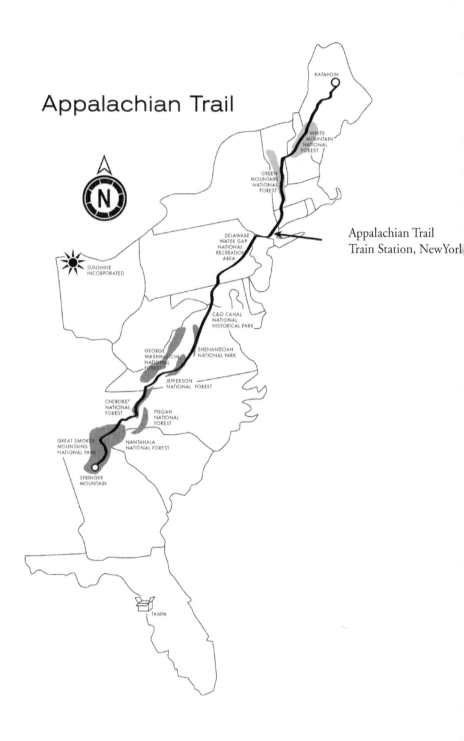

KATAHDIN

WHITE
MOUNTAIN
NATIONAL
FOREST

GREEN
MOUNTAIN
NATIONAL
FOREST

N

DELAWARE
WATER GAP
NATIONAL
RECREATION
AREA

Appalachian Trail
Train Station, New York

SUNSHINE
INCORPORATED

C&O CANAL
NATIONAL
HISTORICAL PARK

GEORGE
WASHINGTON
NATIONAL
FOREST

SHENANDOAH
NATIONAL PARK

JEFFERSON
NATIONAL FOREST

CHEROKEE
NATIONAL
FOREST

PISGAH
NATIONAL
FOREST

GREAT SMOKEY
MOUNTAINS
NATIONAL PARK

NANTAHALA
NATIONAL FOREST

SPRINGER
MOUNTAIN

TAMPA

Chapter 29

That Ain't No Bull

The Appalachian Trail Train Station, New York. June 4, 1998. 1,426 miles from Springer Mountain, Georgia.

The day I blew out my boots, I crossed from New Jersey into New York. The state line was marked with a painted white line on a flat rock high on a mountain ridge with the state initials NJ/NY on its respective sides. Slowly, I was working my way through the New England states. Because I already had been in and out of New York twice, this state crossing didn't feel as exciting as the others had, probably because I was more concerned about my footgear. Foxtrot and I had been leap-frogging each other since Delaware Water Gap. We planned our shelter stops together even though we walked alone throughout the day.

The water in New York looked and tasted disgusting. It had a rust color from the high content of iron and carried the sulphurous smell of rotten eggs. At first I thought the water was contaminated from bad plumbing in the well, but I later learned that iron is so prevalent in the area that it has been mined extensively, dating back to the Revolutionary War for the production of ammunition. Most of the shelters had wells from which to pump water. All through New York, I added Kool-Aid and Gatorade powder to conceal the taste.

The loose, sharp, slab rocks of Pennsylvania were a thing of the past. The AT now climbed along solid rock ridges. Most of the Appalachian Trail has been moved a time or two during rerouting projects. Moving the trail is necessary accommodate new land acquisitions and to prevent erosion.

The New York section of the AT follows some of the original sections of trail. One stretch of the AT that had acquired notoriety was the "lemon squeezer." This section had not been rerouted since the creation of the trail, according to literature. Even the earliest thru-hikers had to pass through this narrow passage. This short span of trail was a bit of an obstacle course that ran between two house-size rock formations that were too narrow to pass through with a full pack. At first, I seemed to fit with my pack on, but then my pack got wedged between the rocks on either side of the trail. Realizing that the basic laws of physics were against me, I pushed back out the way I came, took off my pack, and carried it in my arms sideways.

Later in the day, Foxtrot and I decided to split a hotel room in Fort Montgomery, New York, not far from West Point. We descended the mountain and found that a small section of trail was actually closed. The trail winds through the Appalachian Zoo, which contained caged regional wildlife. The zoo closed at 4:30 p.m., meaning that the AT crossing through the zoo closed also. We had to walk along a very busy road off the AT to Fort Montgomery. We took lodging at a reasonably priced hotel. For twenty-five bucks, we each got our own rooms.

In the morning, we headed north across a half-mile bridge spanning the Hudson River. Every car that passed vibrated our feet. The terrain was not difficult. New York has some of the lowest elevations of the entire trail. We hiked 25 miles, ending the day at a shelter with several section hikers. As I sat writing in my journal and looking at the data books, I realized that I had only one-third of the trail left to go. A total of 750 miles remained.

A few weeks before, I had made arrangements to meet a former college professor of mine. We had become good friends during my studies at Miami University. She was visiting family a short distance from the trail. This time, I gave myself enough latitude so that I would not have to walk ridiculous distances to meet her, as I had done to meet up with others. Still, I needed to pick up my mileage, which meant pushing ahead of Foxtrot.

We did not get an early start out of the shelter, which meant we had to walk later into the evening. Foxtrot and I walked together all day until we reached the shelter where he planned to stay. From there, I continued north, planning to stop at the next shelter, 9 miles ahead.

Connecticut was just 10 miles farther. I had made arrangements to meet my professor in a little town named Kent, just across the state line.

As I was rambling along, I came across a man out for an evening jog. As he passed, I said hello. He didn't even wave but kept on running, holding a can of mace at the ready.

A few miles before the shelter, I came across the Appalachian Trail Train Station. You can actually take the train into New York City. A couple hundred yards north of the train station, a sign posted along a rural highway read "Deli, ½ mile." A New York sub sounded pretty good, so I pounded the gravel alongside the interstate to the deli. Inside, I found a deli counter filled with cold cuts, cheeses, and salads. I ordered two foot-long subs, one to snack on then and one for dinner when I reached the shelter. Along with the sub, I bought a pint of ice cream, pop, and a candy bar. While I stood around eating my ice cream and sandwich, I tried to strike up a friendly conversation with the girl who had made my sandwich.

She said, "Look, I was nice enough to ya. I made your sandwich, now leave me alone." The attitude toward hikers definitely had taken a turn for the worse since I entered New York.

By the time I finished my sandwich, I had the solution for the New York attitude. David Letterman could ride the train to the Appalachian Trail Train Station and have an ice cream eating contest between thru-hikers and Sumo wrestlers. He is always doing some stunt poking fun at someone. The viewers would be amazed as they watched thin, frail thru-hikers polish off more ice cream than big, fat, world-class Sumo wrestlers. Maybe then hikers would get some respect, and locals would act a little nicer to the hearty souls trudging through New York all the way from Georgia. Hmmm! I will have to send this idea into the Late Show producers.

After eating a pint of ice cream and a 12-inch sub, I shouldered my pack and headed back toward the trail with a few miles left to go. The trail left the road and popped out a short while later after crossing another road. The trail markers led over a stile—the small A-frame ladder used to cross barbed-wire fencing—and through a cow pasture.

During my journey, I had walked through many cow pastures and thought nothing of it. Ever since entering Virginia, cow pastures had become a regular fixture. I was always careful and kept the cows in sight. They would usually stare at me for minute then go back to grazing. Stepping into a cow pie was more a concern than being harmed by a cow itself.

This time, things were a little different. A small herd of black-and-white Holstein dairy cows were grazing off the left-hand side of the trail. But shortly after I crossed the stile into the pasture, two rather large bulls with menacing horns separated from the pack and began ambling toward me. Bulls usually were not mixed in with the cattle—at least that had been my experience with all the other pastures I had crossed. As the bulls approached, I figured that I could scare them off. They looked mean, as if I had done something to offend them. It gave a whole new meaning to "mad-cow disease." The distance between us was diminishing.

I yelled. "Back, back!"

They moved closer. Was my red backpack is drawing their attention? Now, all I needed was some matador skills and I would be all set. Unfortunately, I felt as if I were the clown. One of the bulls got within 10 feet. I held one of my hiking poles toward his nose and again yelled, "Back, back!" This just seemed to make him mad. He blew air out of his snout and charged. I was 50 yards from the other side of the pasture. My only option was going back the way I came. Wondering if I could outrun a bull, I turned and ran as fast as I could, 15 yards or so back to the stile. As soon as my feet hit the steps, I jumped, leaping into the air. Bam! I smacked the ground face first on the other side of the fence, my heavy pack landing on top of me. As I lay there, thankful that I made it out of the pasture alive, I heard people laughing. A gold Honda four-door had pulled off the road, across from where I sprawled. A family of four saw the whole event and thought it was hysterical.

The man driving the car yelled out the window, "Are you all right?"

"Yeah," I replied, dragging myself up off the ground.

The man, still laughing, said, "You shouldn't have looked at the heifers." His passengers laughed even harder.

Real funny, I thought. *It must be a farmer thing to be entertained by this.*

"How the heck do I get around this pasture?" I asked.

The drive-by comedians suggested walking the road to the next farmhouse and asking permission to cross the farmer's land around the trail. As I started walking, I noticed blue blaze markings that indicated a trail that led up to the AT. This was an old section of AT that eventually linked back to the current AT route.

A few miles of climbing up away from the road led me to the shelter. After rolling out my sleeping bag, I dug out my sandwich, which just happened to be roast beef. I savored every bite with symbolic pleasure. All night, I dreamt of cows stampeding through my camp.

In the morning, I made the usual coffee and ripped open a Pop-Tart package. Another few miles and I would leave New York. With no regrets, I stuffed my pack, saddled up, and took off. The weather was sunny and warm.

That day, I planned to meet up with my former professor near Kent, Connecticut. She planned on leaving her car in town and walking up the mountain until she met me on the trail. The morning whipped by as I blazed up and down the relatively easy terrain with no bulls to slow me down. Just before noon, I crossed into Connecticut, the tenth state on the trail. Only four more to go.

Dr. VanVliet inspired me during my studies at Miami. Her courses were always enjoyable because she put her heart and excitement into her career as an educator. What really made her a quality professor was that she did not put herself above the students. She let you know that she was human. She always treated everyone with respect and politeness. Her schedule was always hectic, with travel plans to Europe to teach or a project meeting out of town. So when I got word that she had set aside her busy schedule to meet me on the trail, I was inspired by the fact that she didn't forget about me even after I had graduated.

Around noon, I saw someone hiking up the mountain toward me. Sure enough, it was Dr. VanVliet. Hiking pole in hand and a backpack hanging from her shoulders, she was ready to go.

We met up just two miles out of town. We stopped at a shelter a mile from the road and caught up with each other's lives. Of course, I told her that I'd almost met my fate with a bull the day before, and a little distance made it seem a lot funnier to me. Then I showed her my torn boots and explained that I needed to arrange for new ones at the outfitter in town. Dr. VanVliet unbuckled her knap sack and pulled out fresh fruits, vegetables, and granola as a care package for me.

Dr. VanVliet belongs to the Appalachian Trail Conference and has volunteered her time to trail maintenance in previous years. She had a good understanding of what I had been going through for the past 1,440 miles. We slowly worked our way toward town. Dr. VanVliet had reserved a hotel room for the night. The town was a bit pricey, so if I had been traveling through alone, I probably would have stayed out of town at the shelter.

Supposedly, some celebrities live in the area. While I was in the outfitter looking at boots, the shop owner was telling me that Michael J. Fox dropped in occasionally. Someone else told me that Tom Brokaw lived nearby. The gorgeous country with rolling hills and wide-open valleys was perfect for a celebrity hideaway.

My good pair of boots that I had mailed ahead was sitting in a post office a few hundred miles up the trail in Massachusetts, useless to me here. Now, I had a brand new pair of boots that I was able to obtain at the outfitter. Most equipment suppliers are good about replacing gear that breaks down during a thru-hike, and the outfitter simply exchanged my worn-out boots for the new ones. Breaking in a new pair of boots can be damaging to your feet, especially when you're walking 20 miles a day. With this in mind, the outfitter fitted me with a boot that had no break-in time. It was soft leather, with a thick cushioned lining.

Dr. VanVliet seemed to enjoy going along with me through my town chores of the post office package pickup, laundry, and the outfitter. It was a good thing that she had a car because I had five boxes waiting at the post office when I arrived.

After getting all of my chores handled, we went up the street and found an Italian restaurant for dinner. I had my eyes on an ice-cream parlor for dessert. Again, my appetite left a lasting impression.

In the morning, we had breakfast together. Dr. VanVliet planned to spend the rest of her vacation with her sister in New York, and I was heading north. Again, I was inspired by someone who cared enough to meet me along the way to show support.

Appalachian Trail

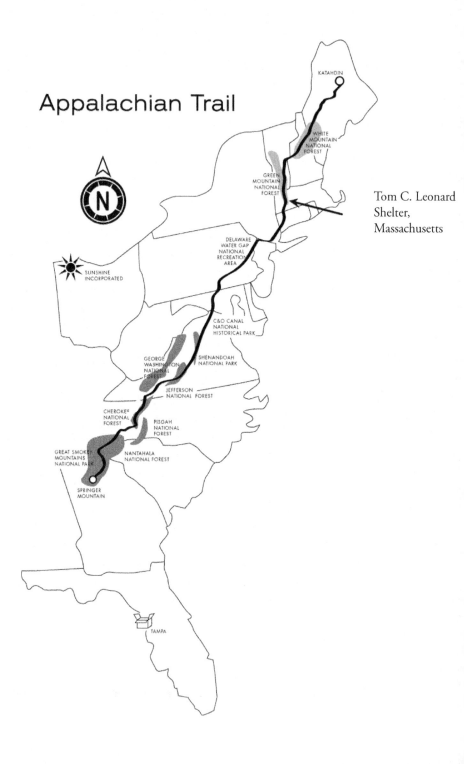

KATAHDIN

WHITE
MOUNTAIN
NATIONAL
FOREST

GREEN
MOUNTAIN
NATIONAL
FOREST

N

SUNSHINE
INCORPORATED

DELAWARE
WATER GAP
NATIONAL
RECREATION
AREA

C&O CANAL
NATIONAL
HISTORICAL PARK

GEORGE
WASHINGTON
NATIONAL
FOREST

SHENANDOAH
NATIONAL PARK

JEFFERSON
NATIONAL FOREST

CHEROKEE
NATIONAL
FOREST

PISGAH
NATIONAL
FOREST

GREAT SMOKEY
MOUNTAINS
NATIONAL PARK

NANTAHALA
NATIONAL FOREST

SPRINGER
MOUNTAIN

TAMPA

Tom C. Leonard
Shelter,
Massachusetts

Chapter 30

No Senior Discounts on the AT

Tom C. Leonard Shelter, Massachusetts. June 6, 1998. 1,506 miles from Springer Mountain, Georgia.

Leaving town with a new pair of boots had pros and cons. The upside was that I had arch support once again, but breaking in a pair of boots on the trail is not recommended. There really is no time to allow for blisters to heal. If you take a day of rest, that's a day off the trail. I hoped that these new tires would work out. I wished that I had never changed boots with my parents.

Dr. VanVliet and I ate a hearty lunch together and then said goodbye. She left for New York, and I headed back for the hills. A few miles into the forest from the road, I came across a young woman sitting against a tree. She seemed to be OK, so I began to walk on.

Before I got 20 yards past her, she called out, "Can I hike along with you?"

With no reason to say no, I cheerfully replied, "Sure!"

As we conversed, I learned that this woman was a music major at a college in New York City. She came out to the trail for the weekend, seeking inspiration to write music. A friend dropped her off at the road and planned to pick her up farther north in a few days. As we trudged up and down the relatively easy terrain together, she would ask me questions about my experiences on the trail. As I responded, she played the harmonica to the rhythm of my speech. At first, I thought this was goofy. Soon, though, I got into the rhythm and began to take each step in sync with her music and my speech.

The trail descended down the mountain and meandered alongside the Housatonic River. It was late in the day when we came across

Stewart Hollow Brook Lean-to. The shelters are called lean-tos in the New England states. Foxtrot, Sunny Daze, and 25 Boy Scouts filled the shelter and camping area. Sunny Daze had decided to hike for a few days and get back into trail shape. He had been driving up and down the AT providing thru-hikers with trail magic, so it was good to see him on the trail hiking instead of driving. Foxtrot apparently had slowed his pace to let me catch up.

Dusk was falling, and I decided to assemble my tent. Julie, the music student, seemed distraught about what to do now that she had reached camp.

"Do you have a tent?" I asked her.

"No," she replied.

"You can sleep in mine if you want since there is no space left in the shelter."

She followed me over to where I chose to put up my tent. I had found a spot along the river, secluded from the large group of Scouts. After the tent was up, I laid down my sleeping pad and threw my sleeping bag on top. Looking over, I noticed Julie was pulling out a sleeping bag. Good, I thought, at least she has that. Then I walked down to the river and filled my pan with water for dinner.

"Julie, did you bring a stove?" I asked.

"No."

With increasing concern for her wilderness preparedness, I asked, "What did you plan to eat, and where did you plan to sleep?"

She explained that she was going to sleep under the stars and eat the vegetables that she brought along. When my couscous was ready, I offered her some. She declined the offer and pulled a carrot from a zip-lock bag, and crunched away. A few minutes went by, and she asked me how my couscous was. I offered her some.

"I just want a bite," she explained, and proceeded to eat half of my dinner.

After dinner we discussed stretching techniques to avoid cramping pain from long days of hiking. Apparently, she's a yoga instructor. She agreed to show me some stretches for my legs in the morning. In the meantime, she massaged my back, which felt magnificent.

In the morning, I boiled water for coffee and polished off a few granola bars. Julie was still lying in my tent. Finally, she began to move about. She declined my offer for some coffee. I asked her if she wouldn't mind getting out of my house so I could pack up my gear.

She helped disassemble my tent, and showed me some basic yoga exercises to stretch out my leg muscles. We exchanged addresses so that I could send her a note when I finished the trail, and I moved on, knowing that I would not see her again. She planned to stay another night in the shelter.

Twenty-four miles later, I rolled into another shelter and found Foxtrot already bunked down. My new boots were causing some pain. As soon as I sat down, off went the boots and socks, revealing bloody toes and missing toenails. Ow! Were the boots too small?

The next day, we both trekked into Massachusetts. Only three more states until the end. The terrain had been increasing in difficulty since leaving New York, but the toughest part of the trail was yet to come—the White Mountains of New Hampshire. Many hikers and trail guides warned of the weather and terrain there. It was an obstacle that I would address when I came to it.

One day as I strolled through Massachusetts, drifting in and out of thoughts, I came across an older woman sitting all alone, smack dab in the middle of the trail. She looked up with a smile from ear to ear and said she was taking a rest. It's not typical to find an older person sitting in the middle of the woods resting, so I became concerned for her well being. You hear of folks wandering off unaware of their surroundings, only to be found dead days later. She explained that the rest of her group was up ahead. As we talked, I noticed some rocks in front of her that were arranged meticulously in the shape of an arrow. It pointed north down the trail.

"What's the arrow for?" I asked.

She explained that she was 74 years old and that her memory needed a kick-start every so often. She didn't want to head down the trail going the wrong way after her break, so she left some directions. *A smart idea*, I thought. It turned out that we were planning to stay at the same shelter, so she asked me to let her group know that she would catch up soon. Before heading on, I encouraged her that the shelter was only another mile or two. Her trail name was High Five. As I prepared to march on, she held up her hand for a high five, which explained the origin of her name.

Seeing High Five reminded me that Earl Shaffer, the first person to walk the entire trail in 1948, was undertaking another thru-hike as a 50-year commemoration in 1998. He was somewhere on the AT hundreds of miles south. He would turn 80 before finishing his expedition. Occasionally, I would leave a note for him in the trail registers to cheer him on for his efforts. When I'm 80 years old, I hope that I have the energy to undertake a thru-hike. He is an inspiration.

When I arrived at the shelter, Foxtrot and two other men were unpacked and settled in for the night. Matt was a college student from Dartmouth in Hanover, New Hampshire, a town on the trail a few hundred miles to the north. The other gentleman was his grandfather. They were traveling with High Five. I let them know that she was OK and how far back she was.

High Five arrived as dusk was setting in. The lower bunks were already claimed, and she didn't want to clamber up a ladder to the top bunks, so she set up her sleeping bag on the floor. After I had dinner, I climbed to an upper bunk to arrange my sleeping gear. The shelter had two sets of bunks adjacent to one another with a middle aisle space. High Five began setting her gear up on the floor in the middle aisle. Somehow, while I was arranging things, I lost my balance and fell from the top bunk all the way to the floor, missing High Five by inches. If my 160-pound body, multiplied by the velocity, had landed on her, she wouldn't have made it. Luckily, no one was hurt. No high five for that move!

We all sat around the fire into the late hours of the night. In the morning, Matt gave me his name and number. He said to call him when I got to Hanover so that I could crash at his fraternity house.

***

A popular stay-over for thru-hikers in Massachusetts is Upper Goose Pond Cabin, which sits on the bank of a glacial pond just off the AT. In the summer months, a live-in volunteer provides hospitality. For a four-dollar donation, hikers can occupy a bunk under a roof with four walls and enjoy an all-you-can-eat pancake breakfast in the morning.

I took a polar dip in the cold pond. While I was soaking myself, a dog ran up the dock behind me, trampling my clothes, and jumped into the pond with a big splash. I had been reading trail register entries signed "Life with Riley." Riley had just introduced himself to me. His owner was studying the fish life in waterways along the trail in hopes of one day publishing a book of fishing along the AT.

The next day, Foxtrot and I hitched a ride into Cheshire, Massachusetts, to resupply. That was where I had mailed my original hiking boots. My first stop was the outfitter, which gladly switched boots with me to a bigger size. With my boot problem handled, I decided to send my bounce box containing my old boots, addresses, and repair kits to the next supply point in Vermont and see how my new boots would work out. That was the last time I saw the box. The box and all of its contents were lost in the U.S. mail. All of the addresses of people I had met along the way were lost with it. To this day, the whereabouts of the box remains a mystery. Every time I had mailed this box before, I had insured it and got a tracking number. I did not insure it this time, and it vanished.

Appalachian Trail

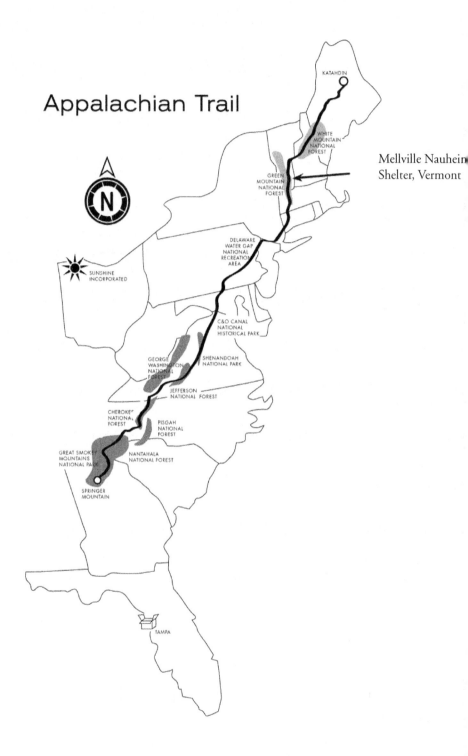

KATAHDIN

WHITE MOUNTAIN NATIONAL FOREST

GREEN MOUNTAIN NATIONAL FOREST

Mellville Nauhein Shelter, Vermont

N

SUNSHINE INCORPORATED

DELAWARE WATER GAP NATIONAL RECREATION AREA

C&O CANAL NATIONAL HISTORICAL PARK

GEORGE WASHINGTON NATIONAL FOREST

SHENANDOAH NATIONAL PARK

JEFFERSON NATIONAL FOREST

CHEROKEE NATIONAL FOREST

PISGAH NATIONAL FOREST

GREAT SMOKEY MOUNTAINS NATIONAL PARK

NANTAHALA NATIONAL FOREST

SPRINGER MOUNTAIN

TAMPA

Chapter 31

Where's The Moose?

Mellville Nauheim Shelter, Vermont. June 16, 1998. 1,600 miles from Springer Mountain, Georgia.

The rain had been relentless. For three days, it poured nonstop. As I awoke one morning, I looked out at the hard-pouring rain from beneath a shelter roof in my cozy, dry sleeping bag and had no motivation to leave. Almost every day of my hike, I had gotten up at first light, made coffee, ate some breakfast, and got on the trail, whether it was raining or snowing. This time, I rolled over and went back to sleep. Eventually, I got the motivation to pack, don my rain parka, and slosh on northward.

Crossing into Vermont was exciting, despite the continuous rain. Only two more states to go, and for 100 miles, the AT combined with the Long Trail, America's first long-distance hiking trail. For 100 miles, AT thru-hikers share the same footpath with Long Trail thru-hikers. The Long Trail eventually splits off from the AT and heads up to Canada. Meeting hikers on a completely different trail was exciting. The Long Trail is only a few hundred miles in length—small compared to the entire AT—but the terrain is severe, and walking it is an accomplishment.

During an afternoon break, I ducked into a shelter to get out of the rain. A young man and woman already were settled in for the evening, out of the rain. They were from the Washington, D.C., area and were thru-hiking the Long Trail. The woman was a very attractive, longhaired brunette with a dark complexion. Her trail name was Kid—like the baby mountain goat. The gentleman was rather tall, with bushy blond hair. He went by the trail name Happy Jo. As we talked, I learned that they used to date but supposedly were just friends now.

After a long rest, I collected my gear, draped the parka back on, and moved on to the next shelter, where Foxtrot said he planned to stop. As I walked, I wondered how a man could take a beautiful woman out into the wilderness and just be friends? How frustrating that would be. When I reached the next shelter, I had trekked 20 miles in the rain. Foxtrot was all settled in. Of course, he had also taken note of the attractive woman, who became the topic of discussion well into the evening. This is what thru-hikers do, we rationalized.

The registers along the trail had only four thru-hiker entries ahead of me. Two of them, Jackrabbit Slim and Filou, consistently had been no more than a day or two up the trail. They had no idea who was behind them or how far. One morning, I stopped at a shelter to sit and eat a snack. As I looked at the trail register, I realized that Jackrabbit Slim and Filou had just left a few hours before. We had come that close to crossing paths. Connecting with other hikers had become an exciting piece of entertainment on the trail.

The mountain characteristics were changing subtly from the last few states. Elevation had been increasing gradually, working toward the rugged White Mountains that lay one state to the north. Vermont seemed to be more abundant with green forest, hence the name Green Mountains. The forest was rich with pine trees, whose dropped needles made each step hit the trail with the comfort of nature's cushion.

Almost immediately after crossing into Vermont, I began to notice moose droppings. These droppings were hard not to notice, in piles the size of softballs, scattered about the trail. Moose droppings have a distinct look. They are shaped like little chocolate Easter eggs without foil wrappings. They looked so identical to chocolates that I considered taking some and using them as an Easter prank. Moose dung has become such a novelty that you can buy them in tourist shops varnished and made into earrings and necklaces.

Moose sightings were common from Vermont all the way to Maine, yet I had been following their droppings for three days without seeing one. So far in my journey, I had many close encounters with wildlife. In Massachusetts, I almost stepped on a porcupine. In New Jersey, I encountered a bear. In Pennsylvania, I ate lunch with a rattlesnake. In Tennessee, I was in a shelter surrounded by coyotes. In addition, I had encountered skunk, mice, grouse, bald eagles, snakes, lizards, deer, and turkeys. How could the biggest wild animal of the eastern United States avoid detection?

Every noise I heard off in the forest roused my suspicions, yet it always turned out to be a creature other than moose. Eventually, I began to question whether I would ever see a moose. Bullwinkle, the childhood cartoon character came to mind. He was a moose that walked around on two legs instead of four. *It's a Bullwinkle conspiracy*, I thought. That's what I labeled it in the trail registers as each day passed without a moose sighting. As I blazed through the forest, I envisioned a moose standing up on his hind legs as it hid behind a tree, sucking in his belly to become as thin as the tree, and chuckling to himself as I passed by without noticing him. It would not be until Maine, thousands of moose tracks later, that I would finally encounter one.

Vermont is a well-known ski destination among New Englanders. As a matter of fact, the AT weaves over the tops of the same mountains that skiers enjoy every winter. At the tops of the ski slopes, there are four-walled, house-like structures used by skiers to get out of the elements. These warming huts are open for hikers to use as shelters during the spring, summer, and fall months.

All day, Foxtrot and I had moved along, putting 20 miles behind us. Then the trail began winding up Stratton Mountain, one of the highest elevations since Virginia. The heavily wooded terrain and rain had not hampered my pace until I started this difficult climb up Stratton Mountain. The trail ascended steadily.

Dusk began to fall, but Foxtrot and I trudged on, motivated by the thought of staying in a ski hut when we reached the top. We donned our headlamps. Even with lights, the trail was difficult to see. Heavy fog had enveloped the mountain, and a hard rain continued to fall. Finally at about 9:00 p.m., 24 miles from where we had started that day, we could see light shining from the windows of the ski hut.

We stumbled onto the porch, finally out of the rain. Since the hut was supposed to be open to hikers, we let ourselves in. As soon as the door swung open, the pleasant smell of vegetables and cooked meat met my nose. Several people already occupied the hut. We stood in the foyer area across the room from a little kitchen. Steam was emitting from a large kettle on the stove. The hut had all the amenities of a house. Several men and women were scattered about on chairs and lying in sleeping bags on the floor.

A young man, 20-something, approached us and belched out, "Sorry, the hut is full."

I had walked 24 miles in the pouring rain up a mountain in the dark and wasn't going to accept his answer. I replied, "Can't you let two soaked hikers throw their sleeping bags on the floor for the night?"

With hesitation in his voice, the young man replied, "OK, but we are hitting the sack shortly and getting up at 3:00 a.m."

Just getting out of the rain was good enough for us. I have slept in hundreds of shelters with snoring hikers and folks with unusual sleeping habits, so their 3:00 a.m. wake-up was fine. I replied, "Thank you for letting us get out of the rain."

Slowly, I removed my wet clothes and put some dry stuff on. Some of the occupants told us that some hikers, calling themselves The Vegetarians, had passed through several days ago and given the group a difficult time. Now I understood why we were treated in such a cold manner about staying.

The current occupants were ornithologists—bird scientists—studying the migration habits of birds. Every morning they would get up and drape large, blanket-size nets between the trees. Birds would fly into the nets; the scientists then clipped radio transmitters to their legs and set them free.

The Vegetarians criticized the scientists' nettings, accusing them of blocking the trail. Foxtrot and I had noticed the nets in our approach to the summit, but they did not inhibit the trail in any way. We did wonder what they were, though.

The Vegetarians were not thru-hiking, so we did not know who they were. Supposedly they had gotten on the trail back in Connecticut. Their register entries were very vulgar, and they had written mean things about other hikers and the Upper Goose Pond caretaker—the cabin with the pancake breakfast and glacial pond. The Vegetarians ridiculed the four-dollar fee and said that the pancakes had sucked. Contrary to the Vegetarians' opinions, every hiker I had talked to raved about the pancakes and enjoyed their inexpensive stay at the cabin.

Foxtrot and I had pushed ourselves physically and mentally into the night, up a difficult climb, with the incentive of lodging in a nice, warm, dry hut, only to be treated with hesitation by the current occupants due to the rudeness that the Vegetarians had displayed.

After conversing with the scientists for a while and sharing our appreciation for their ongoing research, they even offered us some leftover soup. The Vegetarians had left bad impressions with everyone they encountered. Even hikers were leaving notes in the registers complaining that the Vegetarians were being loud and obnoxious into the late hours in the shelters. I did not want to follow in their footsteps having to constantly defend the usual goodness of hikers.

By morning, Foxtrot and I had worked our magic and rekindled the scientists' views of hikers. I trust that the next few thru-hikers passing through wouldn't have to volley so hard for floor space in the ski hut. After a few cups of freshly brewed coffee left by the ornithologists and a granola bar, Foxtrot and I hit the trail.

***

Not only did Vermont offer some of the greenest forest I had ever encountered, but it was also the home state of Ben and Jerry's ice cream. Ice cream, pizza, and beer were the three cravings I had as I rambled through the mountains. One of my supply points was Manchester Center, a small New England town known for its manufacturer retail outlets. The town also had a Ben and Jerry's ice cream parlor.

For a donation, the Zion Episcopal Church in Manchester Center allows hikers to use its recreation room. When Foxtrot and I arrived, a large high school group of hikers had already occupied the recreation room, but there was plenty of room. Not long after arriving, all hikers were asked to vacate the premises temporarily so that the church bridge club could play. Deciding what to do with my time while the bridge club occupied our hostel was easy—I headed for the Ben & Jerry's outlet. It was the first one I had ever visited.

All along the trail, hostels and outfitters sell pints of Ben and Jerry's ice cream, knowing that it's a hiker favorite. Now I was in a manufacturer's outlet. Not only can you buy ice cream by the scoop, factory-second pints are for sale at reduced prices. How can ice cream be labeled factory-second? Ice cream is ice cream. I plowed through two pints. Then I went across the street for my other two cravings, pizza and beer.

Happy Jo and the Kid—the Long Trail thru-hikers—arrived the next morning. Foxtrot and I decided to take the day off the trail and do our town chores. Foxtrot was planning to split off and hike the Long Trail, then shuttle back and continue with the AT, so he was discussing the Long Trail with Happy Jo.

In the morning, Foxtrot saddled up and headed back for the trail. Before I left, I needed to stop at the post office and mail some letters, so I planned to catch up to him later. After mailing my letters, I walked along the road toward the trail with my thumb out. Soon, a truck pulled over and took me five miles up the mountain to the AT.

When we reached the trailhead, I hopped out and thanked the driver for the ride. Two men were sitting on the gravel in the parking lot next to a van. They had hiking gear scattered next to the vehicle. Before heading off into the forest, one of them came over to me and said hello.

It turns out that the one guy, Maineak, had completed the entire AT in less than 56 days. Wow! I had read about him in *Walking the Appalachian Trail*. Now he was part of a support team helping another gentleman break the speed record. They were waiting to supply the speed hiker. Speed hikers typically carry nothing more than water and a few snacks, relying upon an on-hand support team all along the route. As we spoke, another man emerged from the forest. Tears rolled down his cheeks, and he was obviously upset about something. It turned out that the man crying was the speed hiker. He quit his quest right then and there. He had come to the realization that he could not maintain the pace necessary to beat the record. Just before he had emerged from the woods, a car had pulled up. The speed hiker's father was there to greet him and console him.

Realizing that there was nothing I could do to help the situation, I waved goodbye, strapped on my pack, and began following the white blazes north. Everybody hikes the AT for different reasons, but it struck me as odd that someone would quit the trail because they weren't going to beat a record. This made me realize that my goal of just making it the whole way was not good enough for some. Giving the speed hiker my advice to keep going, slow down, and enjoy the trip only would have made matters worse.

A few days later, I began to experience the pesky black flies that the New England states are known for. For months, I had been warned about how horrible these flies are by others who had experienced them.

During late spring and early summer, the flies multiply and become a nuisance. Some hikers had elaborate netting screens to protect themselves. I thought all this screening stuff was for weenies. How could a fly be so bad? I had been bitten just about everywhere on my body by mosquitoes and a few spiders and was still alive.

Shortly after a six-mile ascent to Mount Killington, I came to a four-walled shelter and decided to rest and regain my energy. It was one of those hot, sticky summer days with temperatures in the 80s. Sweat had saturated my body all day, and a film of dirt stuck to my sweat.

All around me, flies swarmed. I began to feel an itchy prick similar to a mosquito bite, followed by a stinging sensation similar to a bee sting. These flies look just like a common housefly, but they were much more annoying. If I stood still for even a minute, I would get bitten several times. Swatting them away didn't help, either. Later, I learned that they are drawn to sweat, which explained why they were swarming me. Even after I stepped inside the shelter, they continued to nail me. After a few minutes of annoyance, I gave up the idea of a rest and kept moving.

The trail followed the ridge along Mount Killington, another popular ski slope, and then the AT began to descend one of the forest-cleared ski runs. Straight ahead, I followed the steepest ski run on Mount Killington, but I lacked the skis that would have gotten me to the bottom of the mountain much quicker. The trail darted into the tree line along the ski run, making the descent a little easier without ski poles.

At the bottom of Mount Killington, the Long Trail separates from the AT after more than a 100 miles. Foxtrot had been walking with me since Pennsylvania, but he was following the Long Trail from here. He planned to shuttle back later to resume the AT. Happy Jo, the Kid, and Foxtrot would split off from the AT here in their pursuit of thru-hiking the LT. Again, I was walking alone. Before leaving, Happy Jo, Foxtrot, and I got a two-room lodge attached to the bar and restaurant at the bottom of the mountain—with free breakfast in the morning—for $21 each. Just after we finished paying for the room, the front door of the lobby swung open, and in walked the Kid. She'd made it. We split our room cost even further, saving all of us more money. Since it was the last night together, we felt just cause in celebrating with a few beers at the bar.

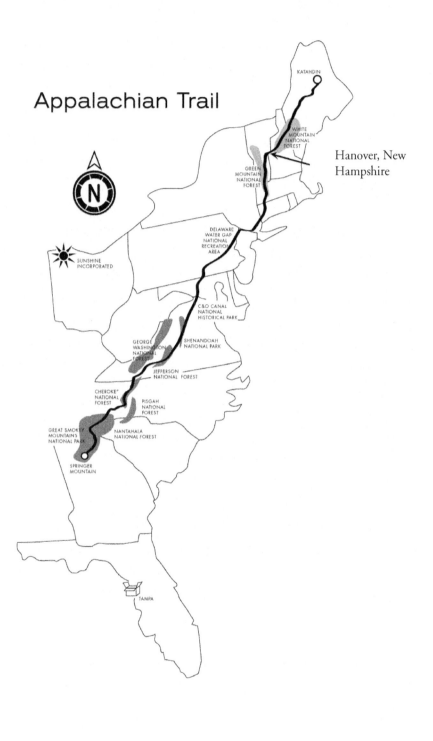

Appalachian Trail

N

KATAHDIN

WHITE MOUNTAIN NATIONAL FOREST

Hanover, New Hampshire

GREEN MOUNTAIN NATIONAL FOREST

DELAWARE WATER GAP NATIONAL RECREATION AREA

SUNSHINE INCORPORATED

C&O CANAL NATIONAL HISTORICAL PARK

GEORGE WASHINGTON NATIONAL FOREST

SHENANDOAH NATIONAL PARK

JEFFERSON NATIONAL FOREST

CHEROKEE NATIONAL FOREST

PISGAH NATIONAL FOREST

GREAT SMOKEY MOUNTAINS NATIONAL PARK

NANTAHALA NATIONAL FOREST

SPRINGER MOUNTAIN

TAMPA

Chapter 32

Vegetarians Don't Pack Meat

Hanover, New Hampshire. June 22, 1998. 1,772 miles from Springer Mountain, Georgia.

Nude hikers on the trail? A trail tradition that has received lots of controversy over the years is Naked Hiker Day. This occurs on the first day of summer, the solstice. It just so happened that solstice fell on Father's Day, Sunday, June 21, 1998. Hundreds of hikers hiked naked in honor of this day. Imagine taking your family for a day hike on Father's Day and running into several thru-hikers sporting their birthday suits. Well, I guess this actually happens every year. A popular hiking magazine even ran a story about the Naked Hiker Day.

I just happened to have spent the eve of Naked Hiker Day with the Kid. Happy Jo emphasized that she was available. He wanted to distance himself from her so that he could meet other women. I don't know what he was thinking. The odds of meeting women in the woods were slim, unless he was setting his sights on an entirely different species.

The opportunity—or should I say fascination—to see an attractive woman naked was front and center in my mind. In the morning, I would continue on the AT while the Kid, Happy Jo, and Foxtrot split off onto the Long Trail. Foxtrot explained to the Kid that participating in Naked Hiker Day would establish her as a true thru-hiker, hoping that she would go along with the spirit. We assured her that we would walk naked, too. But, in the morning, she was still sporting a layer of nylon clothing, with no intentions of joining the nude ranks. Shucks, it was worth a shot!

Of course, I figured she wouldn't go along with the plan, and I hadn't planned to actually walk through the woods naked, either. Thank goodness I didn't. Shortly after saying goodbye to the LT hikers and moving north, I ran into the same coed high-school group with whom I had stayed at the Episcopal church in Manchester Center. If I had gone along with the naked-hiker theme, this group would have met me in my birthday suit, taking away every bit of dignity and privacy I possessed. I ended up walking with them for two days.

A courageous woman led this group of 10. It's not typical to run into one adult leading a group of that size. I was impressed with her control and confidence. The students were well-mannered and fun to be around.

In spite of the well-behaved students and the solid leadership, the young hikers complained to me about a bad experience they'd had with another group in a shelter. Two nights earlier, the students bunked down at a shelter. Some of the students pitched tents to accommodate the size of the group. Another group of four shared the shelter with them. As usual, the students worked together to make the evening meal. After the meal, a few of the students appointed to cleaning detail took their pots and pans down to the nearby stream to wash them. When they were done, they brought the dishes back to camp to let them dry. One of the hikers from the other hiking party went down to the stream to fill up his water container. When he returned to the campsite a few minutes later, he began cussing and swearing like a drunken sailor, complaining that the students polluted the stream with detergent. The students were immediately put on the defensive.

One of the female students broke down in tears from being falsely accused of polluting the stream. As it turns out, the students didn't even have soap for dish cleaning. What the obnoxious hiker observed in the stream was foam residue that occurs after rainstorms. The wealth of pine trees emits a sudsy chemical from the tree sap into the streams from runoff. Either way, the obnoxious stranger yelling at young kids scared the group. Even if the kids had polluted the water, this was not a healthy way to address the issue.

The students, who were actually an environmental group from a high school, could have explained the natural suds process to the obnoxious hiker had he piped down long enough to listen. All night, however, this man taunted the group with obscenities, including writing harsh comments in the trail register.

The students were so shaken up from this encounter that they had decided to slow their pace and let the obnoxious bunch get ahead. This is when I came across them. The students were sitting around a shelter taking a break. As the students were filling me in on their bad experience, I was paging through the shelter's trail register. The rude trail entry left by the obnoxious group was signed "The Vegetarians." Of course.

Listening to these students complain about the Vegetarians upset me. That group had caused enough havoc. They had harassed some retired volunteers who simply tried to provide a memorable experience for hikers with hot pancakes and a nice bunk house; they did not pay the few dollars to camp at Upper Goose Pond; they tormented bird scientists, falsely accusing them of blocking the trail with nets; they had left numerous register entries using brash words about other hikers; they were up until all hours in the shelters, keeping hikers from needed sleep; and now they had upset a group of young students that were on an educational trip in the forest. Enough! My blood was boiling. I felt compelled to catch up to these ruthless Vegetarians and speak for the hikers.

Other than a small contingent of Appalachian Trail volunteers, referred to as ridge runners, there is no police force actively patrolling the AT. The only patrolled AT sections are the national or state parks—The Great Smoky Mountains, Tennessee; the Shenandoah, Virginia; and Baxter Park, Maine. Other than not paying a caretaker fee, the Vegetarians hadn't actually broken any laws, but someone needed to address this group for their bad behavior.

The students described the Vegetarians to me. They were traveling with a pit bull dog; there were three men and a woman. One of the men was outspoken. He had an unhealthy-looking, frail physique, and curly, bushy, blond hair. Apparently, the group goes along with whatever this obnoxious guy says and does. The students said the Vegetarians were up to all hours of the night, talking quite loudly. They'd scattered their gear throughout the shelter, with no consideration for other hikers' space.

After a few days of walking with the student group, I surged ahead, wishing them well on the rest of their journey. I had gotten distracted temporarily from my inspirational journey and was now on the warpath to catch up to those obnoxious Vegetarians. After spending some time with the young students and learning the context in which these Vegetarians had harassed them, I felt a moral obligation to address this bad-mannered bunch.

The weather had been gorgeous for two days. After walking through almost 12 days of rain, the sun was welcome. I was almost to New Hampshire's White Mountains, some of the most demanding terrain of the entire trail.

When I began walking this particular morning, it was still dark. The student group was sound asleep. Quietly, I took down my tent, left them a note expressing how nice it was to meet a well-mannered, educated young group, and pressed on. By noon, I had covered 12 miles. A sign on the trail indicated a shelter .02 miles off the AT on a side trail. I decided to stop and rest for lunch.

Shortly after turning off onto the side trail, I heard the bark of a dog. Fifty yards ahead, a mean-looking pit bull stood on the trail, growling and showing his teeth. This group had to be the Vegetarians. No one was around to call off the dog, and pit bulls have a reputation of being aggressively violent.

I yelled, "Call off your dog!"

Immediately, a male voice rang out from the shelter privy. "Come here!" The pit bull ran off towards the privy.

As I rounded a bend in the trail, I could see a shelter with someone sitting in it. All morning, I anticipated running across the Vegetarians, so I had strategically placed a stick of summer sausage in my front hip-pouch. This way I could eat meat as a show of disrespect when I encountered them. This was a psychological trick that my First Sergeant used in the Army. He ate dog biscuits while conversing to convince the troops that he was a hard-core, animalistic warrior. We all thought he was nuts. I figured the Vegetarians hate meat, so the sausage would have the same effect.

Exhausted and happy to take a break, I sat down on a log near the fire ring in front of the shelter. With my pack still on, I pulled my sausage and Swiss Army knife from my hip pouch. The young woman sitting inside the shelter had her hiking gear strewn from one end to the other. She hollered out to me. "Hi!"

"Hi," I replied, as I sliced a piece of sausage off with my knife. Then I stuck the knife blade into the end of a log, trying to appear as barbaric as possible. By this time, the pit bull had caught scent of my sausage and was dancing before me, expecting a slice. I asked the woman, "Please call off your dog."

"He just wants a piece of your sausage," she replied.

I shouted back, "Feed him your own sausage; this is my lunch."

"You're not very nice," she said.

"Your dog isn't very nice, either. He would have eaten me for lunch if I didn't yell for someone to call him off," I stated.

"Who are you?" the woman asked.

"I'm Wrongfoot. Who are you?" I asked.

A man with curly, blond hair and a frail physique, fitting the description of the obnoxious, vulgar hiker, walked back from the privy and sat down at the edge of the shelter staring at me. The other two men were nowhere in sight.

The woman replied, "We're the Vegetarians."

Pretending that I hadn't realized it was them, I replied, "Ohhh, the Vegetarians."

"What's that supposed to mean? Have you heard of us?" she asked.

"Not only have I heard of you, but I have several complaints about you guys. Personally, I'm mad about the way you've been treating other hikers, especially that young student group in the shelter a few days ago," I responded.

The bushy-haired man stood up and walked toward me. His rib bones pressed through his skin like the malnourished children I have seen in television ads that ask for money to prevent starvation. With clenched fists flaring in the air, he yelled, "F#$% you, and $%# them. Those %$##rs need their a#$% whipped for polluting the stream."

"Those kids don't even have soap. What you thought were soap suds was actually runoff from all the pine trees and the heavy rains," I said.

"I'll beat up the next person that I catch littering or polluting the trail," the obnoxious hiker screamed, now standing inches from me.

No wonder the young hikers were frightened by this group. This guy was borderline psycho. What had I gotten myself into?

"You're in my comfort zone," I replied, unzipping my front hip-belt pouch containing my bear spray. Ever since Georgia, I carried the spray as a precautionary measure for personal protection. Not once did I feel a need to use it until now. The spray canister carried enough of a kick to turn away a grizzly bear. There are no grizzly bears in the Appalachians, so the only reason I carried the spray was for the slim possibility of an attack by another human.

Any moment, I figured this guy was going to swing at me. If I swung back, I was sure the pit bull would defend his master, sinking its teeth into my tender skin and bringing an end to my adventure. With one eye on the dog, and my other eye focused on the obnoxious man's every move, I pulled the canister of pepper spray out. With a flip of my thumb, the safety cap fell to the ground. All I had to do was push my thumb down on the release lever and a powerful spray would emit 10 feet out, canvassing a four-by-four-foot area. At least, that's what the directions on the canister claimed. The obnoxious guy was leaning over me, fists flaring, just inches from touching me as I sat on the log. I looked him straight in the eyes watching for any sudden violent moves on his part. If he got any closer or swung, I planned to spray the pit bull, immediately eliminating that threat, then prod this guy with my hiking pole.

"Scott, back off. Leave the guy alone," the woman yelled out from the shelter. She must have figured out my intentions, observing my pepper spray aimed at the dog. Physically, I was twice the size of this creep despite my weight loss, and my cheeks were red with anger. She realized that I was not intimated by Scott's obnoxious get-in-my-face approach.

Scott backed away and retreated to the shelter, still bitching as he took a seat. Now with their full attention, I continued voicing my concerns. "Hikers can do without your vulgar comments written in the registers. 'Hike your own hike' is the motto for thru-hikers. If you don't like it out here, then get off the trail. People come out here for a lot of different reasons, and I'm sure getting harassed by you isn't one of them. Several hikers not too far behind would also like to give you a piece of their mind. Consider me the calm before the storm."

"What makes you the boss out here?" the woman asked.

"No one. I'm not the boss. There are no bosses out here. That's why no one needs your criticism on the trail," I replied.

"Who behind us has a problem?" Scott asked with a mean look on his face.

"You wouldn't know half of them. They have never met you guys; they have only heard of you and read your vulgar register entries," I responded.

Reaching out, I pulled my knife blade from the end of the log, folded it up, I picked up the safety cap to my pepper spray, and fastened it back on to the canister. A calm sensation swept over my body. My adrenaline had been going at such a rate that every inch of my body felt hot. My heart was racing with anxiety but now began to pulse at a normal rate.

Standing up from the log, I fastened my pepper spray, sausage, and knife back in my hip pouch and picked up my hiking poles. Scott and the woman just stared at me, seemingly wanting to continue preaching their offensive philosophies.

"If you have any vulgar things to say about me, say them to my face. Don't pollute the registers," I said as I began walking off.

"Well, at least you told us what's up," the woman replied.

"See ya," I said. I walked back down the side trail to the AT.

As I walked off, I half expected Scott to sic the pit bull on me, so I pulled the pepper spray out and carried it in my hand for the next few miles. Reflecting back, I had put myself at risk of being chewed by a pit bull and beat up. This was not one of my more intelligent moves, but I managed to walk away without a scratch, and I hoped they would lighten the ruthless way they were treating people. I doubt that they would have been intimidated by my sausage technique had I encountered them on naked hiker day sporting my birthday suit.

That same day, I hiked 24 miles and crossed into New Hampshire, leaving just two more states. The Trail descended a ridge into some quaint middle-class neighborhoods, and then into Hanover, New Hampshire. Dartmouth, an Ivy League college, was nestled in this town. Way back in Massachusetts, a Dartmouth college student had offered me a place to stay when I passed through. Sure enough, a message pinned to a bulletin board for hikers in one of the university buildings had a note for me to call him when I arrived.

Just north of Dartmouth, I would encounter some of the harshest terrain of the entire trail, the White Mountains. For months, I had heard story after story of how dangerous and difficult these mountains are to hike. The trail ascends above the tree line just north of Hanover. I would leave the forest walls, exposing myself to the brutal elements without any trees to block the wind, rain, or snow. As a precautionary measure, I had my parents mail my winter gear to me in my Dartmouth supply box. Many people have died in this next section from exposure, even in the summer.

A hot-tub house in the uptown section of Hanover caught my attention. For eight dollars, I was able to soak my trail-beaten body in the privacy of my own tub, while listening to classical music piped into the cedar-walled room. The college student working at the counter said that they get quite a few hikers passing through that time of year.

After my hot tub experience, I sat on a bench along the street, licking an ice cream cone and reading a newspaper to stay in tune with the world. The president still was in office, and our country was not at war. I hadn't missed too much, according to the paper I was reading. Out of the corner of my eye, I noticed a group of hikers walking south down the street, which is part of the AT. It was the whole group of Vegetarians. They walked by me heading south, the wrong direction if you're headed to Maine.

"Where are you going?" I yelled.

"We're getting off the trail," the woman in the group hollered back.

The Vegetarians were the bullies of the trail, just the same as the bully at school. They were the one bad apple ruining the experience for the rest of us. Even in the simple trail life to which I had grown accustomed, one group's opinions and ideas had influenced others, similar to society on a bigger scale. I couldn't help but wonder if they were quitting the trail because of the conversation that we'd had the previous day. I had just simply informed them of the emotional damage they were causing other hikers. At least no one would have to experience their intimidating behavior any longer.

Appalachian Trail

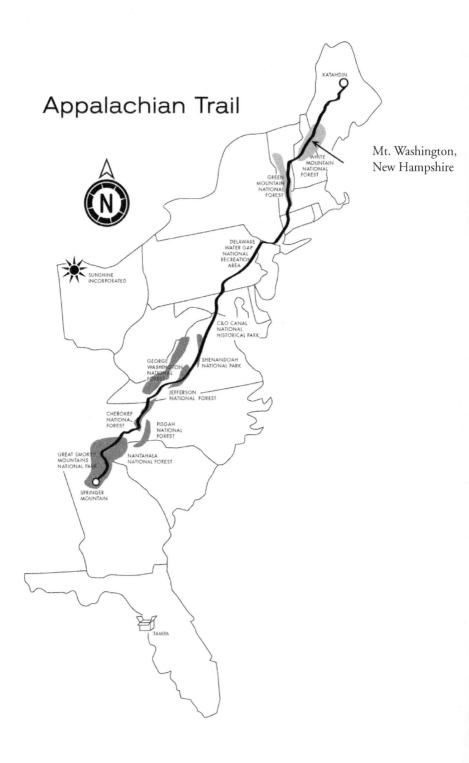

KATAHDIN

Mt. Washington,
New Hampshire

WHITE
MOUNTAIN
NATIONAL
FOREST

GREEN
MOUNTAIN
NATIONAL
FOREST

N

SUNSHINE
INCORPORATED

DELAWARE
WATER GAP
NATIONAL
RECREATION
AREA

C&O CANAL
NATIONAL
HISTORICAL PARK

GEORGE
WASHINGTON
NATIONAL
FOREST

SHENANDOAH
NATIONAL PARK

JEFFERSON
NATIONAL FOREST

CHEROKEE
NATIONAL
FOREST

PISGAH
NATIONAL
FOREST

GREAT SMOKEY
MOUNTAINS
NATIONAL PARK

NANTAHALA
NATIONAL FOREST

SPRINGER
MOUNTAIN

TAMPA

Chapter 33

Sunshine in New Hampshire

6,288 feet. Top of Mount Washington, New Hampshire. June 30, 1998. 1,830 miles from Springer Mountain, Georgia.

With a bulging pack pulling on my hips and shoulders, I embarked northward from Hanover on June 24. Several winter gear items, including a fleece hat, gloves, and long underwear, were crammed into my pack as a precautionary measure for any unexpected weather in the White Mountains. Many people had died from weather exposure—some of these deaths occurred during a typical hot summer.

The White Mountain peaks and ridges are treeless. Due to the harsh weather patterns, very little vegetation can grow. Many trails leading up to the peaks intersect the AT. Every year, tourists are fooled by the blue sky and warm weather and head out onto these trails for afternoon strolls wearing nothing but T-shirts and shorts. Then, without warning, thick clouds settle over the mountain, bringing rain, sleet, and sometimes snow. The tourist, now wet and cold, becomes confused during the early stages of hypothermia. Not being able to see the trail due to dense fog, he gets lost and is later found dead. I was not going to become a statistic.

The shelters north of Hanover were packed full of hikers each night. The White Mountains attract large crowds, similar in numbers to the Great Smoky Mountains National Park in Tennessee. The second day north of Hanover, I took advantage of the terrain before hitting the White Mountains and stomped out a 28-mile day, arriving at the Jeffers Shelter just as the moon replaced the last bit of daylight. Of the six shelter occupants already settled in, one was a southbound hiker, Cool Hand Luke. He started at Mount Katahdin, Maine, just three weeks prior and was heading for Springer Mountain, Georgia. He was the first of many southbound thru-hikers I would meet in the final weeks of my journey. The weather does not allow hikers the option of starting a southbound hike until the end of May, when Mount Katahdin sheds its winter coat.

In the morning, I packed my gear and got onto the trail by 8:00 a.m. Shortly after leaving the shelter, I began my ascent of Mount Moosilauke, elevation 4,802 feet. It would be the first of many peaks above tree line. For five miles, I pulled my body up one of the steepest climbs yet. It took all morning to reach the summit.

As I climbed higher and higher, the hardwood forest became a spruce forest, then the trees became smaller and smaller, until I reached the peak, where the pine trees were nothing more than bushes. The trees had been majestic and towering at the foot of the mountain, but at the summit I felt like a giant, with the pine trees as knee-high shrubs. When I reached the summit, the tiny trees could not shield me from the elements. A strong, chilling gust of wind whistled in my ears and slapped my wet, sweaty shirt against my skin. The temperature had dropped at least 30 degrees since I left the shelter. I had climbed several thousand feet. I stopped and donned my rain parka. The mountain was encased in clouds, offering no view. An old stone foundation stood at the summit, a remnant of a hotel that burnt to the ground some time ago. It now served as a shelter and allowed me to get out of the wind. While I sat behind the foundation wall, I dug through my pack and pulled out my fleece hat and gloves to keep warm.

Because there are no trees to mark the trail, giant stacks of stone called cairns sit about 50 yards apart above tree line. After taking a break from the wind, I stood up and followed the cairns northward. Eventually, the trail descended back below the tree line, offering relief from the unyielding elements. The rest of the afternoon, I slowly descended a very steep mountainside. The trail followed a stream that cascaded down the steep rock mountainside for miles. Some areas were so steep that trail volunteers had fastened wooden blocks into the rock for footing. Handrails were attached to rock in other areas. One slip and I could fall quite a distance.

After a slow, careful descent, I reached Kinsman Notch, a gap between two mountains. U.S. Route 112 rambles through here into

Woodstock, New Hampshire. A hiker who had just completed a few days in the woods offered to drive me into town to the Cascades Lodge, a popular hiker hostel. It had taken me all day to complete nine miles.

Bill and Betty, a very friendly retired couple, ran the hostel. For $15, I had a room with a bed, a hot shower, and a shuttle back to the trail in the morning. Bill offered to help me slack-pack the next day to Franconia Notch, 16 miles north, which would allow me to traverse some difficult terrain without a heavy pack and come back for a second night of domesticated living. It was an easy decision.

After making arrangements for accommodations and unloading my pack in my room, I took my wet clothes across the street to a laundromat and threw them in the dryer. I even threw in my baseball cap. When the dryer stopped, I pulled out the clothes and realized that the plastic snap clips on my baseball cap had melted from the intense dryer heat. This ball cap had been with me since the beginning of my journey, and now it was ruined. The hat had shielded rain, sleet, snow, and bugs from my eyes for 1,774 miles. I had grown attached to it. After a few moments of reflection, I walked up the street to a tourist shop and replaced it with an inexpensive New Hampshire ball cap.

In the morning, Bill, the hostel keeper, drove me back to Kinsman Notch. Bill was slightly overweight, with balding white hair. He was a chain smoker with severe emphysema. During our short car ride, he managed to choke down two cigarettes. Between cigarettes, his head nodded momentarily, and then he perked upright as if everything was OK. Every breath he took was loud and straining.

"Bill, are you OK?" I asked. He seemed light-headed from a lack of oxygen.

"I'm OK," he responded.

I was afraid that he would fall unconscious and drive us into a ditch. What a way to end my journey. He managed to get me to the trail safely, however, and he agreed to pick me up at the end of the day, 16 miles up the trail. I would call him from a pay phone near the trail when I reached Franconia Notch.

Onward I trekked over Kinsman Mountain, carrying just a day's worth of snacks and cold-weather gear. The trail had become much more demanding than it had been. Instead of just walking, I had to climb over rocks and pull myself up using my hands. The poles that

I had been using for balance and endurance were a useless nuisance when climbing up these rocks. They would dangle by the wrist straps as I grabbed rocks and tree roots to pull myself over massive boulders.

Despite the added toughness, the scenery was beautiful. Toward the end of the day, I stopped along Lonesome Lake and sat for a spell on the shore. Across the water, a towering mountain charged up into the clouds. After I called Bill from a pay phone, he picked me up and returned me to Franconia Notch the next day. I wanted to tell him to quit smoking, but his health was not my business.

**

For the next 75 miles, I continued through the White Mountains. Again, I found myself climbing with my hands, holding onto rocks, trees, and roots. During a rest, I collapsed my hiking poles and strapped them to my pack.

The sky was clear all day, and the views were stunning. When I reached the Franconia ridge, I encountered hundreds of tourists perched on rocks, taking in the extraordinary sights all along the trail. Up ahead, I could see the AT marked by cairns as far as my eyes could see. I crossed over Mount Lincoln, Mount Lafayette, and Mount Garfield, each at least 4,500 feet in elevation.

Throughout the White Mountains, the Appalachian Mountain Club has huts, remote cabins where tourists can stay the night. Each hut is staffed with a crew, which provides tourists with hot meals, bunks, and restroom facilities. Bunks in these huts run $65 a night, but they allow two or three thru-hikers a free stay in exchange for a few hours of work. I hoped to arrange for some of the work-for-stays as I passed through. I set my sights on staying at Galehead Hut, 13 strenuous miles from where I had started.

Toward the end of the day, I ran across a group of tourists hiking to Galehead Hut. We were descending a very steep slope, almost straight down. Every step required concentration to maintain balance. The group was full of questions after they discovered that I was a thru-hiker. At the bottom of the descent, one of the hikers pulled a zip-lock bag out of his pack. It was full of burnt french toast, left over from another hut where they had stayed the night before. He offered me a piece.

"No, thanks," I replied.

"What, a thru-hiker turning down food?" he said with a surprised tone. "You must not be a real thru-hiker."

"I'm hungry all the time, but I can't stand burnt food. I have plenty of snacks in my pack. Thanks for the offer," I responded.

By late afternoon, I reached the hut. The hut crew had space for me to do a work-for-stay. My job would be to talk to the tourists about thru-hiking, and in the morning, dust the bunk beds. In exchange, I could eat a hot dinner and breakfast in the morning. Not a bad deal. However, I could not eat until all of the paying tourists had completed their meal. While everyone ate, I sat on the porch trying to ignore the wonderful aroma of fresh bread and stew. Each time I heard a fork and knife hit a plate, I salivated. It seemed as if my turn for dinner would never come.

Finally, a crewmember called out to me on the porch. "Wrongfoot, you can come eat now."

Ahhh yes, I thought as I scrambled inside. The next evening, I arranged another work-for-stay at the Mizpah Hut.

On June 30, I crossed the Presidential Mountain Range within the White Mountains. Each peak is named after a former president or other notable legend. The entire stretch is above tree line, which in good weather can offer spectacular views but in bad weather can be very dangerous. Mount Washington, elevation 6,288 feet, is the highest elevation of all the presidential peaks, and the second highest peak along the Appalachian Trail.

As I neared the summit, I came across a bright yellow sign bolted to a pole that was stuck into the ground on the trail. The sign read, "The area ahead has the worst weather in America. Many people have died here, even in the summer. Turn back now if the weather is bad." Wow, if that isn't a reality check, I don't know what is. A weather station located at the summit of Mount Washington reports conditions year-round. In 1931, the wind speed was measured at 231 mph.

The clouds became thicker as I approached the summit, and I was engulfed. My visibility was reduced to 10 feet. Even the cairns were hard to find. Then, I began to hear voices. I could see a building and people walking around. The climb leveled off to reveal a compound with several buildings. I heard the chugging sound of a slow-moving train and moments later, an old-fashioned train engine burst through the clouds, pushing a passenger car, and screeched to a halt. A few dozen tourists climbed off and began walking around. The Cog Railway delivers tourists to the summit from the base of the mountain. Several of them figured I was a thru-hiker from seeing my scraggly beard and bulky pack. They began bombarding me with questions. After admitting that I had indeed walked there from Georgia, 1,830 miles to the south, and answering a few other questions, I ducked into the Sherman Adams Building on the summit.

On the wall inside the building was a list of those who had died on Mount Washington. The list had room to add to it. A humbling thought. If the weather was bad, you could stay all day in this building. Several amenities were available: a cafeteria, bathrooms, a hiker break room, and even a post office.

Why would the U.S Postal Service have an office at the top of a mountain with the worst weather in America? No one lived up there except for a few meteorologists. Curiosity took over, so I walked over to the post office located near the front entrance of the Sherman Adams Building.

"Hello, sir," I said, greeting the postal worker. "Why is there a post office up here?"

I never got an answer. The man replied, "Would you like me to see if you got any mail?"

"I don't have any mail here," I insisted.

"So you don't want me to check for ya?" he responded.

"Why would I have supplies sent to me here? Then I would have to lug the load across the presidentials." A beat passed. "Go ahead and check just for kicks," I said, handing him my I.D.

The man returned to the counter with a small box and a letter addressed to me.

My jaw dropped. With a grin on his face, the man handed me a sheet to sign, acknowledging receipt of the items. I carried the box and letter over to a bench along the wall and sat down. The box was a care package from Sunshine. Trail magic all the way from Ohio. Here I was on the most dangerous mountain along the toughest stretch of trail, and I was given a strong reminder of the great cause for which I had set out to raise money. The spirit of Sunshine was alive. I had given Douglas a list of addresses to reach me along the trail. I had removed Mount Washington as a supply point, but I must have forgotten to remove it from the list of addresses I gave to Sunshine. The box was filled with cookies, candy, motivational quotes, and throwaway calling cards. My spirit was elevated tenfold.

A letter accompanied the care package from Douglas. He thanked me repeatedly for the successful fundraiser. He reported that to date almost $15,000 had been raised, $5,000 above my original goal. He then asked if I would kick off the Northwest Ohio Special Olympics in August by giving a motivational speech on participation. I sent back a letter that contained an enthusiastic yes. Everyone at Sunshine was cheering for me now; I hoped that I could motivate them in August.

With strong emotions, I trekked on across the Presidential Range. A storm cloud loomed behind me the entire way. Every time I looked back, I would pick up my pace, hoping to avoid getting caught in the open, exposed to all the elements and possible lightning strikes. The rest of the day, the trail led me along the very ridges of the most beautiful mountains I had ever seen. Both sides of the trail angled sharply downward. Miles of boulders were all around me, but no trees were visible.

By late afternoon, I came to a ridge overlooking Madison Hut. This hut marked the end of the Presidential Range. A cloud lingered below me but above the hut. I continued down to the hut and stopped for a break. Several hikers had already checked in for the night. The hut crew offered me a work-for-stay, but I wanted to keep going with several hours of daylight left. I offered the crew a few dollars for some fresh brownies that were sitting on the counter. I'm a sucker for a good brownie. They wouldn't accept any money and let me snack away.

A short while later, I was back on the trail. Just beyond Madison Hut, the trail makes a major descent. In less than three miles, I descended 3,000 feet. On the profile map, it looked as if the trail jumped off a cliff. The trail leveled off, and after several miles, I arrived at Pinkham Notch. An entire tourist compound was nestled in the valley.

I stepped inside a lodge check-in office to see about a room. The clerk in the office said they had some vacancies. As I searched my pack for cash, it dawned on me that I had left my money up at the Madison Hut when I pulled it out to pay for the brownies. All of my cash and credit cards were eight miles south up a treacherous 3,000-foot hand-over-hand climb. Now I was panicked. In the days of Daniel Boone, money wouldn't have helped you much in the woods, but in 1998 on the AT, you wouldn't make it without cash or credit cards.

After explaining the situation to the lodge clerk, she agreed to let me stay and sort out the money in the morning. I couldn't sleep until I knew my wallet was secure. Each hut has a radio for emergencies only. The radio person in Pinkham Notch would not break radio silence to make sure my wallet was at Madison Hut. Over and over, I explained that this was an emergency for me. My journey would abruptly end without my wallet. Finally, the man realized how important it was to me and radioed up to the hut. One of the Madison Hut crewmembers confirmed that they had my money holder. They said they would bring it down in the morning. Luckily for me, the next day was Wednesday, the day that a crewmember straps a Sherpa board on his back and carries the trash down the mountain to Pinkham Notch.

Waiting for someone carrying a load of trash and a wallet on his back down a mountain was a first for me. I was never happier to know that the trash had arrived. With my wallet back again, I thanked the man profusely, paid my room tab, and continued north.

Two more days of rigorous hiking above and below tree line put me at U.S Route 2. Gorham, New Hampshire, was a few miles down the road. I had another supply box waiting there. Without even hanging out my thumb, a red truck pulled over, and a female voice rang out. "You need a ride?" Without hesitation, I nodded my head and thanked her. As I stepped into the passenger seat, I noticed how beautiful she was. She had long blond hair, wore a pair of blue-jean cutoffs, and sported a nice tan on her slender physique. What was a woman like her doing offering grungy hikers rides? She dropped me at the post office. After collecting my supply box, an elderly gentleman in the parking lot offered me a ride. I took him up on the offer and had him drop me at the Hiker's Paradise Hostel in town.

The hostel keepers were very nice. They offered to drive me around town to buy supplies. They had a restaurant in the front of the building, so I ordered the hiker breakfast special. If you finished the whole meal, it only cost two dollars, but if you didn't complete the meal, it cost four dollars. A plate was set before me with four layers of pancakes molded into the shape of a sole of a boot. Chocolate chips were placed on top representing tread, and whipped cream was fluffed on the sides, serving as snow. Needless to say, I only had to pay two dollars.

What an accomplishment that I had completed the White Mountains, the toughest section of the Appalachian Trail! Only one more state to go. Maine also is a very grueling state on the trail, but after blazing through the White Mountains and walking 1,882 miles, I was ready for the last few hundred miles. It was hard to imagine that I had already walked through 13 states. What's one more? My momentum was going strong.

On July 4, I headed northward, hoping to see some fireworks from the top of the mountain. No chance. Rain erupted from the sky by mid-afternoon and never let up. The rocks became slippery, slowing my pace drastically. It wasn't until 9:30 p.m. that I crossed into Maine. A blue sign with white letters nailed to a tree read, "Maine—The Way Life Should Be." With my headlamp focused on the sign, I snapped a picture of my last state crossing.

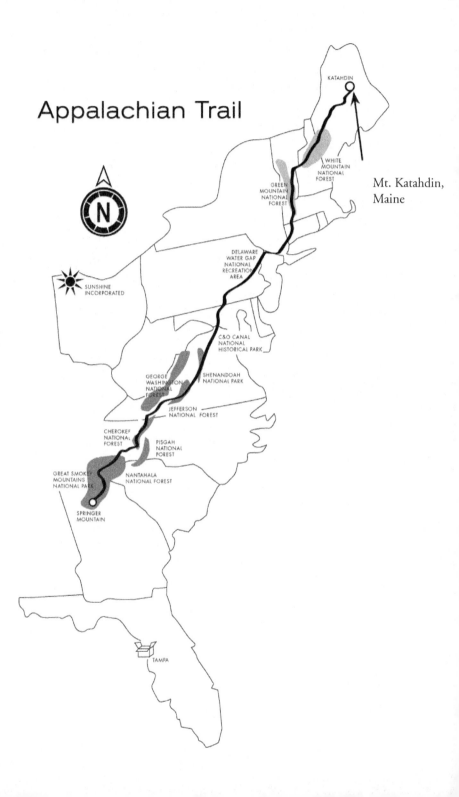

Appalachian Trail

KATAHDIN

Mt. Katahdin,
Maine

N

WHITE
MOUNTAIN
NATIONAL
FOREST

GREEN
MOUNTAIN
NATIONAL
FOREST

DELAWARE
WATER GAP
NATIONAL
RECREATION
AREA

SUNSHINE
INCORPORATED

C&O CANAL
NATIONAL
HISTORICAL PARK

GEORGE
WASHINGTON
NATIONAL
FOREST

SHENANDOAH
NATIONAL PARK

JEFFERSON
NATIONAL FOREST

CHEROKEE
NATIONAL
FOREST

PISGAH
NATIONAL
FOREST

GREAT SMOKEY
MOUNTAINS
NATIONAL PARK

NANTAHALA
NATIONAL FOREST

SPRINGER
MOUNTAIN

TAMPA

Chapter 34

Yahoo!

On top of Mount Katahdin, Maine. July 25, 1998. 147 days and 2,160 miles from Springer Mountain, Georgia.

Maine is definitely the most remote wilderness area of the entire trail. Chances are, most of the wood at your local lumberyard was cut from Maine's vast forests. You might be writing on paper that was manufactured from Maine's fine tree specimens. I was entering the final state of the AT, following a narrow footpath that cuts through the thickest of forests, up and over the state's highest peaks, along lakes and ponds, and abruptly ending on top of the most distinguished mountain of the entire trail, Mount Katahdin.

On the morning of July 5, I woke up inside the comforts of Carlo Col Shelter. Now I could see the faces of everyone on whom I had intruded the night before. Rain continued to fall outside. While I sat sipping my morning coffee, a woman hiked up to the shelter entrance and peered inside. She had a German shepherd with her, and she was hiking south toward Gorham, New Hampshire. After stepping in from the rain, she told us the rocks were dangerous up ahead, due to the rain. Apparently, she had taken a tumble down a slope, dog and all. I had fallen so many times that it had become part of my daily routine. In fact, I had become so accustomed to falling that I would lie there and take a break, sometimes even eating a snack before getting up. So I wasn't too worried by the woman's warnings of the slippery rocks ahead.

Starting the day off in the rain always gave me a yucky feeling, especially in the middle of summer when it was warm. I constantly debated whether I should wear my rain parka or not. My sweat would drench my clothes anyway.

Three miles north of the dry shelter, I discovered what the woman with the dog was talking about. I was traveling over the north peak of Goose Eye Mountain. Most of the trail was eroded to bare rock, creating a slippery, cement-like footpath over the mountain. On my descent from the peak, I lost my footing and fell backward onto my pack. As soon as I hit the ground, I slid down the slick rock slope with nothing available to break the momentum. This I hadn't experienced before. As I lay back on my pack, skidding down a slick, rocky, slope, panic set in. I tried to dig my hiking poles into the rock to stop my slide. Finally, after 20 feet, I managed to wedge a pole into a crevice, which stopped my sled ride. After my panic subsided, I slowly stood up and realized that if I had slid another 10 feet, I would have fallen over a small cliff. Luckily, my pack absorbed the fall. The lower compartment had torn, but better the pack than me.

A few miles north of my fall, I climbed through the ferocious Mahoosuc Notch, considered the hardest mile on the entire trail. The notch descends into a canyon-like valley with sheer rock walls ascending either side. Semi-truck-sized boulders cover the valley floor, creating a natural obstacle course. The trail led over, under, and between the huge boulders. As I crawled under some of them, I encountered snow that was unable to melt from the lack of sun. Several times, I took off my pack and flung it ahead due to the narrow tunnels of rocks wedged together. In other spots, I hugged boulders to pull myself over, hoping that I wouldn't slip back down. This one-mile obstacle course took almost two hours for me to cross. At one point during this mile, I caught my shoulder on a rock, which cut my skin. The abrasion healed into a Z-shaped scar that I still have and refer to as my very own Mahoosuc Notch.

Just north of the notch, I stopped for a much-needed rest. As I quietly celebrated while chewing on a Snickers bar, a group of adolescent boys walking south stopped along the trail near me. They were heading into the notch that I had just completed. They were all wearing matching T-shirts, and several adult men guided them. One of the boys had his map opened and was sitting on a rock, studying it.

"How far to the next shelter?" I asked him.

"I don't know," he replied.

One of the adult guides walked over to him, stooped down, put his face in front of the boy, and shouted, "You will look at your map and tell the man how far until the next shelter."

"Yes, sir," the boy answered as tears began to flow down his face.

"That's OK, I've got a map of my own. It's not that big a deal," I answered, wondering why the group leader was such a jerk. As it turned out, this was a juvenile delinquent organization, referred to in a derogatory way on the trail as Hoods in the Woods. The adolescents are given a chance to reform instead of serving a prison sentence. They were heading toward the Mahoosuc Notch as part of a discipline and team-building exercise. If they were looking for a challenge, they would definitely get it just up ahead on the trail.

Two days later, I hitchhiked off the trail to Andover, Maine. For ten bucks, I was able to stay at the Andover Bunkhouse, which offered showers, a modern kitchen, and inexpensive shuttle rides to and from the trail. I learned from some southbound hikers boarding with me that Jackrabbit Slim and Filou were just one day north. I had been trailing these guys since the beginning of my journey. The hostel keeper offered to shuttle me north so that I could walk back south toward Andover. This would allow me to intercept Jackrabbit Slim and Filou.

The next morning, I packed a day's worth of food and water and caught a ride north to U.S Route 17. At around 10:00 a.m. I encountered a man with long hair pulled back into a ponytail, glasses, a four-month beard, and a pack on his back. He introduced himself as Filou—pronounced "flew." As I explained who I was and how I had shuttled ahead to meet him and his partner, another hiker with a long beard and short hair approached us. He introduced himself as Jackrabbit Slim. We shared hiker stories for quite a while. I told them how I had hiked with Piasa and Comfortably Numb, who had also hiked with Filou and Jackrabbit Slim back in Pennsylvania. Filou said a section hiker had told them that a thru-hiker was not far behind them, but they didn't know who or how far back I was. The suspense of wondering who these guys were was now over. It was nice to meet the hikers whom I had been following for almost 2,000 miles. I never caught up to them again the rest of my journey.

***

The rain had continued for five days since I'd left New Hampshire.

Maine has very few footbridges spanning the abundant streams and rivers. Due to the excessive rain, some of the waterways had become too dangerous to ford. According to a local hiker I met on the trail, rangers and law enforcement officials receive calls from worried families when a hiker fails to arrive on schedule during heavy rains. The authorities explain to the families to wait until the water subsides, and more often than not, the hiker shows up a few days later.

For almost 300 miles, I had been traveling alone, occasionally staying with other hikers in shelters and hostels. Just north of Sugarloaf Mountain, I drastically descended 1,200 feet in less than two miles to the bank of the Carrabassett River. Before my descent, I could see the river in the valley, which looked small and relaxing from 1,200 feet above. But standing on the riverbank, I realized that this was no calm river. My eyes followed the AT markers painted on rocks scattered across the river, spanning 30 yards to the other side. The current was strong, splashing whitewater up onto the rocks as it rushed past. The water was waist deep. There was no way that I would be able to make it across safely.

The one thing I fear most is drowning. When I was three years old, I fell into the deep end of my grandmother's pool. Not knowing how to swim, I sat on the bottom, inhaling water for what seemed like several minutes. Luckily, my Uncle Brian happened to look out my grandma's attic window, which overlooked the pool, and saw me in the water. He rushed down the stairs and out the door, and he dove in, pulling me to safety. After several minutes of CPR, he revived me. Eventually, I learned to swim, but I still fear water. For almost an hour, I paced up and down the river in search of a safer place to cross but could not find one.

I stood there using a few choice words to reflect on my situation. I was startled when a man suddenly appeared next to me along the river. Between my swearing and the sound of the strong flowing river, I didn't hear him approach. He had a jet-black beard, was wearing a backpack, and appeared as grungy as most thru-hikers.

Shouting over the sound of the water, he introduced himself. "I'm Kubiac."

Earlier, I had passed a tent along the trail. It must have been his. I explained the dilemma of the high water as we both looked across the river. "My map shows a road back up on top of Sugarloaf Mountain that will take us across a bridge," I suggested.

"I'm not going back up that mountain," Kubiac stated.

He walked up river, studying possible places to ford. Then he plunged into the water and walked across, with the water level just below his knees. Without hesitation, I followed. We both sat on the other side while I took off my boots and poured out the water. As we talked, I learned that Kubiac attempted a thru-hike in 1997 but became very sick and had to cut his journey short. Now he was back to complete his journey.

In the rain, we climbed up over Crocker Mountain and down the other side. As we talked and walked, we discovered that we kept a similar pace and agreed to hike together for the last 185-mile stretch. At State Route 27, we caught a ride into Stratton, seeking some domestic amenities out of the rain. While in town sipping a beer, I decided to declare the last stretch of trail "Champagne Alley." Why not celebrate the rest of the way? Kubiac liked the declaration. It became official; in every trail register, I mentioned Champagne Alley. After completing the hike, I learned that Piasa had gotten back on the trail where he left off. He read my register entry and misunderstood the name. To go along with the spirit, he bought a bottle of champagne and carried it in his pack all the way to Katahdin. Oops!

For the next two weeks, Kubiac and I shared quite an adventure. It was nice having someone to talk to, sharing thoughts, ideas, and philosophies. We were solving world problems with each mile. We crossed over majestic mountains, traversed bog bridges, walked over beaver dams, and forded many streams and rivers. We caught a canoe ride across the Kennebec River. Over the years, several hikers had drowned trying to ford that river. The canoe ride now is considered an official AT crossing method, which was fine by me. Looking at my map after crossing the Kennebec, I realized that I had walked 2,000 miles. I took off my boots and socks and snapped a picture of my feet. My dogs had taken me quite a distance.

From one extreme to the other, temperatures had topped 100 degrees. Staying hydrated was difficult. All day, I had a headache from heat exhaustion. After fording the mountain streams, Kubiac and I would drop our packs and jump back in to cool off. In the southern states, I had encountered brutally cold temperatures with below-zero wind-chill factors, and now, four and half months and 2,000 miles later, the weather was the opposite extreme.

Monson, a very small logging town, was my last supply point of the trail. Kubiac and I took lodging at Shaw's Boarding House, a well-known hiker hostel. The Shaws refused to take payment from me after learning of the great cause for which I was hiking. The Shaws were very friendly and accommodating to hikers. They offered home-style meals and shuttles to Dover-Foxcroft, a nearby town. It was so nice for hikers at the Shaw place that a southbound hiker who had just embarked on his thru-hike had been lodging with the Shaws for almost two weeks after having walked for only a week. Life was good.

The last hundred miles were spectacular. With fully stocked provisions, including some extra treats that my family members had put into my last supply box, Kubiac and I headed off toward the last bit of wilderness. The trail followed the edge of glacial lakes and ponds. Temperatures remained hot, so we continued to cool off by swimming in the lakes, ponds, and streams. At night, as we camped along the shoreline, the warbling yodel of loons enhanced the evening. The sound that loons make is often used in Hollywood films as background for scary outdoor scenes. But listening to them in their natural environment was not scary at all. It was calming and relaxing.

Kubiac and I stopped for the night at the Carl Newhall Lean-To. In the morning, Kubiac got an earlier start than I did. Starting the morning off on my own, I began ascending Gulf Hagas Mountain.

Not far from the shelter, I heard the brush move off to my left. For 600 miles, I had followed moose poop but had yet to encounter the animal. The sounds of tree branches snapping could only be from this large animal. Assuming that a moose was just beyond the trees, I quietly unzipped my hip pouch and pulled out my camera. With my camera at the ready, I stood waiting for the moose. Then, without warning, a very large black bear charged out of the brush, running full force straight for me. With nowhere to run and shock coursing through me, I froze in my tracks. I could hear my heart stampeding. The bear came within 10 feet of me and stopped. We both stared at each other, wondering what the other's intentions were. Then, as I began to raise my camera to my eye for a picture, I heard the bushes move and twigs snap from where the bear had burst onto the trail. Two little cubs poked out their fuzzy heads, watching their mom staring me down. Oh, no! Mama bear had charged in order to protect her cubs. Thank goodness I wasn't out West in grizzly country where mama bears demonstrate how to eat human flesh. I nervously tried to control my trembling fingers and put the camera away, fearing the flash might provoke her to attack. For what seemed like eternity—but was actually only a moment or two—the bear and I stood staring at each other. Finally, she turned and ambled off into the forest with her cubs.

Still a little shaken, I proceeded. About 100 yards north, I heard the trees move again. Oh, no! This time the bear was coming back for my food. Quickly, I began unfastening my pack straps. If the bear came at me, I planned to drop my pack and back away. As I stood there feeling like a pizza at a Super Bowl party, a huge female moose emerged. In awe, I unzipped my pouch, pulled out my camera, and snapped several shots. Thinking back, I felt way out of control. A force more powerful than I had enjoyed the humor in hiding all of the moose from me— until now. Then, before finally letting me see a moose, He threw in a bear, just for kicks. Some thru-hikers go all the way without seeing a bear or a moose, so despite the fear I had felt, I considered myself lucky.

Soon, I caught up to Kubiac. He had also seen a moose. As a matter of fact, he had to jump off the trail to avoid getting run down by a cow-moose and her calf running down the trail. We trucked 19 miles to Cooper Brook Lean-to.

At some point in the day, my camera battery had died. The battery was lithium, not a standard battery. My chances of getting a new one in the middle of the forest were slim, but I asked the other hikers in camp anyway. Low and behold, a hiker overheard me asking around for this rare battery and hollered out, "I have a lithium battery you can have."

"Thank you very much," I said, and introduced myself.

"Wrongfoot, remember me, Rockdancer? I met you with your parents the day before you started your hike," he said.

Wow, what a coincidence. It's amazing how small the world is on a long, narrow path in the woods. Rockdancer had gotten back on the trail at Katahdin. He planned to hike until October with no specific geographic destination.

A very intense feeling loomed in my mind. From the summit of Chairback Mountain, Kubiac and I were able to get our first glimpse of the final mountain, Mount Katahdin. The terrain leading up to the final mountain leveled off into flatlands that were riddled with glacial lakes, ponds, and forest. This last mountain on the 2,000-mile footpath radiated a majestic energy. Reaching this mountain had been my goal since I started my journey, 14 states to the south. Now, I could see the end. Each day, Katahdin became clearer and more defined. It was like gradually approaching a stoplight. You had a ways to go before you'd come to a complete stop, but you were reminded visually that you would be stopping soon. Every time Kubiac and I came to a clearing or to a mountain peak with a view of Katahdin, we would snap a few pictures and then just sit and stare at it.

With Katahdin in view, the reality that these were my final days on the trail set in. The last few days seemed like slow motion, as I realized that the lifestyle I had experienced for almost five months was about to change abruptly. Each part of my journey became intense: pulling out my stove and boiling water for dinner; taking polar dips in the glacial ponds and streams; sleeping in three-walled shelters; rolling up my sleeping bag and packing my pack; sitting on my pack to take a break along the trail or at a beautiful overlook; falling down and lying there eating a Snickers bar; swatting away mosquitoes and wishing they didn't exist; reading and writing in trail registers; signing my name "Wrongfoot, GA to ME 98;" pumping water from streams twice a day; sharing the spirit of Sunshine with everyone I met; picking up supply boxes; calling home and writing postcards to my brother, friends, and family; taking ibuprofen daily for pain; eating three times the food I normally consume; showering once a week; viewing life from outside the box; walking all day in rain, sleet, or snow; and waking up to yet another day of walking. All of my simple, daily trail routines would soon end.

My family had made arrangements to meet me in Baxter State Park, which surrounds Mount Katahdin. Ron planned to summit the final climb with me. On July 24, my mom and Ron intercepted Kubiac and I on the trail. A five-mile ascent of Mount Katahdin would complete my journey of 2,160 miles. Baxter State Park truly is a wilderness preserve that allows a limited number of vehicles and people inside the park's boundaries each day. My parents were unable to secure a campsite within the park, so they found a commercial campground just outside of the park entrance.

Kubiac accompanied my family and I back to the campground. He planned to meet friends the next day for his final climb. When we pulled up to our campsite, I was puzzled when I saw the number of tents. Three four-man tents were erected. Before I had a chance to ask what all the tents were for, an all-terrain vehicle pulled up. My brother and brother-in-law emerged from the vehicle. They had surprised me and joined the greeting party, with plans to summit Katahdin with me. While they were waiting for me to arrive, they took advantage of the opportunity to go on a guided fishing tour and had just returned. My father and stepmother also had driven from Toledo to celebrate the end of my journey with me. Having family at the end of my journey was inspiring.

On July 25, in the wee hours of morning, around 4:30 a.m., Kubiac, Ron, my brother Larry, and brother-in-law Dan, and I quietly slipped out of our tents and drove to the main gate of Baxter. Several vehicles were ahead of us at 5:00 a.m. Kubiac and I cooked up a trail breakfast next to our vehicle while we waited for the gate to open at 6 a.m. We brought along some bacon to fry, which let an aroma into the morning air that teased every hiker's appetite.

By 7:30, my family and I were packed and ready for the final climb. Kubiac said goodbye and headed off to wait for his friends to arrive. The first mile was easy walking. Then, shortly after crossing a mountain stream, the trail shot straight up. Just like the White Mountains of New Hampshire, we had to pull ourselves up, grabbing onto rocks, roots, and tree branches. I kept pulling ahead of my family, and then I would catch myself and slow down. This was their first five miles and my last of 2,160 miles. I was in better shape than they were.

A few hours later, we emerged above the tree line, with a little over two miles until the summit. Wind gusts tossed our hood straps and hair around as we proceeded. Iron handles pounded into the rocks along the trail provided a safer climb where the trail got difficult. Slowly we emerged from the challenging hand-over-hand section of boulders onto a flat tableland. Day hikers were scattered everywhere, squatting down between rocks to get out of the brisk wind. Knowing that I was near the end, I surged ahead of my family towards the final summit.

Like a horse with blinders, I focused straight ahead. I began ascending rocks that had been assembled into a set of stairs. At the top of the stairs, I could see the sign announcing the end. Here it was, the summit of Mount Katahdin, 5,268 feet above sea level. I broke into a run all the way up to the sign. A handful of day hikers were sitting around enjoying the breathtaking, mile-high views in every direction. I felt scared, happy, sad, excited, and speechless as I stepped up to the sign announcing the northern terminus. I was scared of what life would bring after the Trail; happy that I had completed my dream and fulfilled my fundraising goal; sad that my thru-hike was over; excited to share my journey with everyone; and speechless with thousands of thoughts racing through my mind. For a few minutes I embraced the sign with both hands, trying to make sense of the awesome notion that I had really walked 2,160 miles through 14 states, all the way from Georgia, over some of the most difficult terrain in the United States.

Larry, Dan, and Ron caught up to me at the sign moments later. Everyone was complaining how cold it was. Larry and Ron told me they had discussed turning back the whole way up the mountain, but when an 8-year-old boy zipped by them, their egos kicked in and they continued. I was glad that they hadn't turned back.

Dan reached inside his pocket and pulled out a small white plastic square that unfolded into a big white plastic sheet. Ron and Dan unfolded it and held it across the Katahdin terminus sign. It read "Congratulations Wrongfoot; 2,159 miles in 147 days; Hike for Sunshine; March 1- July 25." My sister Steph and brother Todd could not be there, so they made the sign as their special contribution to the celebration. As I stood behind it and posed for pictures, Ron and Dan held it across the Katahdin sign, while Larry shot video footage, and I yelled out, "Yahoo!"

***

Out of love, I dedicated my hike to my brother Aaron. He cannot walk or speak, but his smile sends a million messages to anyone who has ever known him. I pulled a bottle of champagne from my backpack. Realizing no one would want to drink it up there, with the wind and cold temperatures, I clenched the bottle in my hand and held my arms up in a victory "V." Here's to you, brother! Every step, here's to you!

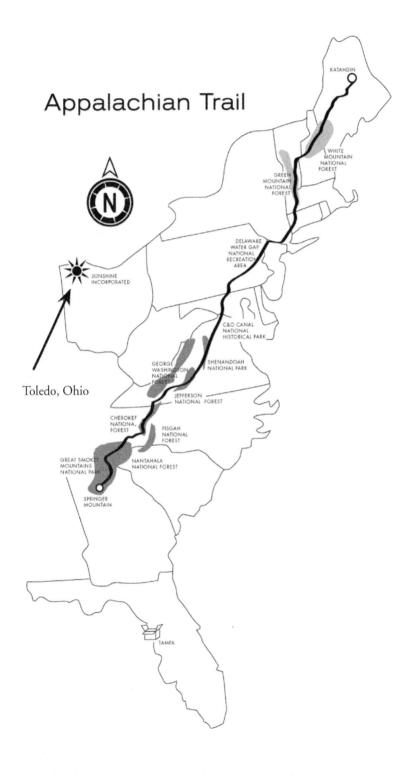

Appalachian Trail

KATAHDIN

WHITE
MOUNTAIN
NATIONAL
FOREST

GREEN
MOUNTAIN
NATIONAL
FOREST

DELAWARE
WATER GAP
NATIONAL
RECREATION
AREA

SUNSHINE
INCORPORATED

C&O CANAL
NATIONAL
HISTORICAL PARK

GEORGE
WASHINGTON
NATIONAL
FOREST

SHENANDOAH
NATIONAL PARK

Toledo, Ohio

JEFFERSON
NATIONAL FOREST

CHEROKEE
NATIONAL
FOREST

PISGAH
NATIONAL
FOREST

GREAT SMOKEY
MOUNTAINS
NATIONAL PARK

NANTAHALA
NATIONAL FOREST

SPRINGER
MOUNTAIN

TAMPA

Chapter 35

We Did It!

Toledo, Ohio. Nowhere near the Appalachian Trail. August 1998.

The day after summiting Mount Katahdin, my family and I gathered for breakfast one last time. Then we said goodbye, going our separate ways—my brother back to Georgia; Ron, Mom, and Dan back to Florida; and Dad, Sue, and I back to Toledo. This last meal symbolized the conclusion of my Sunshine expedition team. Hopefully, the good memories would live on.

After walking all that way, sitting in a car for 13 hours was not a pleasant experience. I felt like the Energizer Bunny stuck up against the wall, trying to move forward. Even though we were flowing with traffic, I felt as if we were traveling faster than the speed of sound, compared to the walking pace that I was used to. As a last request before leaving Maine, we stopped and enjoyed a lobster dinner. Slowly, the terrain leveled out into the flat Midwest that I had known all too well before the trail.

Shortly after arriving in Toledo, I paid a visit to my brother Aaron, to whom I had dedicated my hike. He doesn't speak, but as soon as he saw me, a smile spread across his face from ear to ear. Aaron's smile confirmed in my heart that he understood that I had completed my journey for him. Together, we posed for a picture behind the same sign I used on the final mountain. Symbolically, this signified the end of my hike, with Aaron by my side.

Over the next few weeks, I slowly got used to the domestic routine of hearing lawn mowers, flushing toilets, looking both ways for cars, daily showers, four-walled rooms, street lights drowning out the natural darkness of night, and refrigerated food. I kept my tent set up in the backyard for a place of retreat, but it just wasn't the same.

I gave press interviews, contacted friends and family, and gave speeches and presentations of my journey. I spoke to community organizations that had supported my fundraiser. The Sunshine Home sponsored a dinner and slide show presentation of my journey and had honored me with the Spirit of Sunshine Award. As I presented and shared my trail experiences, I realized the momentum that my dream had created. Hundreds of people attended each presentation and were celebrating in my success. I had relied on my support team for supplies, motivation, and help with the fundraiser. Some hikers choose to hike the AT without a team, but I learned how awesome it was to involve everyone. This involvement led to my success.

Beth, my close friend, came to see me and attended my slide show. Without explanation, our friendship rapidly went to another level. We quickly became more than just friends. We got married the following year.

During my journey, I shared the spirit of Sunshine with everyone I met. Being able to give back to the community left me with a feeling of accomplishment. By the end of my hike, I had raised $16,000 and inspired an annual walk in Toledo, Ohio, which continues to raise money for adaptive equipment.

My journey came full circle when I kicked off the 1998 Northwest Ohio Special Olympics at Sunshine. In August 1998, not long after completing my hike, Aaron and I were up on stage together, wearing identical Sunshine T-shirts and khaki outdoor hats. Aaron sat next to me in his wheelchair while I spoke about the importance of participation.

My voice choked with emotion, as I explained to everyone, "I could not have completed my journey and raised so much money without everyone's involvement. We walked and rolled together in spirit and in step. Thanks to everyone's participation, you walked and rolled with me on May 9 by kicking off the first annual Walk With Sunshine right here in Toledo, Ohio. Your care packages, cards, and words of encouragement carried me the whole way to Maine."

Then, I held the microphone to Aaron, and with guidance, he hit a communication switch that was purchased with funds from my walk. The switch initiated a prerecorded message that was amplified through the microphone: "Let the games begin!"

I had lived my dream and was able to share and inspire others to share their dreams. Although my brother couldn't hike the trail, he celebrated with me. He rolled his chair—assisted by our dad—in the local Walk With Sunshine; he received postcards from me during the journey, and he had a map of the AT on his wall at work. Aaron's spirit was with me every step of the way. When the weather was nasty and cold, or the terrain was extremely difficult, or my spirit was waning, I would think of Aaron back home, rooting me along. Maybe Aaron could not communicate or pursue his dreams, but he sure did motivate me.

After each discussion and presentation of my hike, someone would ask me if I planned to write a book about my experiences. Eventually, I took the question literally and began putting my experiences onto paper. When I finished my journey, my stepfather handed me a photo album with my journals typed and pictures assembled in chronological order from Georgia to Maine. This was an awesome gesture. Despite all the information organized into an easy-to-follow format, I was still processing the most intense experience of my life. On the trail, I began my journey in Georgia and ended in Maine, but my experiences and lessons learned along the way were even bigger than the distance traveled.

As for the other thru-hikers I met along the way, I spoke with a few of them by phone, wrote to others, saw a few at the annual Trail Days Hiker Festival in Damascus, Virginia, the next spring, and never heard from some. Filou, Jackrabbit Slim, Gingerbread Man, and Rob—aka Captain Clammy—summited Katahdin a few days before I did. Kubiac summited Katahdin the day after me, and he hiked the Pacific Crest trail in 2000. Foxtrot completed the Long Trail and went on to finish the AT, chalking up his second thru-hike. Happy Jo completed the Long Trail, but his companion, the Kid, left the trail after a week. Zeb developed allergies and had stepped off the AT for a while. Eventually, he went farther north and thru-hiked the Long Trail. Zeb now lives in northern Georgia and has devoted his spare time to maintaining a stretch of the Appalachian Trail as part of the Georgia Appalachian Trail Club. Briggs, Crash, Magaroni, Piasa, Dharma Bum, Yoon, and Viking all completed their journeys. Crash hiked the AT again in 1999 with his son. The family I met in Virginia that was home-schooling their young son on the trail hiked a good portion of it and intended to go back to complete it in the future. Packrat attempted another thru-hike in 1999 but quit due to the heat. He may set the record for most thru-hike attempts.

The trail was full of magic. The night that lightning struck helped me see that I was not alone on this journey. Just when I felt defeated, something would happen that rejuvenated my spirit or lifted my fear. There was the time I sprained my ankle and thought my journey was over, but the swelling went down and I was able to keep walking. Piasa and I were invited into a stranger's home and given a full-course meal and laundered clothes. Then there was the moment along the Carrabassett River, as I stood fearing possible drowning, when Kubiac showed up and led me across as if the river were a sidewalk. My experience with the moose that I dubbed the Bullwinkle Conspiracy leads me to believe that our Creator has a sense of humor and adventure. I swear the bear was laughing at me as we stood face to face in the forest, as if she knew that the moose I had been expecting was just around the bend in the trail.

For me, the Appalachian Trail was a great opportunity to look at life while removed from the daily hustle and bustle. My life was boiled down to its simplest form, which allowed me to filter out unwanted distractions. I learned that life is as simple or as complicated as you make it. I had chosen to simplify my life to include only the best things: my family, friends, and the mountains.

During my time on the AT, I learned that the American spirit is alive. The Appalachian Trail blazes through many of the original colonies, rich in history. At times, I walked on the same wilderness footpaths where our country's founders marched off to battle in pursuit of freedom. I crossed through the same cow pastures and farm fields that have provided the nation with food for centuries. All along the trail, people routinely offered rides, lodging, food, water, and snacks, which made me feel right at home. This country was founded on patriotism, survival, kindness, trust, and integrity, all of which were very much alive during my journey. To me, the Appalachian Trail is just as much a part of the American spirit as baseball and apple pie.

I learned that the trail was more than a wilderness path. It intertwines with civilization. The people I met along the way were just as much a part of my journey as the wilderness experience. The trail itself would not exist if it weren't for the countless hours that volunteers spend removing fallen trees, painting trail markers, and building and repairing bridges. The towns along the way made it possible for me to receive supplies and stay in contact with friends and family. For six months, my hike and fundraiser had brought together friends and family for a common cause.

Physically, I am no longer on the trail, but my mind often is. I never know what will trigger a thought about the trail: the aroma of coffee, smelly socks, a vegetarian entrée on a restaurant menu, the crunch of a leaf beneath my foot, a rain storm, the sun, a picture of a mountain, cows, or even the simple act of walking. The experiences that I endured and enjoyed remain strong.

My dream was to walk the trail. Yet walking the AT is not appealing to everyone. Everyone has dreams, whether it's to become an actor, run a marathon, get married, or become debt-free. I found that the more I shared my dream with people, the more realistic my dream became. On the whole, people want to be good to their neighbors. I found that the more I shared my hike with others, the more determined I became to follow through. By sharing your dream with your friends, family, and neighbors, you are more likely to see that dream come true.

Walking all that way through rain, snow, heat, humidity, and bugs, over some of the most challenging terrain in the United States, was truly the hardest and most rewarding thing that I have ever done. I have a newfound insight that I have only begun to apply. I know that I can walk anywhere. I learned that anything can be accomplished by breaking it down into daily achievements. I learned to give everything I do all that I have, and if it doesn't work out, trying is good enough. I know that if I make my dreams my goals, I will achieve them with the same passion and perseverance that took me from Georgia to Maine. I learned to set only the biggest of goals and to strive toward them, one day at a time, just by putting one foot in front of the other.

Walking the Extra Mile

Invite everyone in your city, town, school, or office to come along with you on your journey. Whether you're planning an expedition along the Appalachian Trail from Georgia to Maine, the Pacific Crest Trail, the Continental Divide Trail from Canada to Mexico, or a dangerous climb up Mount McKinley, Alaska, you don't have to face the challenge alone. I don't actually mean physically taking an entire city population or office staff with you. Raise money for a good cause while you follow your ambition. If you're someone who likes to give back to the community or help others in need, adding a charity angle to your expedition may be another huge reward for you to consider. Everyone back home, in school, or at the office might not have the same ambition of walking 2,000 miles, but they might contribute to your worthy cause.

If you are considering a long-distance hike or another challenging adventure, including a fundraiser may add some extra motivation and inspiration to give you that burst of energy to go the extra mile when you really need it. A successful fundraiser takes planning, much as the expedition itself. I've outlined some key steps to help you combine a charity with your adventure.

Choose a Charity You Feel Passionate About

A fundraiser can be as fulfilling as the expedition itself. If you are going to take the extra time to raise money for a good cause, choose a charity that means something to you personally. It doesn't necessarily have to involve a family member. When you are out on your adventure, you will feel a sense of accomplishment in addition to your hike or climb, knowing you have impacted the community in a positive way while fulfilling your dream.

Plan Ahead

Planning to hike the Appalachian Trail took me five months. Raising funds for a charity took an equal amount of time. Most nonprofit organizations are excited to receive extra funds, but they need advance notice and might need approval from a governing body regarding your proposal. Nonprofit organizations are continually conducting fundraisers and usually have a systematic process already in place to handle your special event.

Assemble a Support Team for the Expedition and the Charity

Most thru-hikers have a friend or family member acting as a support team, mailing supplies along the journey, and tending to issues as they come up. An additional team member supporting your fundraiser will put you at ease while on your journey. It's a little hard to send thank-you notes, give speeches, and make phone calls from the trail.

Request Sponsorship from Equipment Suppliers

Why not cut some overhead and outfit your expedition for free? Like most businesses, outfitters and equipment manufacturers participate in community-based charities, which enhances public awareness and promotes their products. In addition, equipment suppliers benefit from your feedback regarding their products. Do this four to five months before your expedition. Don't be shy. After deciding what equipment you need, submit written proposals. Be specific about what you are requesting. Provide information about the charity you are raising money for, including tax-exempt information. Be sure to explain how the companies will be recognized for their sponsorship, such as putting their logo on your website or newsletter.

Publicize your Fundraiser

The key to a successful charity event is getting the word out to as many people as possible. Contact the media through news releases. Call businesses and friends. Find out if the organization that you're raising money for has any promotional material to help you out. Schedule speaking engagements with civic organizations such as the Kiwanis, Rotary, or Lions Clubs. Remain flexible, and be creative. Every event and every cause is different.

Offer Incentives For Your Sponsors To Donate

Everyone likes to be recognized for noble deeds. Businesses, friends, and family contributing to your cause will appreciate recognition for their support. Emphasize to potential sponsors that their donation is tax-deductible. Additionally, a webpage can be an effective way to mention everyone who donated. A printed newsletter that names donors is a nice touch if you have the resources. A local printer might even donate the printing costs.

Separate Your Fundraiser from Your Expedition

The last place for advertising is on the trail. Thank goodness! Whether your fundraiser is national or locally based, keep the fundraiser off the trail. Every year, thousands of thru-hikers attempt the Appalachian Trail. If everyone began requesting funds on their journey, the friendly town folks along the way may become weary of hikers asking for handouts. Although I shared my goals with everyone I met, I conducted my fundraising activity in local Ohio communities, far removed from the trail.

Develop a Long-Term Strategy for Your Charity

Is your expedition a one-time event? If so, maybe you could use it as a kickoff for an annual charity event. Perhaps a local walk or run? Of course, you will need a commitment from dedicated volunteers.

Hiking as a fundraiser for Sunshine motivated me to complete my journey. Even more, it was a positive way of promoting awareness of our national wild lands while providing for the community. Reductions in government funding have increased the need for nonprofit organizations to rely on donations more than ever before.

***

The Appalachian Trail is a unit of the National Park system, which has strict rules regarding fundraising within park boundaries that might supercede those of the federal forests and state parks and forest through which it passes. The Appalachian Trail Conservancy (ATC), the keepers of the Appalachian Trail, depends on donations and volunteers to function. As the steward of the Trail, ATC cannot endorse hikers walking the trail to raise funds primarily because it has no means to verify the fundraisers, certify their accounting, or otherwise live up to the expectations that such an endorsement might suggest in the eyes of the general public. Please support the ATC in the following ways: 1.) Become a member; 2.) Donate to the ATC; & 3.) Become an ATC volunteer. For more information, see www.appalachiantrail.org.

***

If you are interested in making a donation to Sunshine, contact the Director of Development, Sunshine Foundation Incorporated, 7223 Maumee-Western Road, Maumee, Ohio 43537; call (419) 865-0251; e-mail: info@Sunshinefnd.com; or visit www.sunshinefnd.com.

Life Lessons from the Trail

Hanging on my wall at home is a framed quotation by Henry David Thoreau: "I went to the woods to live deliberately, to front only the essential facts of life, and see if I could not learn what it had to teach, and not when it came time to die, discover that I had not lived." I identify with that. I knew that stepping away from my modern routine for half of a year and walking more than 2,000 miles would change my life. But I didn't know exactly how things would change or what lessons I would take from the trail. Now, almost ten years since my hike, it's clear to me how walking the Appalachian Trail has changed me, and it has happened in profound, unique, and positive ways.

My readers and those who know me probably would say that I'm never at a loss for words when it comes to describing my adventure. But walking the trail was as much an internal experience as an external one, and it has taken me a while to pinpoint exactly what the trail had to teach and what my 147 days of walking has come to mean. Would the lessons stick with me ten years later? I have been able to apply some valuable lessons to my own life, and I hope that if I share them, you can glean a trail lesson or two—without the blisters, bugs, sweat, and pain of a 2,160-mile journey.

Humor Can Spread a Smile Over the Difficult Times

I wouldn't have lasted even a week on the trail without the ability to laugh. When I discovered that I had put my arch supports into the wrong boots and caused myself horrible blistering, I found the humor in the situation. One blister is painful, but my feet looked like bubble wrap after my first day of carrying a 55-pound pack on a 2,000-mile journey. I took the self-deprecating trail name Wrongfoot, which served as a lasting reminder to laugh and laugh often. I laughed at myself along the entire trail, at situations I encountered, and with other hikers. Sometimes laughing was all I had, and sometimes it was all I needed. A good laugh can remind me that I'm taking things too seriously, and sometimes things are so overwhelming that laughing helps me. I'm happy to report that since completing my hike, I've kept my boots and insoles on the right feet, I haven't slept with any skunks, no one has commented on my awful smell (not to my knowledge, anyway), and I eat normal portions of food in public places. My two-and-a-half-year-old daughter, Madison, is always putting her shoes on the wrong feet. It makes me laugh when I wonder if this is some sort of genetic trait that I've passed along.

The Simplest Things Can Serve as the Biggest Rewards

On the trail, it rained more than the sun shined. At one point, I walked through almost two weeks of continuous rain. I walked and lived in the woods in subzero temperatures. I faced sleet, snow, and frigid weather for nearly a month. It's easy to walk in the woods on a sunny day with views in every direction. But if you had a choice, you probably would head indoors if the weather were bad. Going inside when it rains isn't an option for someone who's walking from Georgia to Maine. I found that, by celebrating something each day, I was able to move beyond the horrible weather. On the trail, I would celebrate a hot cup of coffee or a meal that I'd anticipated as I walked all day in the rain. I fell down a lot, and I would celebrate the chance to take a snack break before even getting up. I learned to appreciate the simple fact that I was able to take time out of my life to go after a goal. By celebrating, I'm still able to navigate difficult situations. Back in the real world, I find something to celebrate each day, and often it's the simplest of things. They're easy to spot when I'm in the right mindset. I celebrate my great wife. I celebrate my daughter's beautiful smile. I still celebrate a hot cup of coffee in the morning. I celebrate at least one accomplishment before leaving work each day. If nothing else, I celebrate the fact that I'm alive and healthy. Life is much more enjoyable when you're celebrating, instead of worrying and stressing.

Go After Your Dreams Now!

I'm so glad that I went to the woods and pursued my Appalachian Trail goal while I was still a healthy young man. I talked recently with a friend and colleague who is struggling with some painful health issues and is taking care of his sick father at the same time. My friend has worked for 30 years as an educator, and he's eligible for a full pension if he chooses to retire. But he said something to me that really brought things into perspective: "Without your health," he said, "nothing else really matters." For decades, he's worked diligently toward that dangling carrot of a full pension, and now that the carrot is within reach, he might not be healthy enough to enjoy the money for which he's worked so long and hard. So many people have told me that they want to hike the Appalachian Trail when they retire, and that's a wonderful end-of-career goal. Based on statistics, though, it's really a crapshoot to see if your health will cooperate with your plans. Money is important, and life sure is easier with money than without it. But when you put off a life goal such as sailing around the world, getting your Ph.D., or walking the Appalachian Trail, you're banking on your health being intact for your endeavor. Many times, that isn't the case. Depending on the situation, I've learned to be flexible with goals based on family issues, work, or finances. Putting one foot in front of the other in pursuit of my goals has opened my mind to the notion that you don't need to wait for retirement to pursue even the loftiest of dreams. You just need to be flexible and creative in how you go about it. Also, make sure that you never take your health for granted.

Self-Motivation Drives Success

I've given hundreds of lectures about my Appalachian Trail journey over the years. I truly enjoy sharing my story. I especially like the discussions that crop up at the end of each presentation. I have a list of answers for some of the common questions that come up over and over. You can guess the questions that elicited these responses: "Two pairs of boots." "I lost 30 pounds." "I averaged 17 miles a day." But one question that keeps coming up has led to some soul-searching on my part: *Is walking the Appalachian Trail more of a physical challenge than a mental one?*

In 1955, at the age of 67 and as a grandmother of 23, Grandma Gatewood walked the entire Appalachian Trail by herself. That's amazing enough, but to top it off, she wore a pair of tennis shoes. In 1998, 79-year-old Earl Shaffer completed his third thru-hike of the entire Appalachian Trail. On two different expeditions, two different men walked the entire trail using prosthetic limbs. Bill Erwin, a blind man, completed the entire Appalachian Trail in 1991 with the help of a seeing eye dog. Whenever someone says, "I'm too old to walk the trail," or, "I can't hike because of bad knees," I can't help but think of Grandma Gatewood, Earl Shaffer, and Bill Erwin. To me, walking the Appalachian Trail blind is accomplishing the impossible. I trip over things on my way to the bathroom at night; I can't even imagine walking along one of the most difficult footpaths in the world without the ability to see where I'm going. So, is walking the trail more mental than physical? I've met hikers who've had all the right equipment and who were in top physical condition but decided to quit walking the Appalachian Trail. I believe that going after any goal as challenging and demanding as walking the AT requires a determined mental commitment. With that positive drive, you can push yourself physically beyond what you ever thought possible. I never thought about quitting my journey. There was one point during my journey where I thought that I had broken my ankle, but I never gave up. I've learned that if I want something bad enough, I will find a way to achieve it. I've become so focused on how to succeed that I never even consider the reasons why I might not. You have to be internally driven to reach challenging goals. Having all the right gear, time, money, and physical ability is useless without the drive to succeed. Above all, determination is what got me from Georgia to Maine.

A Dream Can Be Achieved Through Lots of Small Steps in the Right Direction

Walking the Appalachian Trail has taught me that big dreams can be accomplished by turning them into your goals. After I decided that I really was going to walk the Appalachian Trail, then my dream turned to a process of planning, training, and breaking down my goal into daily steps—5 million of them, to be exact. I made my Appalachian Trail dream tangible by sharing it with others. A rule of thumb is that you need to walk at least 12 miles a day to make it from Georgia to Maine in one season. Twelve miles might seem more doable than 2,000 miles. Any goal can be broken down into daily obtainable steps.

The Most Rewarding Experiences Often are
the Most Challenging

As I stood high atop the Mount Washington summit—the second-highest peak on the Appalachian Trail—and watched forty tourists step off of a train that shuttled people from the base of the mountain to the top, a feeling of accomplishment gelled inside me. I had walked 1,830 miles to where I stood. I had worked all morning to lug my body and pack up the mountain, only to spot an easier way to the top. But for me, my way was far more rewarding. While I'm sure that the tourists on the train enjoyed the excursion—and I would love to ride the Cog Railway myself someday—they didn't have the sweat equity, that feeling of pride earned only by a strenuous hike up the mountain. The things in life that I remember and value the most are the things that I had to work hard to obtain, such as marrying the woman of my dreams, earning a master's degree, and writing an award-winning book. The good things in life come with determination and hard work, and I keep that in the back of my mind when the going gets rough. There is a popular saying on the trail: No pain, no rain, no Maine.

Walking the AT is 2,000 Miles of Problem-Solving

Many Olympic medalists enjoy some amount of fame for their physical abilities, but they tend to blend into the workforce in careers unrelated to their athletic endeavors. That doesn't mean that they have given up their passion. It's that they can apply to their lives many of the principles that earned them medals in the first place. Thru-hiking is by no means an Olympic endeavor, but accomplishing such an adventure requires many of the same skills that an Olympic athlete must possess to be at the top of his or her game. Thru-hiking the AT requires daily problem-solving skills that I've been able to take with me and apply at work, in my marriage, and in virtually all aspects of my life.

Top athletes need to think on their feet. A coach can only provide training; in the actual event, you're on your own. I was my own coach for 2,160 miles. It was up to me to put one foot in front of the other and maneuver through every situation that I encountered. Walking through freezing, wet conditions can be dangerous, and the risk of hypothermia was ever-present. Being caught on a mountain ridge in a snowstorm that brought subzero temperatures required some levelheaded thinking to ensure survival. A torn boot sole miles from a town required some creative repair work. Keeping my water supply topped off in the hot summer months required logistical awareness. Stumbling upon bears, being charged by bulls, and getting swarmed by gnats, black flies, and mosquitoes all required quick responses and well-thought-out solutions. Each day presented a new set of challenges. For each of 147 days, I adapted, solved my dilemmas, and kept moving forward.

I had some initial difficulties adjusting back to domesticated life after living in the woods for nearly five months. It's not often that we get an opportunity to let our minds float for days, weeks, and months. The constant disruptions of schedules, TV, radio, traffic, etc., prevent most of us from allowing ourselves the time to deliberate. I still get Springer Fever—the urge to throw on a pack and walk the Appalachian Trail from Springer Mountain, Georgia—each spring as green returns to the wilderness and the fragrance of fresh blooming flowers permeates the air. When the hustle and bustle becomes overwhelming, I slip in a nature CD, look at a picture of one of my favorite AT views, and take a brief stroll in the nearby park. I revel in letting my mind drift off to that peaceful place on the trail.

What has been fun for me is adapting my problem-solving skills from the trail into my daily life. On the trail, quitting or giving up wasn't an option. Moving forward and overcoming the obstacle or challenge was the only way to get to Maine. When work, family, or life in general presents a problem, my trail prowess kicks in. If I were an employer assembling a troubleshooting task force, I would want a hiker on the team!

What Hiking in the Mountains Does For Me

My hiking philosophy evolved from my long adventure on the AT and my subsequent expeditions. Looking up at a mountain range soothes me. After just a few steps onto a forested mountain trail, I feel my burdens and pressures fall away. I'll gladly exchange a hot shower, a television, and refrigerated beverages for a clear mind. Grit under my fingernails and a layer of dirt on my body don't bother me. I don't mind splashing off with cold mountain stream water and sleeping on the ground. For me, it's all worth the chance to put aside life's distractions and listen to my inner thoughts.

Climbing in the mountains exposes a hiker to many of God's natural beauties and natural dangers. When I get far enough from civilization—physically and mentally—my acuity of all God's creations increases and makes me see my place in the world. It is with this peace that I realize that whatever my thought, situation, or circumstance is, I know that God is there to help me work through it. He has a plan, even when I don't. Sometimes I emerge from the trail with answers to my dilemmas. Sometimes I leave the woods with more questions than I had going in. But I always emerge refreshed and appreciative of this great world.

Experienced hikers know this to be true: the lighter the pack, the more pleasant the journey. On my thru-hike, I discarded items from my backpack that did nothing but weigh me down. I was more efficient and agile with a lighter pack. I return to the mountains often to metaphorically lighten my pack of life. It's easy to get bogged down in our daily lives by taking on extra responsibilities, spending more time on work projects than with family, running in all directions without a focus. Hiking helps me regroup and separate my priorities from the responsibilities that I've shouldered. It's amazing how much more refreshed and successful I am after I realign my focus and goals.

So much research has come out about the physical and mental health benefits of walking. Walking is recommended by physicians for cardiovascular health, weight loss, stress relief, and as a supplement for depression treatment. Take all these good traits of walking, add in the rejuvenating mountain views and the escape from the hustle and bustle, and it really becomes clear to me why hiking is one of the healthiest sports in which you can participate. This is more than a sport. It's a lifestyle.

The People I Meet While Hiking Rekindle My Belief in Human Goodness

Each year, the millions of people who hike parts of the AT and the thousands who attempt thru-hikes make the trail the most populated long-distance footpath in the United States. You are more likely to bump into other hikers than to be alone. Those who want to be alone in the woods can avoid shelters and walk at their own pace. For me, the people I meet on the trail are part of what makes the experience so enriching. They have a similar sense of adventure, so it's easy to make friends, much like belonging to the same gym or civic organization. The social experience along the AT is what life must have been like in rural America in the 1940s when neighbors invited you onto their porches for lemonade, when no one locked the doors at night, and when everyone knew your name. Sleeping in shelters with strangers and sharing the same privy, campfire, and water source has a Mayberry-in-the-woods vibe. There is a natural trust among hikers that removes most people's hardened, leathery shells that are a product of modern society. The small towns along the trail are full of personality, and I left each town with a warm feeling inside that carried me to the next friendly place. Then there's the cherished, mystical trail magic—when strangers offer drinks, rides, meals, and other hospitalities—that makes some of the fondest memories of hiking the AT. I've made it my mantra to try to bring that nostalgic sense of trust with me each time I emerge from the woods.

I've logged many miles on the AT since my epic adventure. I have had some reunions with hikers from my 1998 journey over the years. I continue to hike with my stepfather as he continues his AT section hike. Some of my most memorable hikes are with others.

I Share My Trail Lessons With My Spouse, and it's Been Worth Every Step

I convinced my wife to emerge from the church doors on our wedding day wearing full packs. I had to spend quite a bit of time assuring her that she still looked just as beautiful in her white wedding dress even with a blue backpack attached. Beth had agreed to an overnight backpacking trip in the Great Smoky Mountains as part of our honeymoon adventure. Beth is a marathon runner and enjoyed the hiking part of it. However, she was raised with an appreciation for hot showers and warm beds, so after our honeymoon, Beth declined all offers to overnight hike.

Beth and I have lived in several locations along the southern Appalachian Mountains near the AT. Each place we've lived has fulfilled our simple requirements of being within walking distance of amenities and having a mountain view or forested area. I'm fortunate to have married a woman who is willing to try out a simpler lifestyle than what she experienced growing up in the big city. Beth and I lived in North Carolina, and we later moved to Charlottesville, Virginia, a small university town near the Shenandoah National Park. Nearly every weekend, we enjoyed day-hiking all of the scenic loop trails in the Shenandoah, many of them several times. During my thru-hike, I missed many of the fantastic waterfalls because most of them were situated far enough off the AT to make them impractical for me to visit.

Four years into our marriage, we faced our first major tragedy. Beth's brother died, and she was devastated. In order to help my wife, I turned to nature for help. John Muir, one of the world's most noted naturalists, wrote: "Everyone needs beauty as well as bread, places to play, where nature may heal and cheer and give strength to body and soul." My gut told me to take Beth on a long hike. I know that God helped me convince her to go because she agreed to walk the entire 218-mile John Muir Trail with me. She went for more than half a month without a warm bed or shower—this is the same woman who said "never again" after a one-night backpacking excursion. In the woods, we discovered a new layer of our relationship. The hike brought us together in a holistic way. Our 16-day adventure was romantic and educational. I learned that Beth could eat as much as I can, which is impressive, considering that she's only half my weight. I learned that she doesn't get altitude sickness, whereas I do. I learned that we both could adapt and overcome. We all face struggles in our lifetimes, and on our hike, Beth took positive steps forward. Having a healthy outlet to work through our problems is key to living a full life. Nature has a way of putting the journey of life into perspective. Metaphorically, hiking helps me take the necessary steps forward.

Taking My Children Out Onto the Trail of Life

In 2004, we were blessed with our first baby hiker, and we are expecting our second little one sometime in July 2007. Some thought that my days of trekking would end with the birth of my first child. Not so. I experienced the triumph of completing the Appalachian Trail and John Muir Trail, and I wasn't about to shelve future adventures for fatherhood. In summer 2006, my family and I trekked across a 50-mile swath of Ireland. My then 21-month-old daughter and my four-year old nephew came along. Our journey was no trip up Everest, but I realized that it's worth it to tone down my pursuits a bit if it means that my child can come along. My trail vocabulary changed: "Do you want your sippy cup?" "Where's your pacifier?" "Here, have a goldfish cracker." But taking my family on a safe outdoor adventure was worth the small sacrifices.

Our daughter enjoyed the entire journey. She loved the horses, mules, and cows that would stick their heads over the fences, Mr. Ed-style. Walking as a family was a priceless bonding experience. The trip included nine other family members. Madison traveled with her aunts, uncles, and grandparents, creating some precious memories. We were able to share our hiking passion with our child, and her smile told us that it was worth every step. We hope that letting our child experience our dreams will help guide her to her own.

When I was a young boy, we kids played outside in the forest, in nearby creeks, and on my grandparents' farm. The forest where I once played is now a sprawling housing development. My grandfather's hundred-acre farm is covered with homes, too. The entire country has experienced this trend of housing and shopping centers replacing undeveloped forest and farmland. This has not only ruined wildlife habitat but also has diminished natural outdoor play areas for our children. The Appalachian Trail Conservancy has faced an increasing burden of development that encroaches on the trail corridor. Childhood obesity is at an all-time high. Many children prefer video games to playing outside. Most parents are hesitant to let children run free outside as we did growing up. I've come to realize that it's my role as a parent to help my child appreciate the simple things that only nature can provide. Our national and local parks have become the only resource for our children to discover the wonders of nature. Our parks play a critical role in nurturing in our children an appreciation for the outdoors.

On a recent hike in the Shenandoah National Park with my wife and daughter, we found ourselves splashing in a waterfall instead of following our plan to hike out to a vista. My daughter had a ball, and she couldn't have cared less about the view that we never reached. On my thru-hike, I thought of nothing besides myself and the miles ahead of me, but hiking with children requires an attitude adjustment. Cutting back the distance has actually increased the mileage of happiness. The summit will be there for a future hike. Madison is a potential future Appalachian Trail Conservancy member and steward of our Earth. I want her to have many positive and fun hikes in the woods so that she has a warm foundation to build upon when she thinks back to her outdoor adventures.

The Fragile Appalachian Trail Environment

Amazing volunteerism comes to mind when I think of what makes the Appalachian Trail and the organization that maintains the trail so great. Since my journey, the Appalachian Trail Conference changed its name to the Appalachian Trail Conservancy to better reflect its evolving mission. With only seven miles of trail remaining in private ownership, the ATC is focusing its efforts on expanding the trail corridor to create a buffer for encroaching development. Countless volunteers come together to support the ATC by donating, becoming members, and spending thousands of hours clearing brush, painting trail markers, and building shelters. The original visionary of the Appalachian Trail, Benton MacKaye, sought to create a wilderness sanctuary for people to rejuvenate from city life. His brainchild has become a precious gem. With our unprotected wild lands and farmland rapidly being blanketed with roads and buildings, our children might one day only be able to experience true wilderness in protected areas such as the Appalachian Trail. We should treasure them.

Sharing Your Dream Can Result in Amazing Things

My journey proved that one person's idea could blossom into something huge. My 1998 thru-hike raised $16,000 and inspired an annual 5K walk. As I write this chapter, we are planning our tenth annual Walk With Sunshine. We have raised more than $100,000 for adaptive equipment and animal programming for the residents of Sunshine Inc. of NW Ohio, where my brother Aaron resides. Hundreds of volunteers and friends of Sunshine have planned, organized, and participated in this walk and have made it a huge success. The Sunshine home continues to provide excellent care for those with disabilities who are dependant on others for their daily needs.

Although my brother Aaron's health is fragile, during the ten years since my original hike he has been the healthiest ever. He has rolled along in every walk since my thru-hike. Aaron loves the outdoors. The Sunshine home has a wheelchair-accessible boardwalk that rambles into the forest behind the facility. Aaron beams from ear to ear during strolls in the forest. He is non-verbal, but his enthusiasm for life is strong.

I enjoy sharing my Appalachian Trail journey through an ongoing lecture series and, of course, this book. What's really rewarding to me is when people find their own inspiration to go after their dreams after hearing my talk or reading my book. I've received hundreds of heartfelt letters over the years.

Walking Helped Me Find Perspective
With Enough Time Left to Apply it

When I set out to walk the Appalachian Trail, I had made a decision to simplify my life to include family, friends, and the mountains. Ten years since my hike, that is still my path. Authors, speakers, and clergy have reminded me of some of my trail lessons: humor, determination, internal drive, the importance of family, going after your goals, raising our children, and the impact of nature on our lives. I trust in the positive impact these simple lessons have had on my life. I've sat through many sermons where the pastor discusses a reading from the Bible that everyone in the congregation has heard before. But we sit through the sermon because we want to be reminded of the lesson. Some lessons are harder to apply than others, and that's why I repeatedly return to the trail for a refresher on its simple and profound lessons. My current adventure is raising my children. Children are just as fragile as our environment, and our kids are the key to preserving it. I believe that taking my family on outdoor adventures will develop healthy, well-rounded kids who will grow up to carry the torch of preserving our nation's great trails. My wish is that my children will discover their own dreams and passions, whatever they may be. I hope that one day my children will reach their own Mount Katahdins. In the meantime, we continue to visit various sections of the Appalachian Trail, Benton MacKaye–style, to escape from the hustle & bustle of everyday life. I'm thankful that I took the time to walk the trail and to learn the lessons that I'm able to apply on the journey of life.

For information on the Appalachian Trail contact:

The Appalachian Trail Conservancy
P.O. Box 807,
Hapers Ferry, West Virginia 25425
(304) 535-6331
e-mail: information@appalachiantrail.org
<www.appalachiantrail.org>

Suggested reading

Brill, David. *As Far As The Eye Can See*. Nashville, TN: Rutlidge Hill Press, 1990.

Bruce, Dan "Wingfoot". *The Thru-Hikers Handbook*. Hot Springs, NC: Center For Appalachian Trail Studies, 1998.

Deeds, Jean. *There are Mountains to Climb*. Indianapolis, IN: Silverwood Press, 1996.

Jenkins, Peter. *A Walk Across America*. New York, NY: Harper Collins, 1979

Luxenberg, Larry. *Walking the Appalachian Trail*. Mechanicsburg, Pennsylvania: Stackpole Books, 1994.

Manning, Russ. Jamieson, Sondra. *The Best of the Great Smoky Mountains*. Norris, TN: Mountain Laurel Place, 1991.

Shaffer, Earl V. *Walking With Spring: The First Solo Thru-Hike of the Legendary Appalachian Trail*. Harpers Ferry, WV: Appalachian Trail Conference, 1996.

About the Author

Jeff Alt is a traveling speaker, hiking expert, and award-winning author of the popular Appalachian Trail book, *A Walk for Sunshine* and *Get Your Kids Hiking*. He presents inspiring and entertaining keynotes around the country and hiking seminars in and around National Parks. Alt has been hiking since his youth. He has walked the 2,160-mile Appalachian Trail, the 218-mile John Muir Trail with his wife, and he carried his 21-month old daughter on a family trek across Ireland. Alt has been hiking with his kids since they were infants. He is a member of the Outdoor Writers Association of America (OWAA). Alt lives with his wife and two children in Cincinnati, Ohio.

Contact us

On the web:
www.awalkforsunshine.com
www.jeffalt.com
www.appalachiantrail.org.
visit www.sunshinefnd.com.

E-mail Jeff Alt:
jeffalt@awalkforsunshine.com
or jeff@jeffalt.com

CPSIA information can be obtained at www.ICGtesting.com
Printed in the USA
LVOW04s0845250315

431804LV00003B/3/P

9 780825 307768